Text Mining

Classification, Clustering, and Applications

Chapman & Hall/CRC
Data Mining and Knowledge Discovery Series

SERIES EDITOR

Vipin Kumar
University of Minnesota
Department of Computer Science and Engineering
Minneapolis, Minnesota, U.S.A

AIMS AND SCOPE

This series aims to capture new developments and applications in data mining and knowledge discovery, while summarizing the computational tools and techniques useful in data analysis. This series encourages the integration of mathematical, statistical, and computational methods and techniques through the publication of a broad range of textbooks, reference works, and handbooks. The inclusion of concrete examples and applications is highly encouraged. The scope of the series includes, but is not limited to, titles in the areas of data mining and knowledge discovery methods and applications, modeling, algorithms, theory and foundations, data and knowledge visualization, data mining systems and tools, and privacy and security issues.

PUBLISHED TITLES

UNDERSTANDING COMPLEX DATASETS: Data Mining with Matrix Decompositions
David Skillicorn

COMPUTATIONAL METHODS OF FEATURE SELECTION
Huan Liu and Hiroshi Motoda

CONSTRAINED CLUSTERING: Advances in Algorithms, Theory, and Applications
Sugato Basu, Ian Davidson, and Kiri L. Wagstaff

KNOWLEDGE DISCOVERY FOR COUNTERTERRORISM AND LAW ENFORCEMENT
David Skillicorn

MULTIMEDIA DATA MINING: A Systematic Introduction to Concepts and Theory
Zhongfei Zhang and Ruofei Zhang

NEXT GENERATION OF DATA MINING
Hillol Kargupta, Jiawei Han, Philip S. Yu, Rajeev Motwani, and Vipin Kumar

DATA MINING FOR DESIGN AND MARKETING
Yukio Ohsawa and Katsutoshi Yada

THE TOP TEN ALGORITHMS IN DATA MINING
Xindong Wu and Vipin Kumar

GEOGRAPHIC DATA MINING AND KNOWLEDGE DISCOVERY, Second Edition
Harvey J. Miller and Jiawei Han

TEXT MINING: CLASSIFICATION, CLUSTERING, AND APPLICATIONS
Ashok N. Srivastava and Mehran Sahami

Chapman & Hall/CRC
Data Mining and Knowledge Discovery Series

Text Mining

Classification, Clustering, and Applications

Edited by

Ashok N. Srivastava
Mehran Sahami

CRC Press
Taylor & Francis Group
Boca Raton   London   New York

CRC Press is an imprint of the
Taylor & Francis Group, an **informa** business

A CHAPMAN & HALL BOOK

Chapman & Hall/CRC
Taylor & Francis Group
6000 Broken Sound Parkway NW, Suite 300
Boca Raton, FL 33487-2742

© 2009 by Taylor and Francis Group, LLC
Chapman & Hall/CRC is an imprint of Taylor & Francis Group, an Informa business

Library of Congress Cataloging-in-Publication Data

Text mining : classification, clustering, and applications / Ashok Srivastava, Mehran Sahami.
    p. cm. -- (Chapman & Hall/CRC data mining and knowledge discovery series)
    Includes bibliographical references and index.
    ISBN 978-1-4200-5940-3 (hardcover : alk. paper)
    1. Data mining--Statistical methods. I. Srivastava, Ashok, 1969- II. Sahami, Mehran. III. Title. IV. Series.

QA76.9.D343T393 2009
006.3'12--dc22   2009013047

Visit the Taylor & Francis Web site at
http://www.taylorandfrancis.com

and the CRC Press Web site at
http://www.crcpress.com

To my mom, dad, Lynn, and Leela
for all that you have given me.
−A.N.S.

To Heather, William, and Claire
for always keeping the truly important things in perspective.
−M.S.

Contents

3 Collective Classification for Text Classification   **51**

Galileo Namata, Prithviraj Sen, Mustafa Bilgic, and Lise Getoor

4 Topic Models   **71**

David M. Blei and John D. Lafferty

ix

5 Nonnegative Matrix and Tensor Factorization for Discussion Tracking   **95**
Brett W. Bader, Michael W. Berry, and Amy N. Langville
5.1 Introduction 95
5.1.1 Extracting Discussions 96
5.1.2 Related Work 96
5.2 Notation 97
5.3 Tensor Decompositions and Algorithms 98
5.3.1 PARAFAC-ALS 100
5.3.2 Nonnegative Tensor Factorization 100
5.4 Enron Subset 102
5.4.1 Term Weighting Techniques 103
5.5 Observations and Results 105
5.5.1 Nonnegative Tensor Decomposition 105
5.5.2 Analysis of Three-Way Tensor 106
5.5.3 Analysis of Four-Way Tensor 108
5.6 Visualizing Results of the NMF Clustering 111
5.7 Future Work 116

6 Text Clustering with Mixture of von Mises-Fisher Distributions   **121**
Arindam Banerjee, Inderjit Dhillon, Joydeep Ghosh, and Suvrit Sra
6.1 Introduction 121
6.2 Related Work 123
6.3 Preliminaries 124
6.3.1 The von Mises-Fisher (vMF) Distribution 124
6.3.2 Maximum Likelihood Estimates 125
6.4 EM on a Mixture of vMFs (moVMF) 126
6.5 Handling High-Dimensional Text Datasets 127
6.5.1 Approximating κ 128
6.5.2 Experimental Study of the Approximation 130
6.6 Algorithms 132
6.7 Experimental Results 134
6.7.1 Datasets 135
6.7.2 Methodology 138
6.7.3 Simulated Datasets 138
6.7.4 Classic3 Family of Datasets 140
6.7.5 Yahoo News Dataset 143
6.7.6 20 Newsgroup Family of Datasets 143
6.7.7 Slashdot Datasets 145
6.8 Discussion 146
6.9 Conclusions and Future Work 148

9 Utility-Based Information Distillation   213

Yiming Yang and Abhimanyu Lad

10 Text Search-Enhanced with Types and Entities   233

Soumen Chakrabarti, Sujatha Das, Vijay Krishnan, and Kriti Puniyani

List of Figures

List of Tables

Introduction

Recent years have witnessed an immense growth in the amount of textual information available, both on the World Wide Web and in institutional document repositories. In this context, text mining has become extremely prevalent, giving rise to an age where vast amounts of textual information can be accessed, analyzed, and processed in a fraction of a second. The benefits of text mining go well beyond search and have yielded innovations that help people better understand and make use of the information in document repositories. The development of new technologies to tackle problems such as topic detection, tracking, and trending—where a machine automatically identifies emergent topics in a text corpus—is bound to have wide application in the future. Such applications can be found in ubiquitous consumer-based applications as well as systems focused on banking and finance, health care, aerospace, manufacturing, and the natural sciences.

Indeed, there are numerous applications of text mining, including cutting-edge research in the analysis and classification of news reports, email and spam filtering, hierarchical topic extraction from web pages, automated ontology extraction and management, and competitive intelligence. Each of these applications relies on an appropriate representation of the text corpora and a set of highly scalable, language independent and reliable algorithms for text analysis. Moreover, a systematic framework for incorporating domain knowledge, where available, is often essential for a successful application. Thus, the algorithms need to be flexible enough to learn appropriate patterns from the text corpora but also seamlessly include prior domain information as needed.

At a high level, computational methods to analyze large text corpora fall into two main categories: those based on statistical methods and those based on linguistic methods. Statistical methods usually build on an underlying statistical or probabilistic framework and often do not take meaning, semantics, and other linguistic properties into account. Such methods rely on the development of a mathematical representation of text. The most common representation is the so-called "bag-of-words" matrix, where each document in a corpus is represented as a vector containing the frequency of occurrence of each word in that document. For many real-world applications, this matrix is very large and extremely sparse, thus leading to the development of special methods for working with such matrices. A key point of this representation, however, is that the semantic information in the documents, which humans use to truly understand the meaning of the text, is lost. However, research over the last 25 years has shown that this representation can still yield extremely good results for a variety of applications, and it is still the favored representation in many text mining methods. To wit, an early paper in the field showed that inference methods based on a linear decomposition of these matrices could achieve a passing score on the TOEFL exam!

Linguistic methods, which are often based on natural language processing techniques, attempt to deconstruct documents based on a computer representation of a spoken or written language. These methods facilitate the process of extracting and representing meaning and casual relationships that are naturally expressed in language through the use of language models. This model-based approach can potentially yield a more expressive underlying representation of text, enabling a wide variety of text processing applications. For example, deeper representations of the underlying structure of text can lead to the automatic extraction and representation of an ontology or provide a machine-understandable representation of knowledge. While model-based systems hold great promise, they can also be quite difficult to build, as such models tend to have many built-in assumptions which make them hard to maintain and debug as new needs and applications arise.

The focus of this book is on statistical methods for text mining and analysis. Specifically, we examine methods to automatically cluster and classify text documents as well as the application of these methods in a variety of areas, such as adaptive information filtering, information distillation, and text search. The first three chapters of this book focus on classification of documents into predefined categories, presenting both state-of-the-art algorithms as well as their use in practice. The next four chapters describe novel methods for clustering documents into groups which are not predefined. Such methods seek to automatically determine topical structures that may exist in a document corpus. The final three chapters of the book describe various text mining applications that have significant implications for future research and industrial use. The individual chapters in the book are outlined in more detail below.

The goal of this book is to provide both an overview of various text mining methods and applications at the forefront of current research, while also serving as a reference for many standard technologies on which such systems are based. As a result, this book can provide insights for active researchers in text mining, while also serving as an introduction to more advanced topics for students pursuing graduate work in the area.

Chapter 1 gives a broad view of the field of text analysis using kernel methods, which are a widely used class of advanced algorithms in machine learning. The authors provide a substantial overview of the field by showing how data can be mapped to high, potentially infinite dimensional vector spaces, while maintaining polynomial time computations. Specific kernels are discussed that are relevant for text mining along with the mathematical properties of these kernels. The methods are demonstrated on the problem of modeling the evolution of linguistic sequences.

Chapter 2 shows an innovative application of kernel methods in the area of detecting bias in the news media. The chapter, building on the theoretical discussions in the Chapter 1, focuses on the application of support vector machines and kernel canonical correlation analysis and other statistical methods to detecting bias in four online news organizations: CNN, Al Jazeera, International Herald Tribune, and Detriot News. The authors show how kernel methods and other traditional statistical methods can be used to identify systematic bias in the content of news outlets. The most important terms for discriminating between news outlets are determined using these algorithms, and the results of this analysis are revealing even to the casual news reader.

Realizing that many documents in a corpus may be linked in various ways, such as having similar content, shared authors, or citations of the same works, the authors of Chapter 3 present methods for addressing collective classification problems. In this setting, the information regarding links between documents is explicitly modeled in order to capture the intuition that documents that are linked are more likely to have the same topical content or classification. The problem of collective classification is defined and formal models for this task are presented. The methods are empirically compared, showing that methods making use of the collective classification paradigm tend to outperform those that do not.

As the first chapter of the book focused on document clustering (as opposed to classification), Chapter 4 presents methods for generating topics models. Such techniques use probabilistic methods to analyze the underlying topical structure that may be present in a document collection. Starting with a description of Latent Dirichlet Allocation (LDA), one of the most widely used topic models, the chapter lays a theoretical foundation for topic modeling and then presents state-of-the-art extensions of the basic LDA model. These techniques are applied to model the evolution of topics in the journal *Science*, showing the intriguing evolution of the use of language in describing scientific topics over the span of a century.

Chapter 5 presents models for discussion tracking based on techniques from linear algebra, introducing a new set of algorithms based on factorizing the bag-of-words matrix. The authors provide the mathematical framework for non-negative matrix and tensor factorization (NMF) and discuss its application to the Enron dataset, which contains over 500,000 emails between 150 employees. This text corpus is an ideal dataset to use to discover underlying discussion threads and to evaluate these factorization algorithms. The NMF algorithms operate on positive matrices (i.e., matrices for which all elements are greater than or equal to zero) and yield a matrix factorization where each element in the factorization is also guaranteed to be non-negative. This has been empirically shown to provide highly interpretable results since the factorization better matches the non-negativity constraint of the data. Other factorization approaches such as singular value decomposition and principal components analysis do not share this desirable property. The extension from matrices to tensors allows for a third time dimension to be included in the analysis, again a variation from the standard matrix factorization approaches.

The sixth chapter discusses the classical problem of clustering a collection of documents into a set of k clusters. Although clustering is a standard technique with numerous algorithms (such as k-means, hierarchical methods, and density based methods) this paper explores the use of a probabilistic framework based on the von Mises-Fisher distribution for directional data. When using this method, the document vectors in the bag-of-words matrix are normalized to have unit length. Thus, each vector is effectively a point on a high-dimensional unit sphere. The authors derive the Expectation Maximization algorithm for the von Mises-Fisher distribution, and use their analysis to help explain some of the underlying reasons for the success of the cosine-similarity measure that is widely used in text clustering.

Chapter 7 examines the incorporation of externally defined constraints in document clustering tasks. Specifically, in such a semi-supervised clustering setting, additional information regarding which document pairs should be placed in the same cluster and which should not is available for guiding an algorithm in the formation of clusters. The authors discuss various algorithms that make use of such constraint information, showing experimental results highlighting the power that even a small number of constraints can provide in improving the quality of algorithmically induced clusters.

Shifting the focus from algorithms to applications, Chapter 8 discusses the use of text mining methods in adaptive information filtering, where the user has a stable set of interests and the incoming data to be analyzed are arriving dynamically over time. In many common situations where the in-flow of data is immense, such as tracking information on particular companies in order to gather competitive business intelligence or make more informed stock trades, adaptive filtering is necessary in order to deliver to users only the information that is truly relevant for them. The author covers several classical algorithms and evaluation metrics for information retrieval and filtering, using them to lay a foundation to then further discuss applications in adaptive filtering.

Combining adaptive filtering technology with mechanisms for novelty detection and user feedback is the subject of Chapter 9, which presents systems for utility-based information distillation. Such systems focus on not only delivering relevant documents to users, but also minimizing the amount of redundant information users see. Thereby, such systems have the net goal of maximizing user utility by optimizing the novelty of the relevant information provided to users. Several systems are empirically compared and an analysis is provided of the components which seem to provide the greatest benefit to overall system performance.

Finally, Chapter 10 examines methods for enhancing text search by using information about types of objects and entities in the text to better interpret the intent of the users of information retrieval systems. By inferring information about the type of information that users may be looking for in answer to their queries, the authors show how it is possible to build more powerful retrieval engines. Moreover, an analysis of the practical costs associated with such enhanced systems shows them to be quite reasonable both in terms of storage and performance.

Text mining is a broad and continually expanding research area, which has already had significant impact in the information systems people use on a daily basis, such as search engines and document management systems. We hope that readers find the work presented in this book to capture both the technical depth as well as immense practical potential of this research area. There is no doubt that text mining will continue to play a critical role in the development of future information systems, and advances in research will be instrumental to their success.

The editors are indebted to the chapter authors, without whose contributions this book would not exist. We also thank the teams of reviewers who helped ensure the high quality of the work herein, and also Randi Cohen at Taylor & Francis, who has helped guide this process from beginning to end. A. N. Srivastava wishes to thank the NASA Aviation Safety Program, Integrated Vehicle Health Management project for supporting this work. Mehran Sahami would like to thank Google Inc. and Stanford University for providing the support and flexibility to pursue this project.

About the Editors

Ashok N. Srivastava, Ph.D. is the Principal Investigator of the Integrated Vehicle Health Management research project in the NASA Aeronautics Research Mission Directorate. He also leads the Intelligent Data Understanding group at NASA Ames Research Center. His research interests include data mining, machine learning, and application domains such as systems health management and the earth and space sciences. He has published over 50 technical papers and has won numerous awards, including the NASA Exceptional Achievement Medal, the NASA Distinguished Performance Award, several NASA Group Achievement Awards, the IBM Golden Circle Award, and other awards during graduate school. Ashok holds a Ph.D. in Electrical Engineering from the University of Colorado at Boulder.

Mehran Sahami is an Associate Professor and Associate Chair for Education in the Computer Science Department at Stanford University. His research interests include machine learning, web search, and computer science education. Previously, Mehran was a Senior Research Scientist at Google Inc., and continues to maintain a consulting appointment there. He has published over 35 technical papers, holds four patents, and has helped organize numerous technical conferences and symposia. He received his Ph.D. in Computer Science from Stanford in 1999.

Contributor List

Brett W. Bader
Sandia National Laboratories
Albuquerque, New Mexico

Arindam Banerjee
University of Minnesota
Twin Cities, Minnesota

Sugato Basu
Google Research
Mountain View, California

Michael W. Berry
University of Tennessee
Knoxville, Tennessee

Mustafa Bilgic
University of Maryland
College Park, Maryland

David M. Blei
Princeton University
Princeton, New Jersey

Soumen Chakrabarti
Indian Institute of Technology
Bombay, India

Nello Cristianini
University of Bristol
Bristol, UK

Sujatha Das
University of Pennsylvania
Philadelphia, Pennsylvania

Ian Davidson
University of California, Davis
Davis, California

Inderjit Dhillon
University of Texas at Austin
Austin, Texas

Blaz Fortuna
Institute Jozef Stefan
Slovenia

Carolina Galleguillos
University of California
San Diego, California

Lise Getoor
University of Maryland
College Park, Maryland

Joydeep Ghosh
University of Texas at Austin
Austin, Texas

Vijay Krishnan
Yahoo!
Sunnyvale, California

Abhimanyu Lad
Carnegie Mellon University
Pittsburgh, Pennsylvania

John D. Lafferty
Carnegie Mellon University
Pittsburgh, Pennsylvania

Amy N. Langville
College of Charleston
Charleston, South Carolina

Alessia Mammone
Sapienza University of Rome
Rome, Italy

Galileo Namata
University of Maryland
College Park, Maryland

Kriti Puniyani
Carnegie Mellon University
Pittsburgh, Pennsylvania

Prithviraj Sen
University of Maryland
College Park, Maryland

Suvrit Sra
Max-Planck Institute for Biological
Cybernetics
Tübingen, Germany

Marco Turchi
University of Bristol
Bristol, UK

Yiming Yang
Carnegie Mellon University
Pittsburgh, Pennsylvania

Yi Zhang
University of California
Santa Cruz, California

Chapter 1

Analysis of Text Patterns Using Kernel Methods

Marco Turchi, Alessia Mammone, and Nello Cristianini

1.1 Introduction

The kernel approach offers a very general framework for performing pattern analysis on many types of data and it can be used in a wide variety of tasks and application areas. The kernel technique also enables us to use feature spaces whose dimensionality is more than polynomial in the relevant parameters of the systems even though the computational cost of the pattern analysis algorithm remains polynomial.

Our aim in this chapter is to illustrate the key ideas underlying the proposed approach, by giving a theoretical background on kernels, their main characteristics and how to build them. Then, starting from the representation of a document, we will outline kernel functions that can be used in text analysis.

1.2 General Overview on Kernel Methods

Throughout the chapter we will assume that we have a set of data and that we want to detect interesting relationships within it. Text documents will be our running example. In the following pages we will not assume any restrictions about the data-type.

1

The first step of the kernel approach is to embed the data items (e.g., documents) into a Euclidean space where the patterns can be represented by a linear relation. This step reduces many complex problems to a class of linear problems, and algorithms used to solve them are efficient and well understood. Depending on the data and on the patterns that are to be expected, it is necessary to choose a function that defines an embedding map.

The second step is to detect relations within the embedded data set, using a robust and efficient pattern analysis algorithm. Once again the choice of a particular pattern analysis algorithm depends on the problem at hand.

The strength of the kernel approach is that the embedding and subsequent analysis are performed in a *modular* fashion, so it is possible to consider these two parts as separate and the embedding step does not need to be performed explicitly, as will be described shortly.

Given a general input space $X \subseteq \mathbb{R}^n$ and a linear pattern analysis algorithm, we first embed X into a high dimensional feature space $F \subseteq \mathbb{R}^N$ and then relations are detected in the embedded data using the linear pattern analysis algorithms. The feature space can be defined as

$$F = \{\phi(\mathbf{x}) : \mathbf{x} \in X\}$$

where $\phi : X \rightarrow F \subseteq \mathbb{R}^N$ is the embedding map and $\mathbf{x}$ is a vector containing the feature's value.

Linear algorithms are preferred because of their efficiency and indeed they are well understood, both from a statistical and computational perspective. Since ϕ can be non-linear, any linear relation in F obtained by a linear algorithm can correspond to a non-linear relation in X. Examples include classical methods such as Least Squares, Linear Regression, etc.

Duality. The fundamental observation of the kernel approach is that linear relations can be represented by using inner products $\langle \phi(\mathbf{x}), \phi(\mathbf{z}) \rangle$ between all pairs of observed points $\mathbf{x}, \mathbf{z} \in X$ and without explicitly using their coordinates in $\mathbb{R}^N$. This is called the *dual representation* of linear relations, and has far-reaching consequences for algorithm application. It is possible to apply most linear pattern analysis algorithms given the relative positions of data points in a feature space, without ever needing to know their actual coordinates.

The function that returns the inner product between the images of any two data points in the feature space is called *kernel*. Examples include kernels for text, kernels for images that induce similarity between objects using different aspects of them.

Kernel Function. A *kernel* is a function κ that for all $\mathbf{x}, \mathbf{z} \in X$ satisfies

$$\kappa(\mathbf{x}, \mathbf{z}) = \langle \phi(\mathbf{x}), \phi(\mathbf{z}) \rangle$$

where ϕ is a mapping from X to an (inner product) feature space F

$$\phi : \mathbf{x} \longmapsto \phi(\mathbf{x}) \in F.$$

$\mathbf{x}$ and $\mathbf{z}$ can be elements of any set, and in this chapter they will be text documents. Clearly, the image $\phi(\mathbf{x})$ is a vector in $\mathbb{R}^N$.

Kernel Matrix. The square matrix $\mathbf{K} \in \mathbb{R}^{n \times n}$ such that $\mathbf{K}_{ij} = \kappa(\mathbf{x}_i, \mathbf{x}_j)$ for a set of vectors $\{\mathbf{x}_1, \ldots, \mathbf{x}_n\} \subseteq X$ and some kernel function κ is called *kernel matrix*.

Modularity. As we pointed out, the kernel component is data specific, while the pattern analysis algorithm is general purpose. Similarly, substituting a different algorithm while retaining the chosen kernel leads us to perform a different type of pattern analysis. Clearly, the same kernel function or algorithm can be suitably reused and adapted to very different kinds of problems. Figure 1.1 shows the stages involved in the implementation of a typical kernel approach analysis. The data are processed using a kernel to create a kernel matrix, which in turn is processed by a pattern analysis algorithm to obtain a pattern function. This function will be used to understand unseen examples.

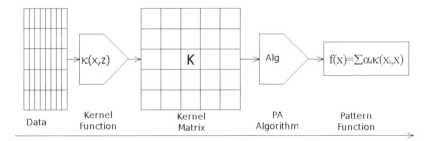

FIGURE 1.1: Modularity of kernel-based algorithms: the data are transformed into a kernel matrix, by using a kernel function; then the pattern analysis algorithm uses this information to find interesting relations, which are all written in the form of a linear combination of kernel functions.

Using efficient kernels, we can look for linear relations in very high dimensional spaces at a very low computational cost. If it is necessary to consider a non-linear map ϕ, we are still provided with an efficient way to discover non-linear relations in the data, by using a linear algorithms in a different space.

If X is not a vector space itself, as is the case of text, the use of kernels enables us to operate on generic entities with essentially algebraic tools. In fact, kernel functions make possible the use of structured input space, i.e., with an exponential or even infinite number of dimensions, and we can produce practical algorithms having computation time that scales polynomially in the number of training examples.

From a computational point of view kernel methods exhibit two fundamental properties; they make it possible to access very high-dimensional and flexible feature spaces at low computational cost, and then pattern analysis algorithms can solve and compute convex optimization problems efficiently without suffering from local minima, no matter the complexity of the resulting function classes.

Example. We now give an example of a kernel function whose complexity is less than the dimension of its corresponding feature space F. Consider a two-dimensional input space $X \subseteq \mathbb{R}^2$ together with the feature map

$$\phi \; : \; \mathbf{x} = (x_1, x_2) \longmapsto \phi(\mathbf{x}) = (x_1^2, x_2^2, \sqrt{2}x_1 x_2) \in F = \mathbb{R}^3.$$

Here, the data are moved from a two-dimensional to a three-dimensional space using the feature map, and the linear relations in the feature space correspond to quadratic relations in the input space. The resulting composition of the feature map with the inner product in the feature space is the following:

$$\begin{aligned} \langle \phi(\mathbf{x}), \phi(\mathbf{z}) \rangle &= \left\langle (x_1^2, x_2^2, \sqrt{2}x_1 x_2), (z_1^2, z_2^2, \sqrt{2}z_1 z_2) \right\rangle \\ &= x_1^2 z_1^2 + x_2^2 z_2^2 + 2x_1 x_2 z_1 z_2 \\ &= (x_1 z_1 + x_2 z_2)^2 = \langle \mathbf{x}, \mathbf{z} \rangle^2. \end{aligned}$$

Hence, the function

$$\kappa(\mathbf{x}, \mathbf{z}) = \langle \mathbf{x}, \mathbf{z} \rangle^2$$

is a kernel function and $F = \mathbb{R}^3$ is the corresponding feature space. Once again we are computing the inner product between the projections of two points into the feature space without explicitly evaluating their coordinates.

It is important to highlight that the feature space is not uniquely determined by the kernel function; the same kernel computes the inner product corresponding to the four-dimensional feature map

$$\phi \; : \; \mathbf{x} = (x_1, x_2) \longmapsto \phi(\mathbf{x}) = (x_1^2, x_2^2, x_1 x_2, x_2 x_1) \in F = \mathbb{R}^4.$$

This property of the kernel function does not affect the algorithms discussed in this chapter.

1.2.1 Finding Patterns in Feature Space

To reinforce the idea that the feature mapping need not be explicit we give examples of how to perform some elementary and often-used calculations in feature space, only using the information provided via the kernel function. The basic relations we measure in the feature space also form the basis of classical linear algorithms from statistics. At the end of this section, we will outline how a linear classifier can be built using dual representation.

Given a finite subset $S = \{\mathbf{x}_1, \ldots, \mathbf{x}_\ell\}$ of an input space X and a kernel $\kappa(\mathbf{x}, \mathbf{z})$ satisfying

$$\kappa(\mathbf{x}, \mathbf{z}) = \langle \phi(\mathbf{x}), \phi(\mathbf{z}) \rangle$$

where ϕ is a feature map into a feature space F, let $\phi(S) = \{\phi(\mathbf{x}_1), \ldots, \phi(\mathbf{x}_\ell)\}$ be the image of S under the map ϕ. Hence $\phi(S)$ is a subset of the inner product space F. Just considering the inner product information contained in the kernel matrix $\mathbf{K}$, significant information about the embedded data set $\phi(S)$ can be obtained. The element

$$\mathbf{K}_{ij} = \kappa(\mathbf{x}_i, \mathbf{x}_j), \quad i, j = 1, \ldots, \ell$$

is a general entry in the kernel matrix.

Working in a kernel-defined feature space means that we are not able to explicitly represent points but despite this handicap there is a surprising amount of useful information that can be obtained about $\phi(S)$.

Norm of Feature Vectors. The simplest example of this is the evaluation of the norm of $\phi(\mathbf{x})$; it is given by

$$\|\phi(\mathbf{x})\|_2 = \sqrt{\|\phi(\mathbf{x})\|^2} = \sqrt{\langle \phi(\mathbf{x}), \phi(\mathbf{x}) \rangle} = \sqrt{\kappa(\mathbf{x}, \mathbf{x})}.$$

The norms of linear combinations of images in the feature space can be evaluated with the following

$$
\left\| \sum_{i=1}^{\ell} \alpha_i \phi(\mathbf{x}_i) \right\|^2 = \left\langle \sum_{i=1}^{\ell} \alpha_i \phi(\mathbf{x}_i), \sum_{j=1}^{\ell} \alpha_j \phi(\mathbf{x}_j) \right\rangle
$$

$$
= \sum_{i=1}^{\ell} \alpha_i \sum_{j=1}^{\ell} \alpha_j \langle \phi(\mathbf{x}_i), \phi(\mathbf{x}_j) \rangle
$$

$$
= \sum_{i,j=1}^{\ell} \alpha_i \alpha_j \kappa(\mathbf{x}_i, \mathbf{x}_j).
$$

Distance between Feature Vectors. The length of the line joining two images $\phi(\mathbf{x})$ and $\phi(\mathbf{z})$ can be computed as

$$\begin{aligned}
\|\phi(\mathbf{x}) - \phi(\mathbf{z})\|^2 &= \langle \phi(\mathbf{x}) - \phi(\mathbf{z}), \phi(\mathbf{x}) - \phi(\mathbf{z}) \rangle \\
&= \langle \phi(\mathbf{x}), \phi(\mathbf{x}) \rangle - 2 \langle \phi(\mathbf{x}), \phi(\mathbf{z}) \rangle + \langle \phi(\mathbf{z}), \phi(\mathbf{z}) \rangle \\
&= \kappa(\mathbf{x}, \mathbf{x}) - 2\kappa(\mathbf{x}, \mathbf{z}) + \kappa(\mathbf{z}, \mathbf{z}).
\end{aligned} \tag{1.1}$$

It is easy to find out that this is a special case of the norm. The algorithms demonstrated at the end of this chapter are based on distance.

Norm and Distance from the Center of Mass. Consider now the center of mass of the set $\phi(S)$. This is the vector

$$\phi_S = \frac{1}{\ell} \sum_{i=1}^{\ell} \phi(\mathbf{x}_i).$$

As with all points in the feature space we have not an explicit vector representation of this point, but in this case there may not exist a point in X whose image under ϕ is ϕ_S. However we can compute the norm of the points of ϕ_S using only evaluations of the kernel on the inputs:

$$\begin{aligned}
\|\phi_S\|_2^2 = \langle \phi_S, \phi_S \rangle &= \left\langle \frac{1}{\ell} \sum_{i=1}^{\ell} \phi(\mathbf{x}_i), \frac{1}{\ell} \sum_{j=1}^{\ell} \phi(\mathbf{x}_j) \right\rangle \\
&= \frac{1}{\ell^2} \sum_{i,j=1}^{\ell} \langle \phi(\mathbf{x}_i), \phi(\mathbf{x}_j) \rangle = \frac{1}{\ell^2} \sum_{i,j=1}^{\ell} \kappa(\mathbf{x}_i, \mathbf{x}_j).
\end{aligned}$$

Hence, the square of the norm of the center of mass is equal to the average of the entries in the kernel matrix. This implies that this sum is equal to zero if the center of mass is at the origin of the coordinate system and greater than zero otherwise. The distance of the image of a point $\mathbf{x}$ from the center of mass ϕ_S is:

$$\begin{aligned}
\|\phi(\mathbf{x}) - \phi_S\|^2 &= \langle \phi(\mathbf{x}), \phi(\mathbf{x}) \rangle + \langle \phi_S, \phi_S \rangle - 2\langle \phi(\mathbf{x}), \phi_S \rangle \\
&= \kappa(\mathbf{x}, \mathbf{x}) + \frac{1}{\ell^2} \sum_{i,j=1}^{\ell} \kappa(\mathbf{x}_i, \mathbf{x}_j) - \frac{2}{\ell} \sum_{i=1}^{\ell} \kappa(\mathbf{x}, \mathbf{x}_i).
\end{aligned} \tag{1.2}$$

Linear Classification. Classification, also called categorization in text analysis, is one of the possible tasks that can be solved using kernel approach. The aim is to assign any input of our training set to one of a finite set of categories; the classification is binary if there are two categories, otherwise we are considering a multi-class problem.

Given a finite subset

$$\mathbf{S} = \{(\mathbf{x}_1, y_1), \ldots, (\mathbf{x}_\ell, y_\ell)\}$$

of points $\mathbf{x}_i \in X \subseteq \mathbb{R}^n$ with labels $y_i \in Y = \{-1, +1\}$, we want to find a classification function

$$g(\mathbf{x}) = sgn\,(\mathbf{w}'\mathbf{x} + b)$$

such that

$$E\,(|g(\mathbf{x}) - y|)$$

is small. Note that for convention $sgn(0) = 1$. Since g is a linear function, it can be regarded as the hyperplane defined by $\mathbf{w}'\mathbf{x} + b$ separating the data according to their labels. The vector $\mathbf{w}$ defines a direction perpendicular to the hyperplane, while varying the value of b moves the hyperplane parallel to itself. We call the vector $\mathbf{w}$ the weight vector.

There are many different algorithms for selecting the weight vector and many of them can be implemented in dual form. Two examples of linear classifiers are Rosenblatt's Perceptron (21) and Regularized Fisher's Discriminant (27). Now, considering the weight vector $\mathbf{w}$ as a function of the training examples

$$\mathbf{w} = \sum_{j=1}^{\ell} \alpha_j y_j \mathbf{x}_j$$

the function $g(\mathbf{x})$ can be rewritten in dual coordinates for the Perceptron:

$$g(\mathbf{x}) = sgn\,(\langle \mathbf{w} \cdot \mathbf{x} \rangle + b) =$$

$$= sgn\left(\left\langle \sum_{j=1}^{\ell} \alpha_j y_j \mathbf{x}_j \cdot \mathbf{x} \right\rangle + b\right) =$$

$$= sgn\left(\sum_{j=1}^{\ell} \alpha_j y_j \langle \mathbf{x}_j \cdot \mathbf{x} \rangle + b\right)$$

where, since the sign of $\mathbf{x}_j$ is given by the classification y_j, the α_j are positive with values proportional to the number of times misclassification of $\mathbf{x}_j$ has caused the weight to be updated; points that have caused fewer mistakes have smaller α_j, whereas difficult points will have large values.

In Regularized Fisher's Discriminant the weight vector $\mathbf{w}$ is chosen to maximize the regularized quotient:

$$F(\mathbf{w}) = \frac{(\mu_\mathbf{w}^+ - \mu_\mathbf{w}^-)^2}{(\sigma_\mathbf{w}^+)^2 + (\sigma_\mathbf{w}^-)^2 + \lambda \|\mathbf{w}\|^2}$$

where $\mu_\mathbf{w}^+$ is the mean of the elements in class $+1$ onto the direction $\mathbf{w}$, $\mu_\mathbf{w}^-$ the mean of the elements in class -1, and the $(\sigma_\mathbf{w}^+)^2$, $(\sigma_\mathbf{w}^-)^2$ the corresponding standard deviations of the function $\{\langle \mathbf{w} \cdot \mathbf{x}_j \rangle + b : y_j = i\}$ for $i = \{1, -1\}$; the term $\lambda \|\mathbf{w}\|^2$ has the aim to regularize the norm of the weight vector. Also in this case, it is possible to rewrite the weight's vector $\mathbf{w}$ as a linear combination of the training examples and the function $g(\mathbf{x})$ in dual coordinates. For an explicit derivation see (27).

Only if there exists an hyperplane that correctly classifies the data, the Perceptron procedure is guaranteed to converge; furthermore, the algorithm may give different results depending on the order in which the elements are processed, indeed several different solutions exist. Fisher's Discriminant does not suffer from these problems because its solution is unique since it finds the hyperplane $(\mathbf{w}, b)$ on which the projection of the data is maximally separated.

Fisher's Linear Discriminant (FDA), Partial Least Squares (PLS), Ridge Regression (RR), Principal Components Analysis (PCA), K-means and Spectral Clustering (SC), Canonical Correlation Analysis (CCA), Novelty Detection (ND), and many others can all be implemented in a dual form following the approaches outlined here. We refer the reader to (25; 18; 29; 6; 19; 1; 27) for more information on these methods, to (3) for a tutorial on kernel methods based on eigenvalue problems (PCA, CCA, PLS, FDA and SC), and to (33; 32) for two nice examples of the use of kernel methods in real life problems.

Owing to the level of maturity already achieved in these algorithmic domains, recently the focus of kernel methods research is shifting towards the design of kernels defined on general data types (such as strings, text, nodes of a graph, trees, graphs,...). Major issues in kernel design are expressive power and efficiency of evaluation (10; 13; 30; 17; 12).

1.2.2   Formal Properties of Kernel Functions

So far, the only way of verifying that the considered function is a kernel is to construct a feature space, for which the function corresponds to first performing the feature mapping and then computing the inner product between the two images. An alternative method of demonstrating that a candidate function is a kernel is Mercer's Theorem; it provides a characterization of when a function $\kappa(\mathbf{x}, \mathbf{z})$ is a kernel. This is an important theoretical tool useful to create new kernels, and combine different kernels to form new ones.

The kernel matrix $K_{ij} = \kappa(\mathbf{x}_i, \mathbf{x}_j)$, formed by evaluating a kernel on all pairs of any set of inputs, is a positive semi-definite matrix.

Finitely Positive Semi-Definite Functions   A function

$$\kappa : X \times X \longrightarrow \mathbb{R}$$

satisfies the finitely positive semi-definite property if it is a symmetric function for which the matrices formed by restriction to any finite subset of the space X are positive semi-definite. Note that this definition does not require the set X to be a vector space.

The finitely positive semi-definite property completely characterizes kernels because it is possible to construct the feature space assuming only this property. The result is stated in the form of a theorem.

THEOREM 1.1 Characterization of kernels
A function

$$\kappa : X \times X \longrightarrow \mathbb{R}$$

can be decomposed

$$\kappa(\mathbf{x}, \mathbf{z}) = \langle \phi(\mathbf{x}), \phi(\mathbf{z}) \rangle$$

into a feature map ϕ into a Hilbert space F applied to both its arguments followed by the evaluation of the inner product in F if and only if it satisfies the finitely positive semi-definite property.

A preliminary concept useful to outline the Mercer's Theorem is the following.

Let $L_2(X)$ be the vector space of square integrable functions on a compact subset X of $\mathbb{R}^n$ with the definitions of addition and scalar multiplication; formally

$$L_2(X) = \left\{ f : \int_X f(x)^2 dx < \infty \right\}.$$

For mathematical details see (27).

THEOREM 1.2 Mercer
Let X be a compact subset of $\mathbb{R}^n$. Suppose κ is a continuous symmetric function such that the integral operator $T_\kappa : L_2(X) \to L_2(X)$,

$$(T_\kappa f)(\cdot) = \int_X \kappa(\cdot, \mathbf{x}) f(\mathbf{x}) d\mathbf{x}$$

is positive, that is

$$\int_{X \times X} \kappa(\mathbf{x}, \mathbf{z}) f(\mathbf{x}) f(\mathbf{z}) d\mathbf{x} d\mathbf{z} \geq 0$$

for all $f \in L_2(X)$. Then we can expand $\kappa(\mathbf{x}, \mathbf{z})$ in a uniformly convergent series (on $X \times X$) in terms of functions ϕ_j, satisfying $\langle \phi_i, \phi_j \rangle = \delta_{ij}$:

$$\kappa(\mathbf{x}, \mathbf{z}) = \sum_{j=1}^{\infty} \phi_j(\mathbf{x}) \phi_j(\mathbf{z}).$$

Furthermore, the series $\sum_{i=1}^{\infty} \|\phi_i\|_{L_2(X)}^2$ is convergent.

The conditions of Mercer's Theorem are equivalent to requiring that for every finite subset of X, the corresponding matrix is positive semi-definite (6).

Kernel Matrix as an Interface.   All the information that is required by the pattern analysis algorithm is inside the kernel matrix. The kernel matrix can be seen as an interface between the input data and the pattern analysis algorithm (see Figure 1.1), in the sense that all the data information passes through the bottleneck. Several model adaptations and selection methods are implemented by manipulating the kernel matrix. This property in some sense is also a limitation, because if the kernel is too general no useful relation can be highlighted in data.

1.2.3   Operations on Kernel Functions

As we pointed out, the positive semi-definiteness property is the core for the characterization of kernel functions. New functions are kernels if they are finitely positive semi-definite. So it is sufficient to verify that the function is a kernel and this demonstrates that there exists a feature space map for which the function computes the corresponding inner product. It is important to introduce some operations on kernel functions which always give as result a new positive semi-definite function. We will say that the class of kernel functions is *closed* under such operations.

The following two propositions can be viewed as showing that kernels satisfy a number of closure properties, allowing us to create more complicated kernels from simpler ones.

PROPOSITION 1.1 Closure properties
Let κ_1 and κ_2 be kernels over $X \times X$, $X \subseteq \mathbb{R}^n$, $a \in \mathbb{R}^+$, $f(\cdot)$ a real-valued function on X, $\phi : X \longrightarrow \mathbb{R}^N$ with κ_3 a kernel over $\mathbb{R}^N \times \mathbb{R}^N$, and $\mathbf{B}$ a symmetric positive semi-definite $n \times n$ matrix. Then the following functions are kernels:

1. $\kappa(\mathbf{x}, \mathbf{z}) = \kappa_1(\mathbf{x}, \mathbf{z}) + \kappa_2(\mathbf{x}, \mathbf{z})$

2. $\kappa(\mathbf{x}, \mathbf{z}) = a\kappa_1(\mathbf{x}, \mathbf{z})$

3. $\kappa(\mathbf{x}, \mathbf{z}) = \kappa_1(\mathbf{x}, \mathbf{z})\kappa_2(\mathbf{x}, \mathbf{z})$

4. $\kappa(\mathbf{x}, \mathbf{z}) = f(\mathbf{x})f(\mathbf{z})$

5. $\kappa(\mathbf{x}, \mathbf{z}) = \kappa_3(\phi(\mathbf{x}), \phi(\mathbf{z}))$

6. $\kappa(\mathbf{x}, \mathbf{z}) = \mathbf{x}'\mathbf{B}\mathbf{z}$ *with* $\mathbf{x}, \mathbf{z} \in X$

PROPOSITION 1.2
Let $\kappa_1(\mathbf{x}, \mathbf{z})$ be a kernel over $X \times X$, where $\mathbf{x}$, $\mathbf{z} \in X$, and $p(x)$ a polynomial with positive coefficients. Then the following functions are also kernels:

1. *Polynomial kernel (4):*
   $$\kappa(\mathbf{x}, \mathbf{z}) = p(\kappa_1(\mathbf{x}, \mathbf{z}))$$

2. *(27):*

   $$\kappa(\mathbf{x}, \mathbf{z}) = \exp(\kappa_1(\mathbf{x}, \mathbf{z}))$$

3. *Gaussian kernel (4):*

   $$\kappa(\mathbf{x}, \mathbf{z}) = \exp(-\|\mathbf{x} - \mathbf{z}\|^2 / (2\sigma^2)) \ \textit{with} \ \mathbf{x}, \mathbf{z} \in X$$

Now we have all necessary tools to discuss kernel applications in text problems.

1.3   Kernels for Text

In the last twenty five-years, the constant growth of the Web has produced an explosion of readily available digital text. This huge amount of data has become one of the main research interests of Artificial Intelligence. Many algorithms and text representations have been developed obtaining successful results. The goal of this section is to introduce some applications of Kernel Methods in this area.

Typically, pattern analysis algorithms are originally developed to be applied to vectorial data. However, for many other types of data it is possible to explicitly or implicitly construct a feature space capturing relevant information from this data. Unfortunately even when it can be expressed explicitly, often this feature space is so high dimensional that the algorithms can not be used in their original form for computational reasons. However many of these algorithms can be reformulated into a kernel version. These kernel versions directly operate on the kernel matrix rather than on the feature vectors. For many data types, methods have been devised to efficiently evaluate these kernels, avoiding the explicit construction of the feature vectors. In this way, the introduction of kernels defined for a much wider variety of data structures significantly extended the application domain of linear algorithms. Now we introduce and discuss various kernels which are commonly used in text.

1.3.1   Vector Space Model

The Vector Space Model (VSM) representation for a document d has been introduced by (23) in 1975. The main idea consists of representing a document as a vector, in particular as a *bag of words*. This set contains only the words that belong to the document and their frequency. This means that a document is represented by the words that it contains. In this representation, punctuation is ignored, and a sentence is broken into elementary elements (words) losing the order and the grammar information. These two observations are crucial, because they show that it is impossible to reconstruct the original document given its bag of words; it means that the mapping is not one to one.

We consider a *word* as a sequence of letters from a defined alphabet. In this chapter we use *word* and *term* as synonyms. We consider a *corpus* as a set of documents, and a *dictionary* as the set of words that appear into the corpus. We can view a document as a bag of terms. This bag can be seen as a vector, where each component is associated with one term from the dictionary

$$\phi : d \longmapsto \phi(d) = (tf(t_1, d), tf(t_2, d), \ldots, tf(t_N, d)) \in \mathbb{R}^N,$$

where $tf(t_i, d)$ is the frequency of the term t_i in d. If the dictionary contains N terms, a document is mapped into a N dimensional space. In general, N is quite large, around a hundred thousand words, and it produces a sparse VSM representation of the document, where few $tf(t_i, d)$ are non-zero.

A corpus of ℓ documents can be represented as a *document-term* matrix whose rows are indexed by the documents and whose columns are indexed by the terms. Each entry in position (i, j) is the term frequency of the term t_j in document i.

$$\mathbf{D} = \begin{pmatrix} tf(t_1, d_1) & \cdots & tf(t_N, d_1) \\ \vdots & \ddots & \vdots \\ tf(t_1, d_\ell) & \cdots & tf(t_N, d_\ell) \end{pmatrix}.$$

From matrix $\mathbf{D}$, we can construct:

- the *term-document* matrix: $\mathbf{D}'$

- the *term-term* matrix: $\mathbf{D}'\mathbf{D}$

- the *document-document* matrix: $\mathbf{D}\mathbf{D}'$

It is important to note that the document-term matrix is the dataset $\mathbf{S}$, while the document-document matrix is our kernel matrix.

Quite often the corpus size is smaller than the dictionary size, so the document representation can be more efficient. Here, the dual description correspond to the document representation view of the problem, and the primal to the term representation. In the dual, a document is represented as the counts of terms that appear in it. In the primal, a term is represented as the counts of the documents in which it appears.

The VSM representation has some drawbacks. The most important is that bag of words is not able to map documents that contain semantically equivalent words into the same feature vectors. A classical example is synonymous words which contain the same information, but are assigned distinct components. Another effect is the complete loss of context information around a word. To mitigate this effect, it is possible to apply different techniques. The first consists in applying different weight w_i to each coordinate. This is quite common in text mining, where uninformative words, called stop words, are removed from the document. Another important consideration is the influence of the length of the document. Long documents contain more words than the short ones, and hence they are represented by feature vectors with greater norm. This effect can be removed by normalizing the kernel (for more details see (27)). Stop word removal and normalization are two examples of operations that can be performed and repeated as a series of successive embedding steps.

1.3.1.1   Vector Space Kernel

We have just defined the function ϕ, which maps a document into a row vector, in which each entry is the term frequency of that term in that document. This vector has a number of entries equal to the number of words inside the dictionary, but few of them have non-zero value.

Matrix $\mathbf{D}$ can be created using this representation. We refer to $\mathbf{X}$ as a matrix of training examples by features. There is a direct correspondence between $\mathbf{X}$ and $\mathbf{D}$, where features become terms, and training examples become documents.

We create a kernel matrix $\mathbf{K} = \mathbf{DD}'$ corresponding to the *vector space kernel*

$$\kappa\left(d_1, d_2\right) = \langle\phi\left(d_1\right), \phi\left(d_2\right)\rangle = \sum_{j=1}^{N} tf\left(t_j, d_1\right) tf\left(t_j, d_2\right).$$

An interesting property of the Vector Space Kernel is the computational cost. In fact, the time to compute the kernel is proportional to the length of the two documents $O(|d_1| + |d_2|)$. This is due to the process of sparse vector representation. Each document is preprocessed, and it is split into a list of terms using spaces as term separators. Each word inside the vocabulary is associated with a unique numeric id. This allows a document to be transformed into a sequence of ids together with term frequencies and sorted in ascending order, according to id. A document d becomes a list $L(d)$ of pairs *(id:term, frequency)*. Now it is a simple and efficient task to compute $\kappa(d_1, d_2) = A(L(d_1), L(d_2))$, where $A(.)$ is an algorithm that traverses the lists, computing products of frequencies whenever the term ids match. This means that when we compute the kernel, it does not involve evaluation of the feature vector $\phi(d)$, but the representation as a list of terms $L(d)$. When we work with high dimensional space, it ensures a cost proportional to the sum of the length of the documents.

1.3.2   Semantic Kernels

An important problem with the bag of words is that it does not contain information about the semantic content of words. An evolution of the Vector Space kernel is *semantic kernels*. They simply try to expand the basic VS kernel using the linear transformation $\tilde{\phi}(d) = \phi(d)\mathbf{S}$. $\mathbf{S}$ is a matrix $N \times k$ and we refer to it as *semantic matrix*. We can rewrite the definition of kernel using the new feature vector $\tilde{\phi}$:

$$\tilde{\kappa}\left(d_1, d_2\right) = \phi\left(d_1\right) \mathbf{S}\mathbf{S}' \phi\left(d_2\right)' = \tilde{\phi}\left(d_1\right) \tilde{\phi}\left(d_2\right)'.$$

Different choices of $\mathbf{S}$ lead to different variants of the VSMs. We can consider $\mathbf{S}$ as a product of successive embeddings. We define it as $\mathbf{S} = \mathbf{R}\mathbf{P}$, where $\mathbf{R}$ is a diagonal matrix giving the *term weightings* and $\mathbf{P}$ is a *proximity* matrix defining semantic spreading between different terms of the corpus.

In Information Retrieval (IR), the term frequency is considered a local feature of the document. In particular tasks, terms need to carry an absolute information across the documents into the corpus or a given topic. Several measures have been proposed for term weighting such as mutual information (8), entropy (26), or term frequency of words across the documents. We consider an absolute measure known as *idf* (11) that weights terms as a function of their *inverse document frequency*. If the corpus contains ℓ documents, and $df(t)$ is the number of documents that contain the term t, the *idf* weight is

$$w\left(t\right) = \ln\left(\frac{\ell}{df\left(t\right)}\right).$$

Idf is implicitly able to downweight the stop words. If a term is present in each document, then $w(t) = 0$. In general it is preferable to create a stop word list, and remove the stop word before computing the vector representation. This helps to decrease the dictionary size.

The *idf* rule is just an example of a kind of term weight. In general, we can develop a new VSM choosing the *term weightings* matrix $\mathbf{R}$ as a diagonal matrix in the following way:

$$\mathbf{R}_{tt} = w\left(t\right).$$

The associated kernel computes the inner product

$$\tilde{\kappa}\left(d_1, d_2\right) = \phi\left(d_1\right) \mathbf{R}\mathbf{R}' \phi\left(d_2\right)' = \sum_t w\left(t\right)^2 tf\left(t, d_1\right) tf\left(t, d_2\right).$$

This kernel merges the *tf* and *idf* representation well known in IR as *tf-idf*. It is implementable by a weighted version A_w of the algorithm A:

$$\tilde{\kappa}\left(d_1, d_2\right) = A_w\left(L\left(d_1\right), L\left(d_2\right)\right).$$

The *tf-idf* representation is able to highlight discriminative terms and downweight irrelevant terms, but it is not able to take into account semantic information about two or more terms or about two or more documents. This semantic information can be introduced into the semantic kernel using the proximity matrix $\mathbf{P}$. This matrix needs to have non-zero off-diagonal entries, $\mathbf{P}_{ij} > 0$ for $i \neq j$, when the term i is semantically correlated with term j. Given $\mathbf{P}$, the vector space kernel becomes

$$\tilde{\kappa}\left(d_1, d_2\right) = \phi\left(d_1\right) \mathbf{P}\mathbf{P}'\phi\left(d_2\right)' \tag{1.3}$$

which corresponds to representing a document by a less sparse vector $\phi\left(d\right)\mathbf{P}$ that has non-zero entries for all terms that are semantically similar to those present in the document $\dot{d}$.

The matrix $\mathbf{P}\mathbf{P}'$ encodes the semantic strength among terms. We can expand the equation (1.3) substituting $\mathbf{P}\mathbf{P}'$ with $\mathbf{Q}$

$$\tilde{\kappa}\left(d_1, d_2\right) = \sum_{i,j} \phi\left(d_1\right)_i \mathbf{Q}_{i,j} \phi\left(d_2\right)_j$$

so that we can view $\mathbf{Q}_{ij}$ as encoding the amount of semantic relation between terms i and j. Note that defining the similarity by inferring $\mathbf{Q}$ requires the additional constraint that $\mathbf{Q}$ be positive semi-definite, suggesting that defining $\mathbf{P}$ will in general be more straightforward. A simple example of semantic similarity mapping is *stemming*, that consists of removing inflection from words.

1.3.2.1 Designing the Proximity Matrix

Extracting semantic information among terms in documents is still an open issue in IR. More techniques have been developed in the last few years. In this part of the chapter, we introduce different methods to compute the matrix $\mathbf{P}$, learning the relationship directly from a corpus or a set of documents. Though we present the algorithms in a term-based representation, we will in many cases show how to implement them in dual form, hence avoiding the explicit computation of the matrix $\mathbf{P}$.

Semantic Information from Semantic Network. Wordnet (9) is a well known example of freely available semantic network. It contains semantic relationship between terms in a hierarchical structure. More general terms occur higher in the tree structure. A semantic proximity matrix can be obtained by the distance between two terms in the hierarchical tree provided by Wordnet, by setting the entry $\mathbf{P}_{ij}$ to reflect the semantic proximity between the terms i and j.

Generalized VSM. The generalized VSM (GVSM) is a variation of the classical VSM, where semantic similarity between terms is used. The main idea of this approach is that two terms are semantically related if they frequently co-occur in the same documents. This implies that two documents can be considered similar also if they do not share any terms, but the terms they contain co-occur in other documents. If the VSM represents a document as bag of words, the GSVM represents a document as a vector of its similarities with the different documents in the corpus. A document is represented by

$$\phi\left(d\right) = \phi\left(d\right)\mathbf{D}',$$

where $\mathbf{D}$ is the document–term matrix, equivalent to taking $\mathbf{P} = \mathbf{D}'$. This definition does not make immediately clear that it implements a semantic similarity, but if we compute the corresponding kernel

$$\tilde{\kappa}\left(d_1, d_2\right) = \phi\left(d_1\right)\mathbf{D}'\mathbf{D}\phi\left(d_2\right)',$$

we can observe that the matrix $\mathbf{D}'\mathbf{D}$ has a non-zero (i, j)-th entry if and only if there is a document in the corpus in which the i-th and j-th terms co-occur, since

$$\left(\mathbf{D}'\mathbf{D}\right)_{ij} = \sum_d tf\left(i, d\right)tf\left(j, d\right).$$

The strength of a semantic relationship between two terms that co-occurs in a document is measured by the frequency and number of their co-occurrences. This approach can be used to reduce the space dimension. In fact, if we have less documents than terms, we map from the vectors indexed by terms to a lower-dimensional space indexed by the documents of the corpus.

Latent Semantic Kernels. Another approach based on the use of co-occurence information is Latent Semantic Indexing (LSI) (7). This method is very close to GSVM, the main difference is that it uses singular value decomposition (SVD) to extract the semantic information from the co-occurrences. SVD of a matrix considers the first k columns of the left and right singular vectors matrices $\mathbf{U}$ and $\mathbf{V}$ corresponding to the k largest singular values. Thus, the word-by-document matrix $\mathbf{D}'$ is factorized as

$$\mathbf{D}' = \mathbf{U}\mathbf{\Sigma}\mathbf{V}'$$

where $\mathbf{U}$ and $\mathbf{V}$ are unitary matrices whose columns are the eigenvectors of $\mathbf{D}'\mathbf{D}$ and $\mathbf{D}\mathbf{D}'$ respectively. LSI now projects the documents into the space spanned by the first k columns of $\mathbf{U}$, using these new k-dimensional vectors for subsequent processing

$$d \longmapsto \phi\left(d\right)\mathbf{U}_k,$$

where $\mathbf{U}_k$ is the matrix containing the first k columns of $\mathbf{U}$. The eigenvectors define the subspace that minimizes the sum-squared differences between the points and their projections, so it defines the subspace with minimal sum-squared residuals. Hence, the eigenvectors for a set of documents can be viewed as concepts described by linear combinations of terms chosen in such a way that the documents are described as accurately as possible using only k such concepts. The aim of SVD is to extract few high correlated dimensions/concepts able to approximately reconstruct the whole feature vector.

The new kernel can be defined as

$$\tilde{\kappa}\left(d_1, d_2\right) = \phi\left(d_1\right)\mathbf{U}_k\mathbf{U}_k'\phi\left(d_2\right)',$$

and the proximity matrix $\mathbf{P}$ is hence equal to $\mathbf{U}_k$. Note that there is a correspondence between the LSI and PCA in the feature space.

1.3.3   String Kernels

A document can be seen in different ways. Often it is modelled as a sequence of paragraphs, or a sequence of sentences. Reducing the granularity, it can be seen as a sequence of words or a string of symbols. In the previous section, we have seen a document viewed as a bag of words. Now we consider a document as a string of letters. This new representation allows different kinds of analysis. In this section, we introduce several kernels that provide an interesting way to compare documents working on substrings.

The p-spectrum Kernel.   Perhaps the most natural way to compare two strings in many applications is to count how many (contiguous) substrings of length p they have in common. We define the *spectrum of order p* (or *p-spectrum*) of a sequence s as the histogram of frequencies of all its (contiguous) substrings of length p. We define the p-spectrum kernel (15) as the inner product of the p-spectra. Formally, the feature space F associated with the p-spectrum kernel is indexed by $I = \Sigma^p$, where Σ denotes the alphabet, and Σ^p is the set of all finite strings of length p, with the embedding given by

$$\phi_u^p\left(s\right) = \left|\{(v_1, v_2) : s = v_1 u v_2\}\right|, \ u \in \Sigma^p$$

and the associated p-spectrum kernel between sequences s and t is defined as

$$\kappa_p\left(s, t\right) = \left\langle \phi^p\left(s\right), \phi^p\left(t\right)\right\rangle = \sum_{u \in \Sigma^p} \phi_u^p\left(s\right)\phi_u^p\left(t\right).$$

The Mismatch Kernel.   When isolated substitutions are likely to occur in a sequence, the p-spectrum kernel might be too stringent to result in a useful similarity measure. In those cases, it makes sense to use a modification of the p-spectrum, where the feature of a sequence s associated to the substring u is equal to the number of contiguous substrings in s that differ by no more than a maximal number m of characters from u. For two substrings u and v of equal length, we use $d\left(u, v\right)$ to denote the number of characters in which u and v differ. The mismatch kernel (16) $\kappa_{p,m}$ is defined by the feature mapping

$$\phi_u^{p,m}\left(s\right) = \left|\{(v_1, v_2) : s = v_1 v v_2 : |u| = |v| = p, \ d\left(u, v\right) \leq m\}\right|.$$

The associated mismatch kernel is defined as

$$\kappa_{p,m}\left(s, t\right) = \left\langle \phi^{p,m}\left(s\right), \phi^{p,m}\left(t\right)\right\rangle = \sum_{u \in \Sigma^p} \phi_u^{p,m}\left(s\right)\phi_u^{p,m}\left(t\right).$$

The Trie-based Implementation.   Direct implementations of these kernels would be very slow to evaluate due to the potentially large dimensionality of the feature space, which is exponential in p. Fortunately, however, much faster implementations of string kernels can be obtained by exploiting an efficient data structure known as a 'trie.' A *trie* over an alphabet Σ is a tree whose edges are labeled with a symbol from Σ. A *complete trie of depth p* is a trie containing the maximal number of nodes consistent with the depth of the tree being p, each parent node having a downward branch for each alphabet symbol from Σ.

In a complete trie there is a one to one correspondence between the nodes at depth k and the strings of length k, the correspondence being between the node and the string on the path to that node from the root. (The string associated with the root node is the empty string ε.) Hence, we will refer to the nodes of a trie by their associated string. The key observation behind the trie-based approach is that one can regard the *leaves* of the complete trie of depth p as the indices of the feature space indexed by the set Σ^p of strings of length p. So the coordinates of the vector $\phi(s)$ (corresponding to the dimensions of the feature space F) are conveniently organized in the trie, which can be used to obtain an efficient search strategy.

The use of this data structure reduces the computational cost of the p-spectrum kernel and mismatch kernel. In both of the kernels, the implementation is based on the traversal of the trie in a depth-first fashion, each time attaching to the explored node a list of substrings of s that match to the substring corresponding to that node. The key difference between p-spectrum kernel and mismatch kernel trie implementation is that in the mismatch kernel when we process a substring it can be added to lists associated with more than one child node. We have an overall complexity of $O\left(p\left(|s| + |t|\right)\right)$ for the p-spectrum kernel and $O\left(p^{m+1}|\Sigma|^m\left(|s| + |t|\right)\right)$ for the mismatch kernel. In this chapter we do not go deep into the implementation of these two kernels using the trie data structure; for more details see (17) and (27).

Computing an Entire Kernel Matrix.   Instead of maintaining a list for two strings s and t at each internal node of the trie, we can maintain a list for a whole set of strings between which we want to compute the kernel functions. Whenever a leaf node is reached, all these kernel functions can be incremented based on the feature values of each of the strings corresponding to that leaf node. This can be carried out efficiently; the traversal of the trie remains linear in the sum of the lengths of all strings, and only the operations at the leaf nodes, where the kernel values are incremented, are inherently quadratic in the number of strings. The result is the full kernel matrix $\mathbf{K}$, containing the kernel function between the ith and jth sequences at position (i, j) and symmetrically at position (j, i). Normalized kernel and distance matrices can then promptly be computed from it.

1.4   Example

At the end this chapter, we want to show by an example the main characteristics of Kernel Methods. In Figure 1.1 in Section 1.2, we have introduced concepts as kernel function, kernel matrix, and pattern analysis algorithm; now we see how they work in practice.

In this example, for more details see (5), we model the evolution of linguistic sequences by comparing their statistical properties. We will see how languages belonging to the same linguistic family have very similar statistical properties. We will use these statistical properties to embed the sequences into a vector space, to obtain their pairwise distances and hypothesize an evolutionary tree. The comparison among languages is performed by p-spectrum kernel and mismatch kernel. Both algorithms demonstrated are based on computing the distance between documents in feature space as defined in equation (1.1) in Section 1.2.1.

We have used the language dataset introduced by (2). Their dataset is made of the translation of the "Universal Declaration of Human Rights" (20) in the most important language branches: Romance, Celtic, German, Slavic, Ugrofinnic, Altaic, Baltic, and the Basque language. Our dataset contains 42 languages from this dataset. Each document has been preprocessed and it has been transformed into a string of the letters belonging to the English alphabet plus the space.

The experiments have been performed with value of $p = 4$, allowing one mismatch. With both the kernels, we have obtained a kernel matrix of size 42×42. From the kernel matrix we have computed the distance matrix using equation (1.1). On the distance matrix, we have applied two different pattern analysis algorithms, neighbor joining (NJ) algorithm (22; 28) and multidimensional scaling (MDS) algorithm (14). NJ is a standard method in computational biology for reconstructing phylogenetic trees based on pairwise distances between the leaf taxa. MDS is a visualization tool for the exploratory analysis of high-dimensional data.

Here we present results relative to the p-spectrum kernel with $p = 4$; there are various elements of interest, both where they match accepted taxonomy and where they (apparently) violate it. The Neighbor Joining tree, see Figure 1.2, correctly recovers most of the families and subfamilies that are known from linguistics. An analysis of the order of branching of various subfamilies shows that our statistical analysis can capture interesting relations, e.g., the recent split of the Slavic languages in the Balkans; the existence of a Scandinavian subfamily within the Germanic family; the relation between Afrikaans and Dutch; the Celtic cluster; and the very structured Romance family. A look at the MDS plot, Figure 1.3, shows that English ends up halfway between Romance and Germanic clusters; and Romanian is close to both Slavic and Turkic clusters.

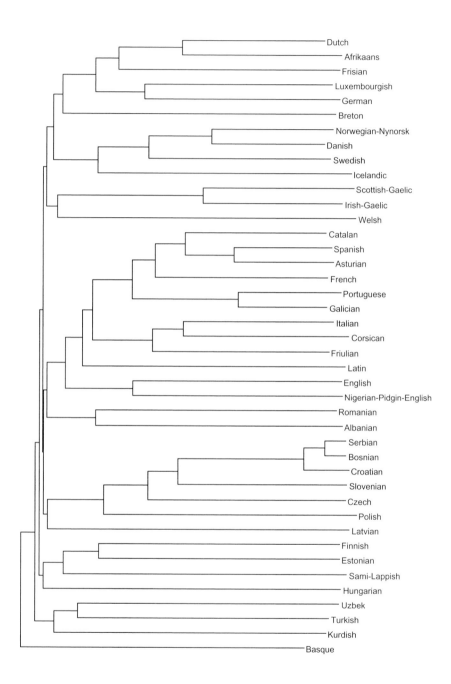

FIGURE 1.2: The evolutionary rooted tree built using a 4-spectrum kernel and the Neighbor Joining algorithm.

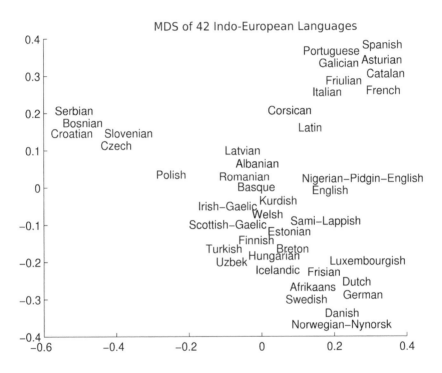

FIGURE 1.3: Multi-dimensional scaling using a 4-spectrum kernel distance matrix.

In this example, we have shown that kernel methods are capable to reveal useful and complex information in linguistics data. Besides, what we have presented here may be regarded as an exposition of the versatility of kernel methods.

1.5   Conclusion and Further Reading

Kernel Methods and Pattern Analysis can be considered two of the most important topics in machine learning in the last few years. Their adaptability and modularity has produced a variety of kernels and algorithms in a number of different topic areas. In particular, well known algorithms have been modified into a kernel version. Thousands of papers have already been published in this field, and accessing the primary literature is becoming increasingly a daunting task. Comprehensive introductions to the field have appeared, particularly the textbooks (27), (6), (24), (31). Many websites are also available, with free software and pointers to recent publications in the field.

In particular `www.kernel-methods.net` and `www.support-vector.net` contain free material, whereas `www.kernel-machines.org` contains updated pointers to all main events in the kernel methods community.

The field of Kernel Methods is a crucial part of modern Pattern Analysis, and a great deal of active research is devoted to do it.

Acknowledgment   Marco Turchi is supported by the EU Project SMART.

References

[1] F. R. Bach and M. I. Jordan. Kernel independent component analysis. *Journal of Machine Learning Research*, 3:1–48, 2002.

[2] D. Benedetto, E. Caglioti, and V. Loreto. Language trees and zipping. *Physical Review Letters*, 88(4), January 2002.

[3] T. De Bie, N. Cristianini, and R. Rosipal. Eigenproblems in pattern recognition. In E. Bayro-Corrochano, editor, *Handbook of Computational Geometry for Pattern Recognition, Computer Vision, Neurocomputing and Robotics*. Springer-Verlag, 2004.

[4] B. E. Boser, I. M. Guyon, and V. N. Vapnik. A training algorithm for optimal margin classifiers. In *COLT '92: Proceedings of the Fifth*

Annual Workshop on Computational Learning Theory, pages 144–152, New York, NY, USA, 1992. ACM.

[5] M. Bresco, M. Turchi, T. Bie, and N. Cristianini. Modeling sequence evolution with kernel methods. *Comput. Optim. Appl.*, 38(2):281–298, 2007.

[6] N. Cristianini and J. Shawe-Taylor. *An Introduction to Support Vector Machines.* Cambridge University Press, Cambridge, U.K., 2000.

[7] S. C. Deerwester, S. T. Dumais, T. K. Landauer, G. W. Furnas, and R. A. Harshman. Indexing by latent semantic analysis. *Journal of the American Society of Information Science*, 41(6):391–407, 1990.

[8] R. Fano. *Transmission of Information: A Statistical Theory of Communications.* MIT Press, Cambridge, 1961.

[9] C. Fellbaum. *WordNet: An Electronic Lexical Database.* MIT Press, 1998.

[10] T. Jaakkola, M. Diekhans, and D. Haussler. Using the fisher kernel method to detect remote protein homologies. In *Proceedings of the Seventh International Conference on Intelligent Systems for Molecular Biology (ISMB99)*, 1999.

[11] K. S. Jones. A statistical interpretation of term specificity and its application in retrieval. *Journal of Documentation*, (28:1):1–21, 1972.

[12] H. Kashima, K. Tsuda, and A. Inokuchi. Kernel methods in computational biology. In B. Schoelkopf, K. Tsuda, and J.P. Vert, editors, *Handbook of Computational Geometry for Pattern Recognition.* Springer-Verlag, 2004.

[13] R. I. Kondor and J. Lafferty. Diffusion kernels on graphs and other discrete structures. In *Proceedings of the International Conference on Machine Learning (ICML02)*, pages 315–322, 2002.

[14] J. B. Kruskal and M. Wish. *Multidimensional Scaling.* Sage Publications, Beverly Hills, CA, 1978.

[15] C. S. Leslie, E. Eskin, and W. S. Noble. The spectrum kernel: A string kernel for svm protein classification. In *Pacific Symposium on Biocomputing*, pages 566–575, 2002.

[16] C. S. Leslie, E. Eskin, J. Weston, and W. S. Noble. Mismatch string kernels for svm protein classification. In K. Obermayer, S. Becker, S. Thrun, editor, *NIPS 2002*, volume 15, pages 1441 – 1448, Cambridge, MA, USA, 2003. MIT Press.

[17] C. S. Leslie and R. Kuang. Fast kernels for inexact string matching. In *Conference on Learning Theory and Kernel Workshop (COLT03)*, pages 114–128, 2003.

[18] S. Mika, G. Ratsch, J. Weston, B. Scholkopf, and K. R. Muller. Fisher discriminant analysis with kernels. In *Proceedings of IEEE Neural Networks for Signal Processing Workshop 1999*, pages 41–48, 1999.

[19] A. Y. Ng, M. I. Jordan, and Y. Weiss. On spectral clustering: Analysis and an algorithm. In *Advances in Neural Information Processing Systems 14 (NIPS01)*, pages 849–856, 2002.

[20] United Nations General Assembly resolution 217 A (III). Universal declaration of human rights. *http://www.unhchr.ch/udhr/navigate/ alpha.htm*, December 1948.

[21] F. Rosenblatt. The perceptron: a probabilistic model for information storage and organization in the brain. *Psychological Review*, 65(6):386–408, 1958.

[22] N. Saitou and M. Nei. The neighbor joining method: A new method for recostructing phylogenetic trees. *Molecular Biology and Evolution, 1987*, (4):406–425, 1987.

[23] G. Salton, A. Wong, and C. S. Yang. A vector space model for automatic indexing. *Commun. ACM*, 18(11):613–620, 1975.

[24] B. Schölkopf and A. Smola. *Learning with Kernels*. MIT Press, Cambridge, MA, 2002.

[25] B. Schölkopf, A. Smola, and K. R. Müller. Nonlinear component analysis as a kernel eigenvalue problem. *Neural Computation*, 10:1299–1319, 1998.

[26] C. E. Shannon. Prediction and entropy of printed English. *Bell Systems Technical Journal*, (30):50–64, 1951.

[27] J. Shawe-Taylor and N. Cristianini. *Kernel Methods for Pattern Analysis*. Cambridge University Press, Cambridge, U.K., 2004.

[28] A. J. Studier and K. J. Keppler. A note on the neighbor joining algorithm of saitou and nei. *Molecular Biology and Evolution*, (5):729–731, 1988.

[29] D. M. J. Tax and R. P. W. Duin. Support vector domain description. *Pattern Recognition Letters*, 20(11-13):1191–1199, 1999.

[30] K. Tsuda, M. Kawanabe, G. Ratsch, S. Sonnenburg, and K. R. Mller. A new discriminative kernel from probabilistic models. *Neural Computation*, 14(10):2397–2414, 2002.

[31] V. N. Vapnik. *Statistical Learning Theory*. Wiley-Interscience, New York, 2nd edition, 1999.

[32] J. P. Vert and M. Kanehisa. Graph-driven features extraction from microarray data using diffusion kernels and kernel CCA. In *Advances in*

Neural Information Processing Systems 15 (NIPS02), pages 1425–1432, 2003.

[33] A. Vinokourov, J. Shawe-Taylor, and N. Cristianini. Inferring a semantic representation of text via cross-language correlation analysis. In *Advances in Neural Information Processing Systems 15*, pages 1473–1480. MIT Press, 2002.

Chapter 2

Detection of Bias in Media Outlets with Statistical Learning Methods

Blaz Fortuna, Carolina Galleguillos, and Nello Cristianini

2.1   Introduction

The international media system plays a crucial role both in reflecting public opinion and events, and in shaping them. Understanding the workings of this complex system is of crucial importance for society, business and democracy, and is one of the research foci of media analysts, anthropologists, and increasingly also of computer scientists.

The traditional way in which the contents of the media system are analyzed has been by human analysts reading each news item, filling a pre-designed questionnaire in the process. This phase of the analysis is termed 'coding.' The questions addressed often have some subjective component, such as the detection of opinions, emphasis, or perspectives. Great care is paid in the design phase of the questionnaire, to make the coding phase as objective as possible. One key limitation of this approach, of course, is that it is very labor intensive, and hence it cannot be scaled up to a global / constant monitoring of the entire system. Indeed, the systems perspective of this analysis cannot be pursued, as long as only small portions of the system can be analyzed at each given time.

Recently, significant attention has been paid to various aspects of text analysis that have relevance to the task of automating media content analysis. Opinion analysis, sentiment analysis, topic categorization, have all reached a reliable level of performance, and most of the main outlets have now a free digital version available over the internet. This creates the opportunity to automatize large part of the media-content analysis process.

From the technical point of view, coding by using a questionnaire is akin to what machine learning researchers call "pattern matching": the detection of a pre-fixed property or pattern in a set of data. This is often done by matching keywords in certain positions, in the context of classical content analysis. What is increasingly becoming possible, however, is the transition to "pattern discovery": the detection of interesting properties in the data, that do not belong to a pre-compiled list of properties. In other words, the questionnaire used by human coders could be replaced by statistical patterns discovered by a machine learning algorithm, if high quality annotated data is available.

In this Chapter, we present a case study where subtle biases are detected in the content of four online media outlets: CNN, Al Jazeera (AJ), International Herald Tribune (IHT), Detroit News (DN). We focus on two types of bias, corresponding to two degrees of freedom in the outlets: the choice of stories to cover, and the choice of terms when reporting on a given story. We will show how algorithms from statistical learning theory (and particularly kernel-based methods, in this case) can be combined with ideas from traditional statistics, in order to detect and validate the presence of systematic biases in the content of news outlets.

We will ask the following questions: can we identify which outlet has written a given news-item? If so, after correcting for topic-choice bias, we would be able to claim that patterns in the language are responsible for this identification. Another - orthogonal - question we will address is: which news-items are more likely to be carried by a given outlet? Technically, we address this question by devising a measure of statistical similarity between two outlets, based on how much they overlap in their choice of stories to cover. Finally, we use a technique from cross-language text analysis, to automatically decompose the set of topics covered in our corpus, in order to find the most polarizing topics, that is those topics where term-choice bias is more evident.

This case study will demonstrate the application of Support Vector Machines (SVM), kernel Canonical, Correlation Analysis (kCCA), Multi Dimensional Scaling (MDS), in the context of media content analysis. After reporting the results of our experiments, and their p-values, we will also speculate about possible interpretations of these results. While the first aspect will contain objective information, the interpretation will necessarily be subjective, and we will alert the reader to this fact.

While the emphasis of this Chapter is to demonstrate a new use of Statistical Learning technology, the experimental results are of interest in their own right, and can be summarized as follows: it is possible to identify which news outlet carried a given news item; it is possible to decompose the space of documents into topics, and detect the most polarizing ones; it is possible to recognize which terms contribute the most to the bias; these quantities can also be used to design two independent measures of similarity between news outlets, one capturing their topic-choice bias, the other capturing their term-choice bias. Maps of the media system could be created based on these metrics, and since every step of this analysis has been done automatically, these could scale up to very large sizes.

This Chapter is organized as follows: in the next section we will give an overview of the experiments we performed; in Section 3 we will describe how we obtained and prepared the data, including the method we used to identify news-items covering the same story in different outlets; in Section 4 we will describe the outlet identification experiments using SVMs; in Section 5 we will describe the kCCA experiments to isolate the topics in which polarization is most present; in Section 6 we will show how similarity measures between outlets can be designed based on the previous experiments; and in Section 7 we will discuss the results, and - importantly - various recent results that are closely related to this study, including work on detecting author's perspective based on the contents of a document.

2.2   Overview of the Experiments

An automatic system based on learning algorithms has been used to create a corpus of news-items that appeared in the online versions of the 4 international news outlets between 31st March 2005 and 14th of April 2006. We have performed three experiments on this dataset, aimed at extracting patterns from the news content that relate to a bias in lexical choice when reporting the same events, or a bias in choosing the events to cover.

The first experiment, using Support Vector Machines (4) and limited to CNN and AJ, demonstrates how it is possible to identify the outlet of a news item based on its content, and identifies the terms that are most helpful in this discrimination. The second experiment, using Canonical Correlation Analysis (14), identifies topics in the CNN/AJ part of the corpus, and then identifies words that are discriminative for the two outlets in each topic. Finally, we have generated maps reflecting the distance separating the 4 outlets, based both on topic-choice and on lexical-choice features.

In order to separate the two effects (choice of topics and of lexicon) we developed an algorithm to identify corresponding news-items in different outlets (based on a combination of date and bag-of-words similarity). This means that any patterns in lexical difference we identify are obtained by comparing different versions of the same stories.

For the first two experiments, we constructed a paired corpus of news-items, much like is done in cross-language content analysis, where each pair is formed by one item from AJ and one item from CNN, reporting on the same story. The corpus was created by extracting the text of each story from HTML pages, using a support vector machine, and later it was paired using an algorithm developed for this purpose. The SVM was necessary as we described each portion of text in the HTML page with a set of features, and we needed to classify these feature vectors in order to identify the portion corresponding to the actual content. Starting from 9185 news-items gathered over a period of 13 months in 2005 and 2006 from those two news outlets, 816 pairs were so obtained, most of which turned out to be related to Middle East politics and events.

The first task for the learning algorithm was to identify the outlet where a given news item had appeared, based only on its content. Furthermore, it has been possible to isolate a subset of words that are crucial in informing this decision. These are words that are used in different ways by the two outlets. In other words, the choice of terms is biased in the two outlets, and these keywords are the most polarized ones. This includes a preference for terms such as '*insurgency*,' '*militants*,' ' *terrorists*' in CNN when describing the same stories in which Al Jazeera prefers using the words '*resistance*,' '*fighters*,' and '*rebels*.'

For the last set of experiments, involving the generation of Maps, we have used the full corpus. Obtained with the same techniques and for the same time interval, it contains 21552 news items: 2142 for AJ, 6840 for CNN, 2929 for DN, and 9641 for IHT. The two news outlets with more regional focus (AJ and DN) have the smallest set of news, as well as having the smallest intersection, resulting in few stories being covered by all 4 newspapers. Most stories that were covered by all four news outlets were mostly Middle East related.

2.3   Data Collection and Preparation

The dataset used in all three experiments was gathered between March 31st 2005 and April 14th 2006 from the websites of AJ, CNN, DN, and IHT. A subset of matching item-pairs was then identified for each pair of news outlets. The acquisition and the matching algorithms are described below. For CNN and Al Jazeera 816 pairs were determined to be matching, and used in the first two experiments. Not surprisingly, these referred mostly to Middle East events.

2.3.1 Article Extraction from HTML Pages

We implemented a system to automatically retrieve every day news items from different news outlets of the web. Some work was done to automatically recognize the content within the HTML page. This was also based on the use of SVMs, in order to create a general-purpose extractor that can work with any outlet, but will not be described here in much detail, due to space limitations.

By using a crawler every day for more than 1 year over the 4 outlets mentioned above, and extracting titles and contents from the HTML pages, we obtained a total of more than 21000 news items, most of which are about Middle East politics and events. For each news item its outlet, date, title, and content are known. The table below gives a precise description of the corpus we created. Further filtering of the news stories will be achieved at a later stage, since the matching algorithm will discard all the news items that cannot be paired reliably.

TABLE 2.1: Number of news items collected from different outlets.

outlet	No. of news
Al Jazeera	2142
CNN	6840
Detroit News	2929
International Herald Tribune	9641

The news collection on which we performed the first part of our analysis consisted of just two outlets, Al Jazeera and CNN, while in the second part of our experiments we use all four news outlets for constructing a map of outlets based on topic similarity and a map based on vocabulary bias.

2.3.2 Data Preparation

The 21552 documents generated by the algorithm described above are purely text files. As part of data preparation we removed stop words and replaced the rest of the words with their appropriate stems. We used a list of 523 stop words and porter stemmer. After the initial cleaning we extracted a list of words, bigrams, and trigrams (or *terms* in short) that appear at least five times in the news collection. We used the extracted list of terms to define the dimensions in the bag-of-words space [see Appendix B]. We also replaced each stemmed word with the most frequent word from the news collection with the same stem, for the purposes of visualization of results at the end of the pipeline.

The implementations of text mining and machine learning algorithms for text preprocessing, Support Vector Machine, Kernel Canonical Correlation Analysis, and Multidimensional scaling which were used in the experiments were all taken from the *Text Garden* (8) software library.

2.3.3   Detection of Matching News Items

We are interested in investigating how different outlets report the same events. To this end, the first step is to identify items from two news outlets, for example Al Jazeera and CNN, that do refer to the same event. We call them "mates," and we call the problem of finding them the "matching problem." Here is an example of two mate articles, the first one is from CNN and the second one is from Al Jazeera:

> UK SOLDIERS CLEARED IN IRAQI DEATH – SEVEN BRITISH SOLDIERS WERE ACQUITTED ON THURSDAY OF CHARGES OF BEATING AN INNO-CENT IRAQI TEENAGER TO DEATH WITH RIFLE BUTTS. A JUDGE AT A SPECIALLY CONVENED MILITARY COURT IN EASTERN ENGLAND OR-DERED THE ADJUDICATING PANEL TO RETURN 'NOT GUILTY' VERDICTS AGAINST THE SEVEN BECAUSE HE DID NOT BELIEVE THERE WAS SUF-FICIENT EVIDENCE AGAINST THEM, THE MINISTRY OF DEFENCE SAID. . . .

> BRITISH MURDERERS IN IRAQ ACQUITTED – THE JUDGE AT A COURT-MARTIAL ON THURSDAY DISMISSED MURDER CHARGES AGAINST SEVEN SOLDIERS, FROM THE 3RD BATTALION, THE PARACHUTE REGIMENT, WHO'RE ACCUSED OF MURDERING IRAQI TEENAGER; CLAIMING THERE'S INSUFFICIENT EVIDENCE TO SECURE A CONVICTION, THE ASSOCIATED PRESS REPORTED THURSDAY. . . .

For finding matching news items we used a method similar to what is used in bioinformatics to detect homologous genes: the method called Best Reciprocal Hit (BRH). Two genes are homologous (respectively, two articles are mates) if they belong to different organisms (respectively, news outlets) and are each other's nearest neighbor (in some appropriate similarity metric).

We represented the documents as bags of words, and used the cosine in the resulting vector space representation as the similarity measure. We also relaxed the method somewhat: our algorithm operates on a list of top n nearest-neighbors for each news item. The nearest-neighbors for a particular news item are only selected from the opposite news outlet and within a 15 days time window around the news item. If two articles appear in each other's nearest-neighbors lists and if they appeared in the news with at most one day difference then the two articles are selected as mates. This ensures that the documents have both word similarity and date similarity (we take advantage of the fact that each news item has an assigned date and use the date to reduce the search space for nearest-neighbors and to eliminate false positives from the detected matches).

Note that by using a nearest-neighbor list with $n > 1$, one news article can have multiple mates. For example: let A be an article from outlet 1 and B and C articles from outlet 2 and let $n \geq 2$. If B and C are on the A's nearest-neighbors list and A is on both B and C nearest-neighbor list, than both articles A and B and articles A and C are selected as mates.

The result is a small subset of news items for each outlet for which we are reasonably sure there is a matching item in the other news outlet. Of course, by tuning the parameter n one can create larger subsets, at the expense of more noise in the matching process. As expected, CNN started with more stories and focuses on more global issues, so only a small fraction of those are present also in Al Jazeera. In turn, Al Jazeera has a more regional focus, and smaller set of news, so a larger fraction of its stories are found to have a mate in CNN.

TABLE 2.2: Number of discovered news pairs and the percentage of the articles from each news outlet that appear in at least in one pair. AJ stands for Al Jazeera.

n	1	2	3	4	5	6	7	8	9	10
pairs	421	816	1101	1326	1506	1676	1865	2012	2169	2339
CNN	6%	9%	13%	14%	16%	17%	18%	19%	20%	21%
AJ	20%	33%	35%	39%	42%	45%	48%	51%	53%	56%

Table 2.2 shows the number of discovered pairs as a function of the parameter n. The last two rows are the percentage of news articles from each of the two outlets that appear in at least one pair. To evaluate the discovered pairs we randomly selected a subset of 100 pairs for $n = 1, 2$ and evaluated them by close inspection. The precision for $n = 1$ was found to be 96% and the precision for $n = 2$ was found to be 86%.

The number of discovered pairs increases significantly by increasing the size of nearest-neighbor list size n. We can use estimated precision to approximate that for $n = 1$ the algorithm found around 400 correct pairs and for $n = 2$ around 700 pairs. From this we can see that by increasing the nearest-neighbor list size to $n = 2$ the precision of discovered pairs drops for 10% but at the same time the recall increases significantly. We can not give an accurate estimate of recall since we do not have a complete list of matchings for out data.

By further increasing the parameter n eventually each news from CNN would be matched with each of the news from Al Jazeera within the time window (15 days). Since we are interested in a large while still accurate set of news article pairs, describing the same event, we will mostly focus on $n = 2$ in the following sections. However, the most important results will be given also for the other values of n.

Another parameter influencing the accuracy of discovered mates is the time window within which the mate search is done. Increase of the time window size also increases the number of candidates for the nearest-neighbor list. This in turn means that in order for two articles being selected as mates they must pass through more strict filters.

We ran the news matching algorithm for different sizes of the time window and the top nearest-neighbor list. The results can be seen in Figure 2.1. From the results we can see that increasing the time window really reduces the number of discovered pairs. Another thing that can be noted from the graph is that the reduction is much more evident when a nearest-neighbor list is large while the reduction hardly affects the smaller nearest-neighbor lists. In the paper we will mostly focus on the case when $n = 2$ and the time window is 15 days. From the graph we can note that further increase of time window for the case of $n = 2$ hardly influences the number of mates which in turn indicates that the selected mates are relatively accurate.

Note finally that this filtering stage is also likely to remove any potential error introduced by the story extraction phase, since it is unlikely that the two outlets would have highly similar text in the navigation menus or banners, that is also time correlated. We have at this point a list of 816 item-pairs collected over 1 year from CNN and Al Jazeera from which we are rather confident

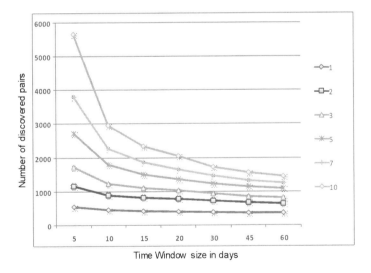

FIGURE 2.1: The window size is on the x axis and the number of discovered mates is on the y axis. The graph number of discovered mates for nearest-neighbor lists of sizes $n = 1, 2, 3, 5, 7, 10$.

that they represent different descriptions of the same events. We will use now various techniques from pattern analysis to extract information about any systematic differences found between the two outlets.

2.4   News Outlet Identification

Given this dataset of 816 pairs of news-items, we can test the hypothesis that each outlet has its own bias in describing the events, which is reflected in the choice of words for the article. We will use Support Vector Machines (SVM) [see Appendix A] to learn a linear classifier capable of identifying the outlet of a news item by just looking at its content. If this is possible in a statistically significant way, then clearly the two documents are distinguishable, or can be modeled as having been generated from a different distribution of probability. Differences between the distributions underlying the two news outlets will be the focus of our investigation.

We trained a SVM with a subset of the data, and tested it on the remaining data. The task of the classifier was to guess if a given news article came from CNN or from Al Jazeera. We used ten-fold cross-validation to evaluate the classifiers. The data were randomly split into 10 folds of equal size and in each turn one fold was held out. A classifier was trained on the remaining 9 folds and then evaluated on the fold that was held out. This was repeated for all 10 folds and the results were averaged over these 10 iterations.

The performance in the task was measured by calculating the break-even-point (BEP) which is a hypothetical point where precision (ratio of positive documents among retrieved ones) and recall (ratio of retrieved positive documents among all positive documents) meet when varying the threshold. Other measures are possible, and can be justified, in this context. Our choice of BEP has advantages when we have imbalanced negative and positive sets, which is the case when we try to assign a news item to a large set of possible outlets, and hence negative examples are more frequent than positive ones.

Before using the 816 pairs that we selected by the matching process, we decided to try by using the *whole* set of 9185 CNN and Al Jazeera news articles, and used ten-fold cross-validation to evaluate the linear SVM classifier trained on the set.

We obtained 91% BEP, a very high score showing that indeed it is very easy to separate the two outlets. This high score can be expected since CNN and AJ cover different topics (e.g., covers the whole world while Al Jazeera mostly focuses on the topics regarding the Middle East). This means that the outlet of an item can be more easily identified as the result of its topic. In order to isolate the effect of term-choice bias, we will have to restrict our analysis only to comparable news-items: those 816 news items that have been matched by the algorithm described above.

The top 20 most important words for determining the outlet, when using the full corpus, are:

> KEYWORDS FOR CNN: ap, insurgency, militants, national, police, troops, china, vote, terrorists, authorities, united, united state, percent, million, protests, suicide, years, allegations, program, day

> KEYWORDS FOR AL JAZEERA: iraq, israel, iraqis, israeli, occupation, americans, nuclear, aljazeera, palestinians, resistance, claim, withdraw, attacks, guantanamo, mr, gaza stripped, war, shia, stripped, iranian

From the keywords we can see that the topics about the Middle East (*'iraq,'* *'israel,'* *'gaza'*) are more significant for Al Jazeera while business (*'percent,'* *'million,'*) elections (*'vote'*), and topics about other parts of the world (*'china'*) are more significant for CNN. We can also see some difference in the vocabulary, for example *'insurgency,'* *'militants,'* and *'terrorists'* versus *'resistances.'*

These keywords are the result of using the full corpus. As mentioned above, we want to isolate the effect due to lexical bias to the effect due to topic bias, by focussing only on those stories that are covered by both outlets.

For this new comparison of the two news outlets we used the set of news pairs which we obtained automatically with the news matching algorithm. Finding a correct news outlet for these articles is now a much harder task since we remove any clues due to topic-choice, and we force the system to rely solely on term-choice bias for distinguishing the two outlets. If we can train a classifier which is better than random, then we can confidently state that there is a significant and consistent difference in the vocabulary used by the news outlets.

Results for ten-fold cross-validation on the news pairs are given in Table 2.3 and 2.4. We can see that the BEP slowly increases to 87% when n increases and decreases to 79% when time window increases. This matches our observations from previous section that increasing n also increases noise in the data while increasing window size decreases noise.

TABLE 2.3: Results for outlet identification of a news item, using different sizes of nearest-neighbor list. Time windows size is fixed to 15 days.

n	1	2	3	4	5	6	7	8	9	10
BEP	73%	81%	84%	84%	85%	85%	85%	86%	87%	87%

The high result for low values of n and large sizes of time window indicates that there is a bias in the choice of vocabulary used by the two news outlets when covering the same events. To assess the significance of the results from

TABLE 2.4:   Results for news outlet identification of a news item from the set of news item pairs for different sizes of time window. Nearest-neighbor list size is fixed to 2.

window size	5	10	15	20	30	45	60
BEP	85%	83%	81%	81%	80%	79%	79%

Table 2.3 we compared them against results obtained on randomly mixed news article pairs (where the distinction between outlets was effectively removed). The randomized pair sets were obtained by taking each pair of news articles and swapping their outlets with probability 0.5. This generated a set where each story pair was the same as before, but the ordering of the pair was essentially random.

The permutation test was run on 300 random sets for $n = 1, \ldots, 10$ and it never returned a result better than the one from Table 2.3. For a sample distribution of BEP obtained on 300 random sets for $n = 2$ see Figure 2.2. Comparing outlet identification results against random runs gives us a p-value of 0.3% and therefore it is very unlikely that the outlet identification results would be due to chance since they need to reflect a true distinction in the distribution of probability over words associated to each news outlet. This, as we already argued before, indicates that there is a significant bias in the vocabulary that Al Jazeera or CNN use to describe the same events.

To put some light on the vocabulary bias we extracted the most important words from the linear SVM classifier for $n = 2$. These are the words associated with the largest coefficient of the primal weight vector w of the SVM, and hence the terms that mostly affect the decision made by the classifier. We obtain the following two lists:

> KEYWORDS FOR CNN: insurgency, militants, troops, hussein, iran, baghdad, united, terrorists, police, united state, suicide, program, al qaeda, national, watching, qaeda, baghdad iraq, wounded, palestinians, al

> KEYWORDS FOR AL JAZEERA: iraq, attacks, army, shia, occupation, withdraw, demanded, americans, claim, mr, nuclear, muslim, saddam, resistance, agency, fighters, rebels, iraqis, foreign, correspondent

While the experimental findings above are significant and reproducible, we believe it can also be useful to attempt an interpretation of these figures, based on an inspection of the specific terms isolated by this analysis. This is of course based on a subjective analysis of our objective results. Comparing the lists we can notice that CNN is more inclined to use words like '*insurgency*,' '*militants*,' '*terrorists*' when describing Iraqis, that might be argued to have negative connotation. On the other hand, Al Jazeera seems more likely to use words like '*resistance*,' '*fighters*,' and '*rebels*' when describing the same events.

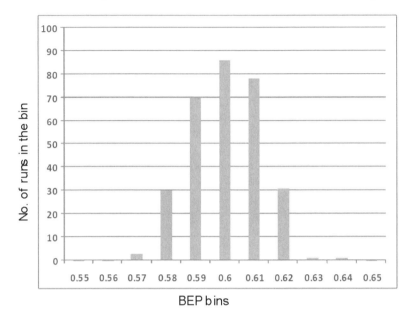

FIGURE 2.2: Distribution of BEP for 300 random sets.

We can also see that CNN uses terrorist related words such as '*al-qaeda*' or '*suicide*' more often than Al Jazeera. Al Jazeera apparently focuses more on '*withdraw.*' There is also an interesting observation that the word '*Hussein*' is more characteristic for CNN while the word '*Saddam*' is more characteristic for Al Jazeera. Both words refer to the same person.

2.5   Topic-Wise Comparison of Term Bias

Using a method borrowed from statistical cross-language analysis, we can compare the data generated by the two news outlets as if it was written in different languages. Kernel Canonical Correlation Analysis (kCCA) [see Appendix C] (14) is a method for correlating two multidimensional random variables, that is how our documents are modelled in the vector space approach. It has been used to analyze bilingual corpora, extracting both topics from the corpora and semantically related pairs of words in the two languages (15) (7). We are interested in discovering if there are specific term-choice biases in certain topics, but we want to discover these topics automatically.

In our experiments we used the set of news pairs obtained with $n = 2$ as a paired dataset for kCCA. Both news outlets use the same language so we could use the same bag-of-words space for each view. The output of kCCA is a set of pairs of vectors along which the news article pairs are highly correlated. Each pair of vectors corresponds to one of the topics from the news collection; this can be observed by checking the most important keywords in the vectors.

For each pair of vectors we took Al Jazeera vector and subtracted it from the CNN vector. We then sorted the words according to the weight they had in this vector. If the word had a highly positive weight, then it was more biased towards CNN and vice versa. Again, this is a way to compare specific differences between the two distributions of probabilities underlying the generation of words in CNN and Al Jazeera.

From each pair of vectors we also composed a set of outlet-independent main keywords describing that topic. This was done by taking the union of the top 5 keywords from each of the two vectors.

In Table 2.5 we present a list of the top 10 topics discovered by kCCA. For each topic there is a set of keywords that describe the topic and a set of topic related keywords specific for CNN and Al Jazeera.

The difference in vocabulary that can be seen from the Table 2.5 is similar to the one we already discovered in the previous section, using the support vector machine. This is of course encouraging, as it suggests we detected a real signal in the data. An important advantage of analysis based on kCCA is that it adds a crucial extra piece of information: namely how the lexical bias is dependent on the topics being discussed. kCCA automatically identifies the main topics, and for each topic the lexical bias between outlets discussing it. Notice that the 'topics' identified by kCCA (or by any other factor analysis method) do not need to correspond to topics that are meaningful in the human sense, although they often are. Attributing a human-topic to a coherent set of keywords found by kCCA analysis involves some amount of interpretation of results, and so it can be considered as a subjective step. However it has to be noticed that - while we do attempt to interpret the topics found by kCCA - this is not necessary for any step of the analysis.

The topics common to AJ and CNN, as separated by CCA analysis, seem to be fairly coherent and cover essentially all the key issues in the Middle East in 2005 (although some topics are a little less focused) - [see Table 2.5]: 1) Iran's nuclear program; 2) Iraq's insurgency; 3) Palestinian question and Gaza; 4) Iran's nuclear program; 5) Iraq and Palestine; 6) Lebanon and Syria; 7) Afghanistan, Guantanamo, Pakistan; 8) Iraq and Saddam's trial; 9) Human right abuses; 10) Sharm el Sheik's terror attack.

The table gives an idea of the main differences in lexicon used to report on the same events, between AJ and CNN. A good example is perhaps Topic 3, where CNN mentions more often words like 'militants,' 'missiles,' 'launch' while AJ mentions more often words like 'settlers,' 'barriers,' 'farms,' and 'suffer,' suggesting a difference in focus.

TABLE 2.5: Main topics covered by the news pairs and keywords characteristic for CNN or Al Jazeera.

TOPIC	Iran, nuclear, Palestinian, Israel, Gaza, EU, enrichment, IAEA
CNN	EU, Iran, Rice, militant, Aceh, diplomats, monitoring, encouraging
AJ	resume, Rafsanjani, research, atomic, Russian, sanctions, reference
TOPIC	Iraq, Baghdad, Hussein, Shiite, trials, insurgents, troops
CNN	insurgents, Hussein, attorney, Kember, family, British
AJ	shia, Sunnis, occupation, Saddam, rebels, attack, killed, car
TOPIC	Palestinian, Gaza, Israel, Sharon, Hamas, Abbas, militant
CNN	militant, Israel, pullout, missiles, launch, Putin, Beirut, jews
AJ	settlers, Hamas, barriers, Israeli, clashes, Hezbollah, farms, suffer
TOPIC	Iran, nuclear, enrichment, IAEA, program, uranium, EU, council
CNN	EU, Aceh, offered, monitoring, Iran, united, Bush, Britain, mission
AJ	Tehran, resume, research, atomic, Rafsanjani, Ahmadinejad, reference
TOPIC	Iraqi, Palestinian, Baghdad, Iran, Gaza, nuclear, shiite, Hamas
CNN	militant, insurgents, terrorists, forces, cross, outlet, Hussein
AJ	shia, Israeli, fighters, Sunnis, squad, farms, occupation, gunmen
TOPIC	Lebanon, Syria, Hariri, assassination, beirut, opposition
CNN	Rafik, cooperation, son, rice, Hezbollah, Syria, Hussam, form
AJ	Lebanese, Rafiq, Christian, opposition, Aoun, Baath, assassination
TOPIC	Afghanistan, London, Pakistan, Egyptian, Muslim, Guantanamo
CNN	Reuters, Taliban, friends, helicopter, investigate, Quran
AJ	Zarqawi, Zawahri, village, Sharm, channel, Pakistani, rocket
TOPIC	Baghdad, Iraq, Saddam, Sunnis, Shiite, trials, Sharon, vote
CNN	Hussein, insurgents, Baquba, troops, attorney, turnout, rocket
AJ	shia, Mosul, marine, interior, raids, Olmert, violence, toppled
TOPIC	prisoners, Guantanamo, detainees, Saddam, court, judge, torture
CNN	Hussein, detainees, camp, Ghraib, bay, prisoners, witnessed, Quran
AJ	judge, Pentagon, mr, detention, responsibility, refuses, holy
TOPIC	bombs, attack, police, blasts, killed, Egyptian, Sharm, explosion
CNN	insurgents, Aziz, suicide, Jordanian, kilometers, helicopter
AJ	toll, striking, Romanian, town, fighters, hit, army, ambassador

2.6 News Outlets Map

In the second set of experiments we used all four news outlets: Al Jazeera (AJ), CNN, Detroit News (DN), and International Herald Tribune (IHT), gathered in the same time interval.

The goal of this experiment was to represent news outlets as points on a map so that 'similar' news outlets would appear closer to each other on the map than 'not-so-similar' news outlets. We wanted the distance to reflect the bias of the news outlet, either in lexical choices or in the overall choice of topics to cover. This led to two approaches: the first defined a distance based on the lexical choices while the second approach was based on the topics covered. The definitions of these two distances will be given below. Once we obtained the distance scores between two news outlets we used the multi-dimensional scaling (MDS) [see Appendix D] algorithm to calculate the map with the optimal positions of the news outlets.

Like in Section 2.4, we ran the matching algorithm on all news outlet pairs. The time window size was 15 days and the size of the nearest-neighbor list was 2. The following table shows the number of discovered pairs:

TABLE 2.6:   Number of discovered pairs.

	AJ	CNN	DN	IHT
AJ	–	816	447	834
CNN	816	–	1103	2437
DN	447	1103	–	895
IHT	834	2437	895	–

The intersection that we find between the various outlet pairs varies considerably. This can be better seen by calculating the conditional probability of a story appearing in an outlet given that it appears in another one, reported in the following table. For example, we can note that more AJ stories feature in CNN than vice versa ($P(AJ|CNN) = 0.1193$ while $P(CNN|AJ) = 0.3810$), which is perhaps explained by the regional focus of one outlet and the global focus of the other. Similar relations apply - for example - to the relation between DN and CNN, or IHT.

TABLE 2.7:   Conditional probabilities of a story from one news outlet appearing in another outlet.

$P(X|Y)$	AJ	CNN	DN	IHT
AJ	1.0000	0.3810	0.2087	0.3894
CNN	0.1193	1.0000	0.1613	0.3563
DN	0.1526	0.3766	1.0000	0.3056
IHT	0.0865	0.2528	0.0928	1.0000

For the purpose of comparing the vocabulary of news outlets we extracted the news events which were covered by all four news outlets. We did that by taking all the news articles that have mates in all other news outlets. The number of news taken from each outlet can be found in Table 2.8.

Note that the number of news articles differs slightly between news outlets with IHT having the largest number of articles and Detroit News the lowest.

TABLE 2.8:   Number of news articles covered by all four news outlets.

outlet	No. of news
Al Jazeera	170
CNN	169
Detroit News	161
International Herald Tribune	175

This happens because a news article from one news outlet can have two mates from an opposite news outlet since the size of the nearest-neighbor list was set to two.

From the upper table we can speculate that IHT covered events with more news articles than other news outlets or that for example Detroit News had more 'digestive' news articles where one article covers more events which other outlets covered in separate articles (this might also confuse the matching algorithm, of course).

2.6.1   Distance Based on Lexical Choices

Our first approach for calculating the distance was based on the difference in lexicon when reporting on the same events. In this part of the experiment we only used the portion of news articles talking about events which were covered by all four news outlets. For each pair of news outlets we trained and evaluated a SVM classifier on the discovered pairs of stories and averaged the BEP using ten-fold cross-validation (the setup used here was exactly the same as in Section 2.3). We used the average BEP between news outlets to define the distance.

Break-even point (BEP) reflects the separability between two classes, or how easy it is to distinguish the news outlets based on the lexical content of their news items. We use it as a distance measure between news outlets, so that nearby outlets are those harder to distinguish based on lexical bias. This allowed us to draw a map based on this distance, shown in Figure 2.3. Note that Al Jazeera is distant from the 3 US-based outlets, and this cannot be attributed to its regional focus. As a matter of fact, the comparison was done only on events reported by all four outlets, so this map shows the (perhaps not surprising) fact the AJ has a rather different perspective on those same events than the other 3 outlets examined here.

The table below shows the distances obtained for each pair of outlets, and the Figure 2.3 shows the same information as a map.

TABLE 2.9: BEP metric distances.

	AJ	CNN	DN	IHT
AJ	–	0.6165	0.6709	0.6852
CNN	0.6165	–	0.5682	0.5735
DN	0.6709	0.5682	–	0.4663
IHT	0.6852	0.5735	0.4663	–

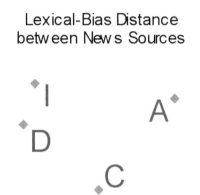

Lexical-Bias Distance between News Sources

FIGURE 2.3: This plot shows the relative distance between news outlets, using the BEP metric described in the text.

2.6.2 Distance Based on Choice of Topics

The second approach for calculating the distance was based on the intersection of topics which were covered by each of the news outlets. To discover these intersections we described each news outlet by a vector of binary features where each feature corresponds to one news article from our collection. A feature in the vector of a news outlet has value 1 if the article corresponding to that feature originates from the news outlet or if the article is a mate of an article from the news outlet. Otherwise the value of the feature is 0. We then used the cosine similarity to calculate the similarity between the vectors.

The effect of such representation is that we effectively compare two news outlets based on their choice of which events to cover. If news outlets A and B both covered the same event then there is a news article a_1 from A and b_1 from B which both covered that event. If our matching algorithm discovered that these two articles are mates, then both news outlets A and B will have a value of 1 for the features corresponding to the a_1 and b_1 and therefore will be more similar. If there is a news outlet C which also covered the event with article c_1 and our algorithm only managed to discover that c_1 is a mate with b_1, then this approach will still manage to match news outlets A and C on this event since they both have mate articles to the article b_1. However, the score of matching will be lower than between A and B or B and C. Results of the mapping based on this distance can be seen in Figure 2.4.

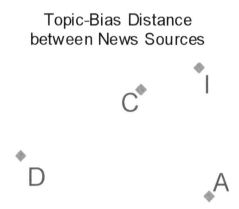

FIGURE 2.4: This plot shows the relative distance between news outlets, using the topic similarity described in the text.

Again, here Al Jazeera is distant from the others. A possible interpretation could be that this reflects the effect of regional focus.

2.7   Related Work

In recent years there has been significant attention to various problems of text analysis that are related to the ones discussed here. Three papers appearing in 2006 (roughly at the same time in which the experiments reported here were under way) are worth mentioning, as they have both significant connections and interesting differences.

The articles (10) and (11), partly involving the same authors, focus on the concept of 'perspective' from which an article is written. In the first article, the authors use a dataset created using the "bitterlemons" website: a debate website set up to contribute to mutual understanding between Palestinians and Israelis by publishing two views of each topic.

In the second article, two of the same authors analyze the same 'bitterlemons' dataset as well as another dataset, formed by "transcripts of the three Bush-Kerry presidential debates in 2004, provided by the Commission on Presidential Debates. Each document is roughly an answer to a question or a rebuttal."

One elegant feature of these studies is that by construction the two datasets are already paired, and the two elements of each pair are definitely written by authors adopting different perspectives. This makes the signal stronger and the analysis very interesting. In both cases, it is found that statistical learning algorithms (both generative models, and discriminative models) can be used to identify the perspective from which an article has been written.

By contrast, in our study we have a somewhat opposite situation. Not only the articles are not naturally paired, but they are also not on a specific topic (as those in bitterlemons), or written by a specific author (as in the case of presidential debates). Furthermore there is no obvious reason to assume that any two news outlets should show a measurable bias in their choice of terms, when reporting on the same events. This makes the signal much harder to isolate, and indeed the automatic identification of topics by using kCCA is very helpful in showing the most biased topics. From a methodological point of view, our use of concepts from machine translation and cross-language retrieval can provide a complementary position to the methods purely based on text categorization that have been so far proposed.

Somewhat related to the above is also the paper (12) where the task involved is to analyze the transcripts of U.S. Congressional floor debates to determine whether the speeches represent support of or opposition to proposed legislation. Rather than paired documents, here we just have labelled documents, but the label somehow relates to the attitude of the speaker. This is again cast as a text categorization task, where the authors use SVM classifiers, again showing that statistical discrimination algorithms can capture the subtle signals contained in the choice of words and relating opinion.

A more indirect relation to this theme can also be found within the growing literature on sentiment analysis, or opinion analysis, where the author's attitude towards a topic or a product is extracted. In these studies, it is typically the presence of specific key-words that is used to determine the attitude of the writer towards a certain issue. Projecting documents onto a subspace spanned by polarized words may be a way to simplify and direct the search for lexical bias in news outlets.

Author identification literature is also indirectly related, as in our experiments we establish the presence of a lexical or stylistic bias by identifying the outlet (author) based on a text.

2.8 Conclusion

We have presented a fully automatic method for the analysis of term-choice bias in media outlets, using state of the art technology in information extraction and pattern analysis. Our automated analysis has uncovered the existence of a statistically significant lexical difference between CNN and Al

Jazeera in the way they report the same events. Although this finding is far from surprising, the fact that it could be done in an automatic way by using statistical learning algorithms has many implications: a large scale implementation of this system could easily be used to monitor a large number of news outlets, and perhaps cluster them according to their similarity in topic / term biases. This in turn could help us to identify different accounts of the same story, that is accounts coming from news outlets that have a significantly different bias. Having access to different versions of the same story is of course a valuable opportunity, as it can help us to form an opinion as independent as possible about current events. Then we have also presented a method to compute distances between media outlets, based on their term-choice and topic-choice biases.

Recent related work, discussed above, points in the same direction. The detection of different political perspectives in authors, groups, or speakers has attracted significant attention of the NLP community, and is also partly related to the task of opinion analysis. Its large scale application to media analysis can truly change that field of scholarship.

Despite the small scale of this case study, we feel that modern AI technology has an important role to play in media content analysis, as well as in the social sciences. When scaled up to include hundreds or thousands of media outlets, a goal easily achievable also with standard equipment, these methods can lead to informative maps showing the relation between media outlets based on the analysis of statistical patterns in their content.

References

[1] Aljazeera News, http://english.aljazeera.net/

[2] Brank, J., Grobelnik, M., Milic-Frayling, N., and Mladenic, D. *Feature selection using support vector machines*. Proc. of the Third International Conference on Data Mining Methods and Databases for Engineering, Finance, and Other Fields, 2002.

[3] CNN News, http://www.cnn.com

[4] Cristianini, N. and Shawe-Taylor, J. *An Introduction to Support Vector Machines and Other Kernel-Based Learning Methods*. Cambridge University Press, 2000.

[5] Detroit News, http://www.detroitnews.com

[6] Fortuna, B., Grobelnik, M., and Mladeni, D. *Visualization of Text Document Corpus*. Informatica 29 (2005), 497–502.

[7] Fortuna, B., Cristianini, N., and Shawe-Taylor, J. *A Kernel Canonical Correlation Analysis For Learning The Semantics Of Text.* Kernel methods in bioengineering, communications and image processing, edited by G. Camps-Valls, J. L. Rojo-Alvarez & M. Martinez-Ramn.

[8] Grobelnik, M. and Mladenic., D. *Text Mining Recipes.* Springer-Verlag, Berlin; Heidelberg; New York (to appear), 2006 (accompanying software available at `http://www.textmining.net`).

[9] International Herald Tribune, http://www.iht.com

[10] Lin, W.-H., Wilson, T., Wiebe, J., and Hauptmann, A. *Which Side are You on? Identifying Perspectives at the Document and Sentence Levels,* Proceedings of the Tenth Conference on Computational Natural Language Learning (CoNLL-2006), 2006.

[11] Lin, W.-H. and Hauptmann, A. *Are These Documents Written from Different Perspectives? A Test of Different Perspectives Based on Statistical Distribution Divergence,* Proceedings of the 21st International Conference on Computational Linguistics and 44th Annual Meeting of the Association for Computational Linguistics, 2006.

[12] Thomas, M., Pang, B., and Lee, L. *Get out the vote: Determining support or opposition from Congressional floor-debate transcripts* Proceedings of EMNLP, 2006.

[13] Joachims, T. *Text categorization with support vector machines: learning with many relevant features.* In Claire Nédellec & Céline Rouveirol, editors, Proceedings of ECML-98, 10th European Conference on Machine Learning, numéro 1398 in Lecture Notes in Computer Science, pages 137–142, Chemnitz, DE, 1998. Springer Verlag, Heidelberg, DE.

[14] Shawe-Taylor, J. and Cristianini, N. *Kernel Methods for Pattern Analysis.* Cambridge University Press, 2004.

[15] Vinokourov, A., Shawe-Taylor, J., and Cristianini, N. *Inferring a semantic representation of text via cross-language correlation analysis.* Advances of Neural Information Processing Systems 15, 2002.

Acknowledgments

Part of the infrastrucure was developed with a grant from Fair Isaac Co. and UC Davis. Blaz Fortuna was partly supported by the Slovenian Research Agency and the IST Programme of the European Community under SEKT

Semantically Enabled Knowledge Technologies (IST-1-506826-IP) and PASCAL Network of Excellence (IST-2002-506778). This publication only reflects the authors' views.

2.9   Appendix A: Support Vector Machines

Support vector machine is a family of algorithms that has gained a wide recognition in the recent years as one of the state-of-the-art machine learning algorithms for tasks such as classification, regression, etc. In the basic formulation they try to separate two sets of training examples by hyperplane that maximizes the margin (distance between the hyperplane and the closest points). In addition one usually permits few training examples to be misclassified; this is know as the soft-margin SVM. The linear SVM is known to be one of the best performing methods for text categorization, e.g., in (2).

The linear SVM model can also be used for feature selection. In (13), the hyperplane's normal vector is used for ranking the features. In this paper we use this approach to find which features (in our case words) are the most important for a news article being classified in to one of the two outlets.

2.10   Appendix B: Bag of Words and Vector Space Models

The classic representation of a text document in Information Retrieval is as Bag of Words (a bag is a set where repetitions are allowed), also known as Vector Space Model, since a bag can be represented as a (column) vector recording the number of occurrences of each word of the dictionary in the document at hand.

A document is represented, in the vector-space model, by a vertical vector $\mathbf{d}$ indexed by all the elements of the dictionary (i-th element from the vector is the frequency of i-th term in the document TF_i). A corpus is represented by a matrix D, whose columns are indexed by the documents and whose rows are indexed by the terms, $D = (\mathbf{d}_1, \ldots, \mathbf{d}_N)$. We also call the data matrix D the term-document matrix.

Since not all terms are of the same importance for determining similarity between the documents we introduce term weights. A term weight corresponds to the importance of the term for the given corpus and each element from the document vector is multiplied with the respective term weight. The most widely used weighting is called TFIDF weighting.

A IDF weight for term i from the dictionary is defined as $w_i = \log(N/\mathrm{DF}_i)$ where DF_i is the number of documents from the corpora which contain word i. A document's TFIDF vector is a vector with elements: $w_i = \mathrm{TF}_i \log(N/\mathrm{DF}_i)$.

2.11   Appendix C: Kernel Canonical Correlation Analysis

Canonical Correlation Analysis is a method of correlating two multidimensional variables. It makes use of two different views of the same semantic object (e.g., the same text document written in two different languages or news event described by two different news agencies) to extract representation of the semantic.

Input to CCA is a *paired dataset* $S = \{(u_i, v_i); u_i \in U, v_i \in V\}$, where U and V are two different views on the data; each pair contains two views of the same document. The goal of CCA is to find two linear mappings into a common semantic space W from the spaces U and V. All documents from U and V can be mapped into W to obtain a view- or in our case language-independent representation.

The criterion used to choose the mapping is the correlation between the projections of the two views across the training data for each dimension in W. This criterion leads to a generalized eigenvalue problem whose eigenvectors give the desired mappings.

CCA can be kernelized so it can be applied to feature vectors only implicitly available through a kernel function. There is a danger that spurious correlations could be found in high dimensional spaces and so the method has to be regularized by constraining the norms of the projection weight vectors. The kernelized version is called Kernel Canonical Correlation Analysis (KCCA).

2.11.0.0.1   Example   Let the space V be the vector-space model for English and U the vector-space model for French text documents. A paired dataset is then a set of pairs of English documents together with their French translation. The output of KCCA on this dataset is a semantic space where each dimension shares similar English and French meaning. By mapping English or French documents into this space, a language independent-representation is obtained. In this way standard machine learning algorithms can be used on multi-lingual datasets.

2.12   Appendix D: Multidimensional Scaling

Multidimensional Scaling (MDS) is a set of related statistical techniques often used in data visualization for exploring similarities and dissimilarities in data. An MDS algorithm starts with the matrix of item-item similarities and then assigns a location in a low-dimensional space to each item making it suitable for visualization. In this paper we used MDS developed for visualizing textual data presented in (6).

Chapter 3

Collective Classification for Text Classification

Galileo Namata, Prithviraj Sen, Mustafa Bilgic, and Lise Getoor

3.1   Introduction

Text classification, the classification of text documents according to categories or topics, is an important component of any text processing system. There is a large body of work which makes use of content – the words appearing in the documents, the structure of the documents – and external sources to build accurate document classifiers. In addition, there is a growing body of literature on methods which attempt to make use of the link structure among the documents in order to improve document classification performance.

Text documents can be connected together in a variety of ways. The most common link structure is the citation graph: e.g., papers cite other papers and webpages link to other webpages. But links among papers can be constructed from other relationships such as co-author, co-citation, appearance at a conference venue, and others. All of these can be combined together to create a interlinked collection of text documents.

In these cases, we are often not interested in determining the topic of just a single document, but we have a collection of unlabeled (or partially labeled) documents, and we want to correctly infer values for all of the missing labels.

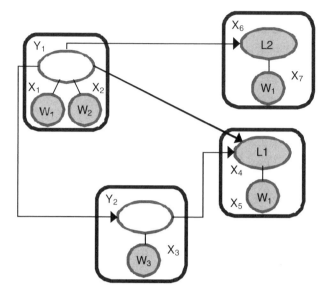

FIGURE 3.1: A small text classification problem. Each box denotes a document, each directed edge between a pair of boxes denotes a hyperlink, and each oval node denotes a random variable. Assume the smaller oval nodes within each box represent the presence of the words, w_1, w_2, and w_3, in the document and the larger oval nodes the label of the document where the set of label values is $\mathcal{L} = \{L1, L2\}$. A shaded oval denotes an observed variable whereas an unshaded oval node denotes an unobserved variable whose value needs to be predicted.

This is straightforward when we consider only document content; the problem is somewhat complicated when we consider the links among the missing labels. In this case, we want to *jointly* or *collectively* optimize the labels, and we refer to the problem as *collective classification*.

Collective classification methods range from simple local influence propagation algorithms to more complex global optimization algorithms. At their heart, they try to model the combined correlations among labels of neighboring documents. Some models assume that neighboring labels are likely to be the same or similar (homophily, or autocorrelation), while others are capable of learning more complex dependencies.

In this chapter, we present several of the common algorithms for collective classification. Our collection of algorithms is not exhaustive, and we are not presenting some of the most advanced algorithms. Instead, we try to provide the reader with a simple tutorial introduction to the methods, with a focus on the algorithms rather than the mathematical justification.

3.2 Collective Classification: Notation and Problem Definition

Collective classification is a combinatorial optimization problem, in which we are given a set of documents, or nodes, $\mathcal{V} = \{V_1, \ldots, V_n\}$ and a neighborhood function $\mathcal{N}$, where $\mathcal{N}_i \subseteq \mathcal{V} \setminus \{V_i\}$, which describes the underlying network structure. Each node in $\mathcal{V}$ is a random variable that can take a value from an appropriate domain. $\mathcal{V}$ is further divided into two sets of nodes: $\mathcal{X}$, the nodes for which we know the correct values (observed variables) and $\mathcal{Y}$, the nodes whose values need to be determined. Our task is to label the nodes $Y_i \in \mathcal{Y}$ with one of a small number of labels, $\mathcal{L} = \{L_1, \ldots, L_q\}$; we'll use the shorthand y_i to denote the label of node Y_i.

We explain the notation further using a document classification example shown in Figure 3.1. In this example, we will use the words (and phrases) contained in the documents as local attributes. Each document is indicated by a box, the corresponding topic of the webpage is indicated by an ellipse inside the box, and each word that appears in the document is represented using a circle inside the box. The observed random variables $\mathcal{X}$ are shaded whereas the unobserved ones $\mathcal{Y}$ are not. We will assume that the domain of the unobserved label variables is $\mathcal{L}$. Figure 3.1 shows a network with two unobserved variables (Y_1 and Y_2), which require prediction, and seven observed variables (X_3, X_4, X_5, X_6, X_7, X_8 and X_9). Note that some of the observed variables happen to be labels of webpages (X_6 and X_8) for which we know the correct values.

As mentioned in the introduction, due to the large body of work done in this area of research, we have a number of approaches for collective classification. At a broad level of abstraction, these approaches can be divided into two distinct types, the first where we use a collection of unnormalized local conditional classifiers and the second, where we define the collective classification problem as one global objective function to be optimized. We next describe these two approaches and, for each approach, we describe two approximate inference algorithms.

3.3 Approximate Inference Algorithms for Approaches Based on Local Conditional Classifiers

Two of the most commonly used approximate inference algorithms following this approach are the *iterative classification algorithm* (ICA) and *Gibbs sampling* (GS), and we next describe these in turn.

Algorithm 1 Iterative classification algorithm

Iterative Classification Algorithm (ICA)

    for each node $Y_i \in \mathcal{Y}$ **do** {bootstrapping}

        {c}ompute label using only observed nodes in $\mathcal{N}_i$

        compute $\vec{a}_i$ using only $\mathcal{X} \cap \mathcal{N}_i$

        $y_i \leftarrow f(\vec{a}_i)$

    repeat {iterative classification}

        generate ordering $\mathcal{O}$ over nodes in $\mathcal{Y}$

        for each node $Y_i \in \mathcal{O}$ **do**

            {c}ompute new estimate of y_i

            compute $\vec{a}_i$ using current assignments to $\mathcal{N}_i$

            $y_i \leftarrow f(\vec{a}_i)$

    until all class labels have stabilized or a threshold number of iterations have elapsed

---

3.3.1   Iterative Classification

The basic premise behind ICA is extremely simple. Consider a node $Y_i \in \mathcal{Y}$ whose value we need to determine and suppose we know the values of all the other nodes in its neighborhood $\mathcal{N}_i$ (note that $\mathcal{N}_i$ can contain both observed and unobserved variables). Then, ICA assumes that we are given a local classifier f that takes the values of $\mathcal{N}_i$ as arguments and returns a label value for Y_i from the class label set $\mathcal{L}$. For local classifiers f that do not return a class label but a goodness/likelihood value given a set of attribute values and a label, we simply choose the label that corresponds to the maximum goodness/likelihood value; in other words, we replace f with $\text{argmax}_{l \in \mathcal{L}} f$. This makes the local classifier f an extremely flexible function and we can use anything ranging from a decision tree to an SVM in its place. Unfortunately, it is rare in practice that we know all values in $\mathcal{N}_i$ which is why we need to repeat the process iteratively, in each iteration, labeling each Y_i using the current best estimates of $\mathcal{N}_i$ and the local classifier f, and continuing to do so until the assignments to the labels stabilize.

Most local classifiers are defined as functions whose argument consists of one fixed-length vector of attribute values. A common approach to circumvent such a situation is to use an aggregation operator such as `count`, `mode`, or `prop`, which measures the proportion of neighbors with a given label.

Algorithm 1 depicts the ICA algorithm as pseudo-code where we use $\vec{a}_i$ to denote the vector encoding the values in $\mathcal{N}_i$ obtained after aggregation. Note that in the first ICA iteration, all labels y_i are undefined and to initialize them we simply apply the local classifier to the observed attributes in the neighborhood of Y_i; this is referred to as "bootstrapping" in Algorithm 1.

3.3.2   Gibbs Sampling

Gibbs sampling (GS) (12) is widely regarded as one of the most accurate approximate inference procedures. It was originally proposed in (10) in the context of image restoration. Unfortunately, it is also very slow and one of the common issues while implementing GS is to determine when the procedure has converged. Even though there are tests that can help one determine convergence, they are usually too expensive or complicated to implement.

Researchers in collective classification (29; 22; 24) have developed a version of Gibbs sampling that is easy to implement and faster than traditional GS. The basic idea behind this algorithm is to assume, just like in the case of ICA, that we have access to a local classifier f that can sample for the best label estimate for Y_i given all the values for the nodes in $\mathcal{N}_i$. We keep doing this repeatedly for a fixed number of iterations (a period known as "burn-in"). After that, not only do we sample for labels for each $Y_i \in \mathcal{Y}$ but we also maintain count statistics as to how many times we sampled label l for node Y_i. After collecting a predefined number of such samples we output the best label assignment for node Y_i by choosing the label that was assigned the maximum number of times to Y_i while collecting samples. The pseudo-code for GS is shown in Algorithm 2. For all our experiments that we report later, we set burn-in to 200 iterations and collected 800 samples.

3.3.3   Local Classifiers and Further Optimizations

One of the benefits of both ICA and GS is the fact that it is fairly simple to make use of any local classifier. Some of the classifiers used included: naïve Bayes ((7; 28)), logistic regression ((21)), decision trees (14) and weighted-vote ((22)). There is some evidence to indicate that discriminatively trained local classifiers such as logistic regression tend to produce higher accuracies than others; this is consistent with results in other areas.

Other aspects of ICA that have been the subject of investigation include the ordering strategy to determine in which order to visit the nodes to relabel in each ICA iteration. There is some evidence to suggest that ICA is fairly robust to a number of simple ordering strategies such as random ordering, visiting nodes in ascending order of diversity of its neighborhood class labels and labeling nodes in descending order of label confidences (11). However, there is also some evidence that certain modifications to the basic ICA procedure tend to produce improved classification accuracies. For instance, both (28) and (24) propose a strategy where only a subset of the unobserved variables are utilized as inputs for feature construction. More specifically, in each iteration, they choose the top-k most confident predicted labels and use only those unobserved variables in the following iteration's predictions, thus ignoring the less confident predicted labels. In each subsequent iteration they increase the value of k so that in the last iteration all nodes are used for prediction.

Algorithm 2 Gibbs sampling algorithm

Gibbs Sampling ICA (GS)

   for each node $Y_i \in \mathcal{Y}$ **do** {bootstrapping}
      {c}ompute label using only observed nodes in $\mathcal{N}_i$
      compute $\vec{a}_i$ using only $\mathcal{X} \cap \mathcal{N}_i$
      $y_i \leftarrow f(\vec{a}_i)$
   for n=1 to B **do** {burn-in}
      generate ordering $\mathcal{O}$ over nodes in $\mathcal{Y}$
      for each node $Y_i \in \mathcal{O}$ **do**
         compute $\vec{a}_i$ using current assignments to $\mathcal{N}_i$
         $y_i \leftarrow f(\vec{a}_i)$
   for each node $Y_i \in \mathcal{Y}$ **do** {initialize sample counts}
      for label $l \in \mathcal{L}$ **do**
      $c[i, l] = 0$
   for n=1 to S **do** {collect samples}
      generate ordering $\mathcal{O}$ over nodes in $\mathcal{Y}$
      for each node $Y_i \in \mathcal{O}$ **do**
         compute $\vec{a}_i$ using current assignments to $\mathcal{N}_i$
         $y_i \leftarrow f(\vec{a}_i)$
         $c[i, y_i] \leftarrow c[i, y_i] + 1$
   for each node $Y_i \in \mathcal{Y}$ **do** {compute final labels}
      $y_i \leftarrow \text{argmax}_{l \in \mathcal{L}} c[i, l]$

McDowell et al. report that such a "cautious" approach leads to improved accuracies.

3.4 Approximate Inference Algorithms for Approaches Based on Global Formulations

An alternate approach to performing collective classification is to define a global objective function to optimize. In what follows, we will describe one common way of defining such an objective function and this will require some more notation.

We begin by defining a *pairwise Markov random field* (pairwise MRF) (34). Let $G = (\mathcal{V}, E)$ denote a graph of random variables as before where $\mathcal{V}$ consists of two types of random variables, the unobserved variables, $\mathcal{Y}$, which need to be assigned values from label set $\mathcal{L}$, and observed variables $\mathcal{X}$ whose values we know. Let Ψ denote a set of *clique potentials*. Ψ contains three distinct types of functions:

- For each $Y_i \in \mathcal{Y}$, $\psi_i \in \Psi$ is a mapping $\psi_i : \mathcal{L} \to \Re_{\geq 0}$, where $\Re_{\geq 0}$ is the set of non-negative real numbers.

- For each $(Y_i, X_j) \in E$, $\psi_{ij} \in \Psi$ is a mapping $\psi_{ij} : \mathcal{L} \to \Re_{\geq 0}$.

- For each $(Y_i, Y_j) \in E$, $\psi_{ij} \in \Psi$ is a mapping $\psi_{ij} : \mathcal{L} \times \mathcal{L} \to \Re_{\geq 0}$.

Let $\mathbf{x}$ denote the values assigned to all the observed variables in G and let x_i denote the value assigned to X_i. Similarly, let $\mathbf{y}$ denote any assignment to all the unobserved variables in G and let y_i denote a value assigned to Y_i. For brevity of notation we will denote by ϕ_i the clique potential obtained by computing $\phi_i(y_i) = \psi_i(y_i) \prod_{(Y_i, X_j) \in E} \psi_{ij}(y_i)$. We are now in a position to define a pairwise MRF.

DEFINITION 3.1 *A pairwise Markov random field (MRF) is given by a pair $\langle G, \Psi \rangle$ where G is a graph and Ψ is a set of clique potentials with ϕ_i and ψ_{ij} as defined above. Given an assignment $\mathbf{y}$ to all the unobserved variables $\mathcal{Y}$, the pairwise MRF is associated with the probability distribution $P(\mathbf{y}|\mathbf{x}) = \frac{1}{\mathcal{Z}(\mathbf{x})} \prod_{Y_i \in \mathcal{Y}} \phi_i(y_i) \prod_{(Y_i, Y_j) \in E} \psi_{ij}(y_i, y_j)$ where $\mathbf{x}$ denotes the observed values of $\mathcal{X}$ and $\mathcal{Z}(\mathbf{x}) = \sum_{\mathbf{y}'} \prod_{Y_i \in \mathcal{Y}} \phi_i(y_i') \prod_{(Y_i, Y_j) \in E} \psi_{ij}(y_i', y_j')$.*

Given a pairwise MRF, it is conceptually simple to extract the best assignments to each unobserved variable in the network. For instance, we may adopt the criterion that the best label value for Y_i is simply the one corresponding to the highest marginal probability obtained by summing over all other variables from the probability distribution associated with the pairwise MRF. Computationally, however, this is difficult to achieve since computing one marginal probability requires summing over an exponentially large number of terms which is why we need approximate inference algorithms.

Algorithm 3 Loopy belief propagation

Loopy Belief Propagation (LBP)

   for each $(Y_i, Y_j) \in E(G)$ s.t. $Y_i, Y_j \in \mathcal{Y}$ **do**
      for each $y_j \in \mathcal{L}$ **do**
         $m_{i \to j}(y_j) \leftarrow 1$
   repeat {perform message passing}
      for each $(Y_i, Y_j) \in E(G)$ s.t. $Y_i, Y_j \in \mathcal{Y}$ **do**
         for each $y_j \in \mathcal{L}$ **do**
$$m_{i \to j}(y_j) \leftarrow \alpha \sum_{y_i} \psi_{ij}(y_i, y_j) \phi_i(y_i)$$
$$\prod_{Y_k \in \mathcal{N}_i \cap \mathcal{Y} \setminus Y_j} m_{k \to i}(y_i)$$
   until all $m_{i \to j}(y_j)$ stop showing any change
   for each $Y_i \in \mathcal{Y}$ **do** {compute beliefs}
      for each $y_i \in \mathcal{L}$ **do**
$$b_i(y_i) \leftarrow \alpha \phi_i(y_i) \prod_{Y_j \in \mathcal{N}_i \cap \mathcal{Y}} m_{j \to i}(y_i)$$

We describe two approximate inference algorithms in this chapter and both of them adopt a similar approach to avoiding the computational complexity of computing marginal probability distributions. Instead of working with the probability distribution associated with the pairwise MRF directly (Definition 3.1) they both use a simpler "trial" distribution. The idea is to design the trial distribution so that once we fit it to the MRF distribution then it is easy to extract marginal probabilities from the trial distribution (as easy as reading off the trial distribution). This is a general principle which forms the basis of a class of approximate inference algorithms known as *variational methods* (15).

We are now in a position to discuss *loopy belief propagation* (LBP) and *mean-field relaxation labeling* (MF).

3.4.1 Loopy Belief Propagation

Loopy belief propagation (LBP) applied to pairwise MRF $\langle G, \Psi \rangle$ is a message passing algorithm that can be concisely expressed as the following set of equations:

$$m_{i \to j}(y_j) = \alpha \sum_{y_i \in \mathcal{L}} \psi_{ij}(y_i, y_j) \phi_i(y_i)$$

$$\prod_{Y_k \in \mathcal{N}_i \cap \mathcal{Y} \setminus Y_j} m_{k \to i}(y_i), \quad \forall y_j \in \mathcal{L} \qquad (3.1)$$

$$b_i(y_i) = \alpha \phi_i(y_i) \prod_{Y_j \in \mathcal{N}_i \cap \mathcal{Y}} m_{j \to i}(y_i), \ \forall y_i \in \mathcal{L} \qquad (3.2)$$

where $m_{i \to j}$ is a message sent by Y_i to Y_j and α denotes a normalization constant that ensures that each message and each set of marginal probabilities sum to 1, more precisely,

---

Algorithm 4 Mean-field relaxation labeling

Mean Field Relaxation Labeling (MF)

  for each $Y_i \in \mathcal{Y}$ **do** {initialize messages}
    for each $y_i \in \mathcal{L}$ **do**
      $b_i(y_i) \leftarrow 1$
  repeat {perform message passing}
    for each $Y_j \in \mathcal{Y}$ **do**
      for each $y_j \in \mathcal{L}$ **do**
        $b_j(y_j) \leftarrow \alpha \phi_j(y_j) \prod_{Y_i \in \mathcal{N}_j \cap \mathcal{Y}, y_i \in \mathcal{L}} \psi_{ij}^{b_i(y_i)}(y_i, y_j)$
  until all $b_j(y_j)$ stop changing

$\sum_{y_j} m_{i \to j}(y_j) = 1$ and $\sum_{y_i} b_i(y_i) = 1$. The algorithm proceeds by making each $Y_i \in \mathcal{Y}$ communicate messages with its neighbors in $\mathcal{N}_i \cap \mathcal{Y}$ until the messages stabilize (Eq. (3.1)). After the messages stabilize, we can calculate the marginal probability of assigning Y_i with label y_i by computing $b_i(y_i)$ using Eq. (3.2). The algorithm is described more precisely in Algorithm 3.

LBP has been shown to be an instance of a variational method. Let $b_i(y_i)$ denote the marginal probability associated with assigning unobserved variable Y_i the value y_i and let $b_{ij}(y_i, y_j)$ denote the marginal probability associated with labeling the edge (Y_i, Y_j) with values (y_i, y_j). Then (44) showed that the following choice of trial distribution,

$$b(\mathbf{y}) = \frac{\prod_{(Y_i, Y_j) \in E} b_{ij}(y_i, y_j)}{\prod_{Y_i \in \mathcal{Y}} b_i(y_i)^{|\mathcal{Y} \cap \mathcal{N}_i| - 1}}$$

and subsequently minimizing the Kullback-Leibler divergence between the trial distribution from the distribution associated with a pairwise MRF gives us the LBP message passing algorithm with some qualifications. Note that the trial distribution explicitly contains marginal probabilities as variables. Thus, once we fit the distribution, extracting the marginal probabilities is as easy as reading them off.

3.4.2 Relaxation Labeling via Mean-Field Approach

Another approximate inference algorithm that can be applied to pairwise MRFs is *mean-field relaxation labeling* (MF). The basic algorithm can be described by the following fixed point equation:

$$b_j(y_j) = \alpha \phi_j(y_j) \prod_{Y_i \in \mathcal{N}_j \cap \mathcal{Y}} \prod_{y_i \in \mathcal{L}} \psi_{ij}^{b_i(y_i)}(y_i, y_j), \quad y_j \in \mathcal{L}$$

where $b_j(y_j)$ denotes the marginal probability of assigning $Y_j \in \mathcal{Y}$ with label y_j and α is a normalization constant that ensures $\sum_{y_j} b_j(y_j) = 1$. The algorithm simply computes the fixed point equation for every node Y_j and keeps doing so until the marginal probabilities $b_j(y_j)$ stabilize. When they do, we simply return $b_j(y_j)$ as the computed marginals. The pseudo-code for MF is shown in Algorithm 4.

MF can also be justified as a variational method in almost exactly the same way as LBP. In this case, however, we choose a simpler trial distribution:

$$b(\mathbf{y}) = \prod_{Y_i \in \mathcal{Y}} b_i(y_i)$$

We refer the interested reader to (40; 44) for more details.

3.5   Learning the Classifiers

One aspect of the collective classification problem that we have not discussed so far is how to learn the various classifiers described in the previous
sections. Learning refers to the problem of determining the parameter values for the local classifier, in the case of ICA and GS, and the values in the
clique potentials, in the case of LBP and MF, which can then be subsequently
used to classify unseen test data. For all our experiments, we learned the parameter values from fully labeled datasets using gradient-based optimization
approaches. Unfortunately, a full treatment of this subject is not possible
within this article and we refer the interested reader to various other works
that discuss this in more depth such as (34), (31), (32).

3.6   Experimental Comparison

In our evaluation, we compared the four collective classification algorithms
(CC) discussed in the previous sections and a content-only classifier (CO),
which does not take the link structure into account, along with two choices
of local classifiers on document classification tasks. The two local classifiers
we tried were naïve Bayes (NB) and Logistic Regression (LR). This gave us
8 different classifiers: CO with NB, CO with LR, ICA with NB, ICA with
LR, GS with NB, GS with LR, MF and LBP. The datasets we used for the
experiments included both real-world and synthetic datasets.

3.6.1   Features Used

For CO classifiers, we used the words in the documents for observed attributes. In particular, we used a binary value to indicate whether or not
a word appears in the document. In ICA and GS, we used the same local
attributes (i.e., words) followed by count aggregation to count the number of
each label value in a node's neighborhood. Finally, for LBP and MF, we used
pairwise Markov Random Fields with clique potentials defined on the edges
and unobserved nodes in the network.

3.6.2   Real-World Datasets

We experimented with three real-world datasets: Cora and CiteSeer (two
bibliographic datasets), and WebKB (a hypertext dataset). For the WebKB
experiments, we only considered documents which link to or are linked to by
at least one other webpage in the corpus. This gave us a corpus of size 877

documents divided into the four standard university splits (after discarding the "other" split) containing webpages from Cornell, Texas, Wisconsin and Washington. We also performed stemming and stop word removal to obtain a vocabulary with 1703 distinct words. There are 1608 hyperlinks in the dataset with 5 class labels. Note that webpages from one university do not link to webpages from the other universities, which means that while performing four-fold cross-validation using the university splits, we can only use the words in the webpages to seed the inference process with. There are no observed labels to bootstrap the inference. This is not the case with Cora and CiteSeer datasets.

The Cora dataset contains a number of Machine Learning papers divided into one of 7 classes while the CiteSeer dataset has 6 class labels. For both datasets, we performed stemming and stop word removal besides removing the words with document frequency less than 10. The final corpus has 2708 documents, 1433 distinct words in the vocabulary and 5429 links, in the case of Cora, and 3312 documents, 3703 distinct words in the vocabulary and 4732 links in the case of CiteSeer.

Unlike WebKB, the Cora and CiteSeer datasets do not have natural splits in the data for use as test and training sets. To create splits, we use two sampling strategies, random sampling and snowball sampling. Random sampling (RS) is accomplished using the traditional k-fold cross-validation methodology where we choose nodes randomly to create splits. In snowball sampling (SS), we sample with a bias toward placing neighboring nodes in the same split. We construct the splits by randomly selecting an initial node and expanding around it. We do not expand randomly. We instead select nodes based on the class distribution of the dataset; that is, the test data is stratified. Selected nodes are used as the test set while the rest are used in the training set. We repeat the sampling k times to obtain k test-train pairs of splits. We note that when using SS, unlike in RS, some objects may appear in more than one test splits. Consequently, we need to adjust accuracy computation so that objects appearing multiple times are not over counted. We choose a simple strategy where we first average the accuracy for each instance and then take the averages of the averages. Also, to help the reader compare the results between SS and RS strategies, we provide accuracies averaged per instance across only instances which appear in test sets for both SS and RS (i.e., instances in at least one SS test split). We denote these numbers using the term matched cross-validation (M).

For each dataset, we performed both random sampling evaluation (with 10 splits) and snowball sampling evaluation (averaged over 10 runs).

3.6.2.1 Results

The accuracy results for the real world datasets are shown in Table 3.1, Table 3.2 and Table 3.3. The accuracies are separated by sampling method and base classifier. The highest accuracy at each partition is in bold. We

TABLE 3.1: Accuracy results for WebKB. CC algorithms outperformed their CO counterparts significantly, and LR versions outperformed NB versions significantly. The differences between ICA-NB and GS-NB, and the differences between ICA-LR and GS-LR, are not statistically significant. Both LBP and MF outperformed ICA-LR and GS-LR significantly.

Algorithm	4-fold
CO-NB	0.7030
ICA-NB	0.7215
GS-NB	**0.7234**
CO-LR	0.7734
ICA-LR	0.7956
GS-LR	**0.7969**
LBP	**0.8446**
MF	**0.8446**

performed t-test (paired where applicable, and Welch t-test otherwise) to test statistical significance between results. Here are the main results:

1. Do CC algorithms improve over CO counterparts?

   In all three datasets, CC algorithms outperformed their CO counterparts, in all evaluation strategies (SS, RS and M). The performance differences were significant for all comparisons except for the NB (M) results for CiteSeer.

2. Does the choice of the base classifier affect the results of the CC algorithms?

   We observed a similar trend for the comparison between NB and LR. LR (and the CC algorithms that used LR as a base classifier) outperformed NB versions in all datasets, and the difference was statistically significant for both WebKB and Cora.

3. Is there any CC algorithm that dominates the other?

   The results for comparing CC algorithms are less clear. In the NB partition, the difference between ICA-NB and GS-NB was not significant for WebKB, ICA-NB outperformed GS-NB significantly for Cora using SS and M, and GS-NB outperformed ICA-NB for CiteSeer SS. Thus, there was no clear winner between ICA-NB and GS-NB in terms of performance. In the LR portion, again the differences between ICA-LR and GS-LR were not significant for all datasets. As for LBP and MF, they outperformed ICA-LR and GS-LR most of the time, but the differences were not significant for Cora and CiteSeer.

4. How do SS results and RS results compare?

TABLE 3.2:   Accuracy results for the Cora dataset. CC algorithms outperformed their CO counterparts significantly. LR versions significantly outperformed NB versions. ICA-NB outperformed GS-NB for SS and M, the other differences between ICA and GS were not significant (both NB and LR versions). Even though MF outperformed ICA-LR, GS-LR, and LBP, the differences were not statistically significant.

Algorithm	SS	RS	M
CO-NB	0.7285	0.7776	0.7476
ICA-NB	**0.8054**	**0.8478**	**0.8271**
GS-NB	0.7613	0.8404	0.8154
CO-LR	0.7356	0.7695	0.7393
ICA-LR	0.8457	0.8796	0.8589
GS-LR	**0.8495**	**0.8810**	**0.8617**
LBP	0.8554	0.8766	0.8575
MF	**0.8555**	**0.8836**	**0.8631**

Finally, we take a look at the numbers under the columns labeled M. First, we would like to remind the reader that even though we are comparing the results only on instances appearing in at least one test set in both sampling strategies (SS and RS), different training data could have been potentially used for each test instance, thus the comparison can be questioned. Nonetheless, we expected the matched cross-validation results (M) to outperform SS results simply because each instance had more labeled data around it from RS splitting. The differences were not big (around 1% or 2%); however, they were significant. These results tell us that the evaluation strategies can have a big impact on the final results, and care must be taken while designing an experimental setup for evaluating CC algorithms on network data (9).

3.6.3   Practical Issues

In this section, we discuss some of the practical issues to consider when applying the various CC algorithms. First, although MF and LBP perform consistently better than ICA and GS, they were also the most difficult to work with in both learning and inference. Choosing the initial weights so that the weights will converge during training is non-trivial. Most of the time, we had to initialize the weights with the weights we got from ICA in order to get the algorithms to converge. Thus, the MF and LBP had unfair advantages in the above experiments. We also note that of the two, we had the most trouble with MF being unable to converge, or when it did, not converging to the global optimum. Our difficulty with MF and LBP is consistent with previous work (39; 27; 43) and should be taken into consideration when choosing to apply these algorithms.

Second, ICA and GS parameter initializations worked for all datasets we

TABLE 3.3:   Accuracy results for the CiteSeer dataset. CC algorithms significantly outperformed their CO counterparts except for ICA-NB and GS-NB for matched cross-validation. CO and CC algorithms based on LR outperformed the NB versions, but the differences were not significant. ICA-NB outperformed GS-NB significantly for SS; but, the rest of the differences between LR versions of ICA and GS, LBP and MF were not significant.

Algorithm	SS	RS	M
CO-NB	0.7427	0.7487	0.7646
ICA-NB	0.7540	**0.7683**	**0.7752**
GS-NB	**0.7596**	0.7680	0.7737
CO-LR	0.7334	0.7321	0.7532
ICA-LR	**0.7629**	**0.7732**	0.7812
GS-LR	0.7574	0.7699	**0.7843**
LBP	**0.7663**	**0.7759**	0.7843
MF	0.7657	0.7732	**0.7888**

used and we did not have to tune the initializations for these two algorithms. They were the easiest to train and test among all the collective classification algorithms evaluated.

Third, ICA and GS produced very similar results for almost all experiments. However, ICA is a much faster algorithm than GS. In our largest dataset, CiteSeer, for example, ICA-NB took 14 minutes to run while GS-NB took over 3 hours. The large difference is due to the fact that ICA converges in just a few iterations, whereas GS has to go through significantly more iterations per run due to the initial burn-in stage (200 iterations), as well as the need to run a large number of iterations to get a sufficiently large sampling (800 iterations).

3.7   Related Work

Even though collective classification has gained attention only in the past five to seven years, the general problem of inference for structured data has received attention for a considerably longer period of time from various research communities including computer vision, spatial statistics and natural language processing. In this section, we attempt to describe some of the work that is most closely related to the work described in this article; however, due to the widespread interest in collective classification our list is sure to be incomplete.

One of the earliest principled approximate inference algorithms, *relaxation labeling* (13), was developed by researchers in computer vision in the context of object labeling in images. Due to its simplicity and appeal, relaxation labeling was a topic of active research for some time and many researchers developed different versions of the basic algorithm (20). Mean-field relaxation labeling (39; 44), discussed in this article, is a simple instance of this general class of algorithms. (4) also considered statistical analysis of images and proposed a particularly simple approximate inference algorithm called *iterated conditional modes* which is one of the earliest descriptions and a specific version of the *iterative classification algorithm* presented in this article. Besides computer vision, researchers working with an iterative decoding scheme known as "Turbo Codes" (3) came up with the idea of applying Pearl's belief propagation algorithm (30) on networks with loops. This led to the development of the approximate inference algorithm that we, in this article, refer to as *loopy belief propagation* (LBP) (also known as *sum product* algorithm) (17; 25; 18).

Of course, the focus of this chapter is on collective classification techniques for document classification. (7) was one of the first to apply collective classification to a corpora of patents linked via hyperlinks and reported that considering attributes of neighboring documents actually hurts classification performance. (33) also considered the problem of document classification by constructing features from neighboring documents using an *Inductive Logic Programming* rule learner. (42) conducted an in-depth investigation over multiple datasets commonly used for document classification experiments and identified different patterns. Since then, collective classification has also been applied to various other applications such as part-of-speech tagging (19), classification of hypertext documents using hyperlinks (34), link prediction in friend-of-a-friend networks (37), optical character recognition (36), entity resolution in sensor networks (8), predicting disulphide bonds in protein molecules (35), segmentation of 3D scan data (2) and classification of email "speech acts" (6).

Besides the four approximate inference algorithms discussed in this article, there are other algorithms that we did not discuss such as graph-cuts based formulations (5), formulations based on linear programming relaxations (16; 38) and expectation propagation (26). Other examples of approximate inference algorithms include algorithms developed to extend and improve loopy belief propagation (LBP) to remove some of its shortcomings such as alternatives with convergence guarantees (46) and alternatives that go beyond just using edge and node marginals to compute more accurate marginal probability estimates such as the cluster variational method (45), junction graph method (1) and region graph method (44).

More recently, there have been some attempts to extend collective classification techniques to the semi-supervised learning scenario (41; 23).

3.8 Conclusion

In this chapter, we gave a brief description of four popular collective classification algorithms. We explained the algorithms, showed how to apply them to various applications using examples and highlighted various issues that have been the subject of investigation in the past. Most of the inference algorithms available for practical tasks relating to collective classification are approximate. We believe that a better understanding of when these algorithms perform well will lead to more widespread application of these algorithms to more real-world tasks and that this should be a subject of future research.

3.9 Acknowledgments

This material is based upon work supported in part by the National Science Foundation under Grant No.0308030.

References

[1] S. M. Aji and R. J. McEliece. The generalized distributive law and free energy minimization. In *Proceedings of the 39th Allerton Conference on Communication, Control and Computing*, 2001.

[2] D. Anguelov, B. Taskar, V. Chatalbashev, D. Koller, D. Gupta, G. Heitz, and A. Ng. Discriminative learning of markov random fields for segmentation of 3d scan data. In *IEEE Computer Society Conference on Computer Vision and Pattern Recognition*, 2005.

[3] C. Berrou, A. Glavieux, and P. Thitimajshima. Near Shannon limit error-correcting coding and decoding: Turbo codes. In *Proceedings of IEEE International Communications Conference*, 1993.

[4] J. Besag. On the statistical analysis of dirty pictures. *Journal of the Royal Statistical Society*, 1986.

[5] Y. Boykov, O. Veksler, and R. Zabih. Fast approximate energy minimization via graph cuts. *IEEE Transactions on Pattern Analysis and Machine Intelligence*, 2001.

[6] V. Carvalho and W. W. Cohen. On the collective classification of email speech acts. In *Special Interest Group on Information Retrieval*, 2005.

[7] S. Chakrabarti, B. Dom, and P. Indyk. Enhanced hypertext categorization using hyperlinks. In *International Conference on Management of Data*, 1998.

[8] L. Chen, M. Wainwright, M. Cetin, and A. Willsky. Multitarget-multisensor data association using the tree-reweighted max-product algorithm. In *SPIE Aerosense conference*, 2003.

[9] B. Gallagher and T. Eliassi-Rad. An evaluation of experimental methodology for classifiers of relational data. In *Workshop on Mining Graphs and Complex Structures, IEEE International Conference on Data Mining (ICDM)*, 2007.

[10] S. Geman and D. Geman. Stochastic relaxation, gibbs distributions and the bayesian restoration of images. *IEEE Transactions on Pattern Analysis and Machine Intelligence*, 1984.

[11] L. Getoor. *Advanced Methods for Knowledge Discovery from Complex Data*, chapter Link-based classification. Springer, 2005.

[12] W. R. Gilks, S. Richardson, and D. J. Spiegelhalter. *Markov Chain Monte Carlo in Practice*. Interdisciplinary Statistics. Chapman & Hall/CRC, 1996.

[13] R. Hummel and S. Zucker. On the foundations of relaxation labeling processes. In *IEEE Transactions on Pattern Analysis and Machine Intelligence*, 1983.

[14] D. Jensen, J. Neville, and B. Gallagher. Why collective inference improves relational classification. In *Proceedings of the 10th ACM SIGKDD International Conference on Knowledge Discovery and Data Mining*, 2004.

[15] M. I. Jordan, Z. Ghahramani, T. S. Jaakkola, and L. K. Saul. An introduction to variational methods for graphical models. *Machine Learning*, 1999.

[16] J. Kleinberg and E. Tardos. Approximation algorithms for classification problems with pairwise relationships: Metric labeling and markov random fields. In *IEEE Symposium on Foundations of Computer Science*, 1999.

[17] F. R. Kschischang and B. J. Frey. Iterative decoding of compound codes by probability progation in graphical models. *IEEE Journal on Selected Areas in Communication*, 1998.

[18] F. R. Kschischang, B. J. Frey, and H. A. Loeliger. Factor graphs and the sum-product algorithm. In *IEEE Transactions on Information Theory*, 2001.

[19] J. D. Lafferty, A. McCallum, and F. C. N. Pereira. Conditional random fields: Probabilistic models for segmenting and labeling sequence data. In *Proceedings of the International Conference on Machine Learning*, 2001.

[20] S. Z. Li, H. Wang, and M. Petrou. Relaxation labeling of markov random fields. In *Proceedings of International Conference Pattern Recognition*, volume 94, 1994.

[21] Q. Lu and L. Getoor. Link based classification. In *Proceedings of the International Conference on Machine Learning*, 2003.

[22] S. Macskassy and F. Provost. Classification in networked data: A toolkit and a univariate case study. *Journal of Machine Learning Research*, 2007.

[23] S. A. Macskassy. Improving learning in networked data by combining explicit and mined links. In *Proceedings of the Twenty-Second Conference on Artificial Intelligence*, 2007.

[24] L. K. McDowell, K. M. Gupta, and D. W. Aha. Cautious inference in collective classification. In *Proceedings of AAAI*, 2007.

[25] R. J. McEliece, D. J. C. MacKay, and J. F. Cheng. Turbo decoding as an instance of Pearl's belief propagation algorithm. *IEEE Journal on Selected Areas in Communication*, 1998.

[26] T. Minka. Expectation propagation for approximate bayesian inference. In *Proceedings of the Annual Conference on Uncertainty in Artificial Intelligence*, 2001.

[27] J. M. Mooij and H. J. Kappen. Validity estimates for loopy belief propagation on binary real-world networks. In *NIPS*, 2004.

[28] J. Neville and D. Jensen. Iterative classification in relational data. In *Workshop on Statistical Relational Learning, AAAI*, 2000.

[29] J. Neville and D. Jensen. Relational dependency networks. *Journal of Machine Learning Research*, 2007.

[30] J. Pearl. *Probabilistic Reasoning in Intelligent Systems*. Morgan Kaufmann, San Francisco, 1988.

[31] P. Sen and L. Getoor. Empirical comparison of approximate inference algorithms for networked data. In *ICML workshop on Open Problems in Statistical Relational Learning (SRL2006)*, 2006.

[32] P. Sen and L. Getoor. Link-based classification. Technical Report CS-TR-4858, University of Maryland, February 2007.

[33] S. Slattery and M. Craven. Combining statistical and relational methods for learning in hypertext domains. In *International Conference on Inductive Logic Programming*, 1998.

[34] B. Taskar, P. Abbeel, and D. Koller. Discriminative probabilistic models for relational data. In *Proceedings of the Annual Conference on Uncertainty in Artificial Intelligence*, 2002.

[35] B. Taskar, V. Chatalbashev, D. Koller, and C. Guestrin. Learning structured prediction models: A large margin approach. In *Proceedings of the International Conference on Machine Learning*, 2005.

[36] B. Taskar, C. Guestrin, and D. Koller. Max-margin markov networks. In *Neural Information Processing Systems*, 2003.

[37] B. Taskar, M. F. Wong, P. Abbeel, and D. Koller. Link prediction in relational data. In *Neural Information Processing Systems*, 2003.

[38] M. J. Wainwright, T. S. Jaakkola, and A. S. Willsky. Map estimation via agreement on (hyper)trees: Message-passing and linear-programming approaches. In *IEEE Transactions on Information Theory*, 2005.

[39] Y. Weiss. Comparing the mean field method and belief propagation for approximate inference in MRFs. In *Advanced Mean Field Methods*, M. Opper and D. Saad, eds., MIT Press, 2001.

[40] Y. Weiss. *Advanced Mean Field Methods*, chapter Comparing the mean field method and belief propagation for approximate inference in MRFs. MIT Press, 2001.

[41] L. Xu, D. Wilkinson, F. Southey, and D. Schuurmans. Discriminative unsupervised learning of structured predictors. In *Proceedings of the International Conference on Machine Learning*, 2006.

[42] Y. Yang, S. Slattery, and R. Ghani. A study of approaches to hypertext categorization. *Journal of Intelligent Information Systems*, 2002.

[43] C. Yanover and Y. Weiss. Approximate inference and protein-folding. In *Neural Information Processing Systems*, 2002.

[44] J. S. Yedidia, W. T. Freeman, and Y. Weiss. Constructing free-energy approximations and generalized belief propagation algorithms. In *IEEE Transactions on Information Theory*, 2005.

[45] J. S. Yedidia, W. T.Freeman, and Y. Weiss. Generalized belief propagation. In *Neural Information Processing Systems*, 2000.

[46] A. L. Yuille. CCCP algorithms to minimize the bethe and kikuchi free energies: Convergent alternatives to belief propagation. In *Neural Information Processing Systems*, 2002.

Chapter 4

Topic Models

David M. Blei and John D. Lafferty

4.1 Introduction

Scientists need new tools to explore and browse large collections of scholarly literature. Thanks to organizations such as JSTOR, which scan and index the original bound archives of many journals, modern scientists can search digital libraries spanning hundreds of years. A scientist, suddenly faced with access to millions of articles in her field, is not satisfied with simple search. Effectively using such collections requires interacting with them in a more structured way: finding articles similar to those of interest, and exploring the collection through the underlying topics that run through it.

The central problem is that this structure—the index of ideas contained in the articles and which other articles are about the same kinds of ideas—is not readily available in most modern collections, and the size and growth rate of these collections preclude us from building it by hand. To develop the necessary tools for exploring and browsing modern digital libraries, we require *automated* methods of organizing, managing, and delivering their contents.

In this chapter, we describe *topic models*, probabilistic models for uncovering the underlying semantic structure of a document collection based on a hierarchical Bayesian analysis of the original texts (10; 18; 11; 20; 12). Topic models have been applied to many kinds of documents, including email (42), scientific abstracts (18; 10), and newspaper archives (38). By discovering patterns of word use and connecting documents that exhibit similar patterns, topic models have emerged as a powerful new technique for finding useful structure in an otherwise unstructured collection.

computer	chemistry	cortex	orbit	infection
methods	synthesis	stimulus	dust	immune
number	oxidation	fig	jupiter	aids
two	reaction	vision	line	infected
principle	product	neuron	system	viral
design	organic	recordings	solar	cells
access	conditions	visual	gas	vaccine
processing	cluster	stimuli	atmospheric	antibodies
advantage	molecule	recorded	mars	hiv
important	studies	motor	field	parasite

FIGURE 4.1: Five topics from a 50-topic LDA model fit to *Science* from 1980–2002.

With the statistical tools that we describe below, we can automatically organize electronic archives to facilitate efficient browsing and exploring. As a running example, we will analyze JSTOR's archive of the journal *Science*. Figure 4.1 illustrates five "topics" (i.e., highly probable words) that were discovered automatically from this collection using the simplest topic model, latent Dirichlet allocation (LDA) (10) (see Section 4.2). Further embellishing LDA allows us to discover connected topics (Figure 4.7) and trends within topics (Figure 4.9). We emphasize that these algorithms have no prior notion of the existence of the illustrated themes, such as neuroscience or genetics. The themes are automatically discovered from analyzing the original texts

This chapter is organized as follows. In Section 4.2 we discuss the LDA model and illustrate how to use its posterior distribution as an exploratory tool for large corpora. In Section 4.3, we describe how to effectively approximate that posterior with mean field variational methods. In Section 4.4, we relax two of the implicit assumptions that LDA makes to find maps of related topics and model topics changing through time. Again, we illustrate how these extensions facilitate understanding and exploring the latent structure of modern corpora.

4.2   Latent Dirichlet Allocation

In this section we describe latent Dirichlet allocation (LDA), which has served as a springboard for many other topic models. LDA is based on seminal work in latent semantic indexing (LSI) (12) and probabilistic LSI (20). The relationship between these techniques is clearly described in (33). Here, we develop LDA from the principles of generative probabilistic models.

4.2.1 Statistical Assumptions

The idea behind LDA is to model documents as arising from multiple topics, where a *topic* is defined to be a distribution over a fixed vocabulary of terms. Specifically, we assume that K topics are associated with a collection, and that each document exhibits these topics with different proportions. This is often a natural assumption to make because documents in a corpus tend to be heterogeneous, combining a subset of main ideas or themes that permeate the collection as a whole.

JSTOR's archive of *Science*, for example, exhibits a variety of fields, but each document might combine them in novel ways. One document might be about genetics and neuroscience; another might be about genetics and technology; a third might be about neuroscience and technology. A model that limits each document to a single topic cannot capture the essence of neuroscience in the same way as one which addresses that topics are only expressed in part in each document. The challenge is that these topics are not known in advance; our goal is to learn them from the data.

More formally, LDA casts this intuition into a *hidden variable model* of documents. Hidden variable models are structured distributions in which observed data interact with hidden random variables. With a hidden variable model, the practitioner posits a hidden structure in the observed data, and then learns that structure using posterior probabilistic inference. Hidden variable models are prevalent in machine learning; examples include hidden Markov models (30), Kalman filters (22), phylogenetic tree models (24), and mixture models (25).

In LDA, the observed data are the words of each document and the hidden variables represent the latent topical structure, i.e., the topics themselves and how each document exhibits them. Given a collection, the *posterior distribution* of the hidden variables given the observed documents determines a hidden topical decomposition of the collection. Applications of topic modeling use posterior estimates of these hidden variables to perform tasks such as information retrieval and document browsing.

The interaction between the observed documents and hidden topic structure is manifest in the probabilistic generative process associated with LDA, the imaginary random process that is assumed to have produced the observed data. Let K be a specified number of topics, V the size of the vocabulary, $\vec{\alpha}$ a positive K-vector, and η a scalar. We let $\mathrm{Dir}_V(\vec{\alpha})$ denote a V-dimensional Dirichlet with vector parameter $\vec{\alpha}$ and $\mathrm{Dir}_K(\eta)$ denote a K dimensional symmetric Dirichlet with scalar parameter η.

1. For each topic,
    (a) Draw a distribution over words $\vec{\beta}_k \sim \mathrm{Dir}_V(\eta)$.
2. For each document,
    (a) Draw a vector of topic proportions $\vec{\theta}_d \sim \mathrm{Dir}(\vec{\alpha})$.
    (b) For each word,

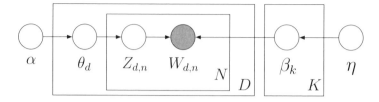

FIGURE 4.2: A graphical model representation of the latent Dirichlet allocation (LDA). Nodes denote random variables; edges denote dependence between random variables. Shaded nodes denote observed random variables; unshaded nodes denote hidden random variables. The rectangular boxes are "plate notation," which denote replication.

    i. Draw a topic assignment $Z_{d,n} \sim \mathrm{Mult}(\vec{\theta}_d)$, $Z_{d,n} \in \{1, \ldots, K\}$.

    ii. Draw a word $W_{d,n} \sim \mathrm{Mult}(\vec{\beta}_{z_{d,n}})$, $W_{d,n} \in \{1, \ldots, V\}$.

This is illustrated as a directed graphical model in Figure 4.2.

The hidden topical structure of a collection is represented in the hidden random variables: the topics $\vec{\beta}_{1:K}$, the per-document topic proportions $\vec{\theta}_{1:D}$, and the per-word topic assignments $z_{1:D,1:N}$. With these variables, LDA is a type of *mixed-membership model* (14). These are distinguished from classical mixture models (25; 27), where each document is limited to exhibit one topic. This additional structure is important because, as we have noted, documents often exhibit multiple topics; LDA can model this heterogeneity while classical mixtures cannot. Advantages of LDA over classical mixtures have been quantified by measuring document generalization (10).

LDA makes central use of the Dirichlet distribution, the exponential family distribution over the simplex of positive vectors that sum to one. The Dirichlet has density

$$p(\theta \mid \vec{\alpha}) = \frac{\Gamma\left(\sum_i \alpha_i\right)}{\prod_i \Gamma(\alpha_i)} \prod_i \theta_i^{\alpha_i - 1}. \tag{4.1}$$

The parameter $\vec{\alpha}$ is a positive K-vector, and Γ denotes the Gamma function, which can be thought of as a real-valued extension of the factorial function. A *symmetric Dirichlet* is a Dirichlet where each component of the parameter is equal to the same value. The Dirichlet is used as a distribution over discrete distributions; each component in the random vector is the probability of drawing the item associated with that component.

LDA contains two Dirichlet random variables: the topic proportions $\vec{\theta}$ are distributions over topic indices $\{1, \ldots, K\}$; the topics $\vec{\beta}$ are distributions over the vocabulary. In Section 4.4.2 and Section 4.4.1, we will examine some of the properties of the Dirichlet, and replace these modeling choices with an alternative distribution over the simplex.

contractual	employment	female	markets	criminal
expectation	industrial	men	earnings	discretion
gain	local	women	investors	justice
promises	jobs	see	sec	civil
expectations	employees	sexual	research	process
breach	relations	note	structure	federal
enforcing	unfair	employer	managers	see
supra	agreement	discrimination	firm	officer
note	economic	harassment	risk	parole
perform	case	gender	large	inmates

FIGURE 4.3: Five topics from a 50-topic model fit to the *Yale Law Journal* from 1980–2003.

4.2.2 Exploring a Corpus with the Posterior Distribution

LDA provides a joint distribution over the observed and hidden random variables. The hidden topic decomposition of a particular corpus arises from the corresponding *posterior distribution* of the hidden variables given the D observed documents $\vec{w}_{1:D}$,

$$p(\vec{\theta}_{1:D}, z_{1:D,1:N}, \vec{\beta}_{1:K} \mid w_{1:D,1:N}, \alpha, \eta) = \tag{4.2}$$
$$\frac{p(\vec{\theta}_{1:D}, \vec{z}_{1:D}, \vec{\beta}_{1:K} \mid \vec{w}_{1:D}, \alpha, \eta)}{\int_{\vec{\beta}_{1:K}} \int_{\vec{\theta}_{1:D}} \sum_{\vec{z}} p(\vec{\theta}_{1:D}, \vec{z}_{1:D}, \vec{\beta}_{1:K} \mid \vec{w}_{1:D}, \alpha, \eta)}.$$

Loosely, this posterior can be thought of as the "reversal" of the generative process described above. Given the observed corpus, the posterior is a distribution of the hidden variables which generated it.

As discussed in (10), this distribution is intractable to compute because of the integral in the denominator. Before discussing approximation methods, however, we illustrate how the posterior distribution gives a decomposition of the corpus that can be used to better understand and organize its contents.

The quantities needed for exploring a corpus are the posterior expectations of the hidden variables. These are the topic probability of a term $\widehat{\beta}_{k,v} = \mathrm{E}[\beta_{k,v} \mid w_{1:D,1:N}]$, the topic proportions of a document $\widehat{\theta}_{d,k} = \mathrm{E}[\theta_{d,k} \mid w_{1:D,1:N}]$, and the topic assignment of a word $\widehat{z}_{d,n,k} = \mathrm{E}[Z_{d,n} = k \mid w_{1:D,1:N}]$. Note that each of these quantities is conditioned on the observed corpus.

Visualizing a topic. Exploring a corpus through a topic model typically begins with visualizing the posterior topics through their per-topic term probabilities $\widehat{\beta}$. The simplest way to visualize a topic is to order the terms by their probability. However, we prefer the following score,

$$\text{term-score}_{k,v} = \widehat{\beta}_{k,v} \log \left(\frac{\widehat{\beta}_{k,v}}{\left(\prod_{j=1}^{K} \widehat{\beta}_{j,v} \right)^{\frac{1}{K}}} \right). \tag{4.3}$$

This is inspired by the popular TFIDF term score of vocabulary terms used in information retrieval (3). The first expression is akin to the term frequency; the second expression is akin to the document frequency, down-weighting terms that have high probability under all the topics. Other methods of determining the difference between a topic and others can be found in (34).

Visualizing a document. We use the posterior topic proportions $\widehat{\theta}_{d,k}$ and posterior topic assignments $\widehat{z}_{d,n,k}$ to visualize the underlying topic decomposition of a document. Plotting the posterior topic proportions gives a sense of which topics the document is "about." These vectors can also be used to group articles that exhibit certain topics with high proportions. Note that, in contrast to traditional clustering models (16), articles contain multiple topics and thus can belong to multiple groups. Finally, examining the most likely topic assigned to each word gives a sense of how the topics are divided up within the document.

Finding similar documents. We can further use the posterior topic proportions to define a topic-based similarity measure between documents. These vectors provide a low dimensional simplicial representation of each document, reducing their representation from the $(V-1)$-simplex to the $(K-1)$-simplex. One can use the Hellinger distance between documents as a similarity measure,

$$\text{document-similarity}_{d,f} = \sum_{k=1}^{K} \left(\sqrt{\widehat{\theta}_{d,k}} - \sqrt{\widehat{\theta}_{f,k}} \right)^2. \tag{4.4}$$

To illustrate the above three notions, we examined an approximation to the posterior distribution derived from the JSTOR archive of *Science* from 1980–2002. The corpus contains 21,434 documents comprising 16M words when we use the 10,000 terms chosen by TFIDF (see Section 4.3.2). The model was fixed to have 50 topics.

We illustrate the analysis of a single article in Figure 4.4. The figure depicts the topic proportions, the top scoring words from the most prevalent topics, the assignment of words to topics in the abstract of the article, and the top ten most similar articles.

4.3   Posterior Inference for LDA

The central computational problem for topic modeling with LDA is approximating the posterior in Eq. (4.2). This distribution is the key to using LDA for both quantitative tasks, such as prediction and document generalization, and the qualitative exploratory tasks that we discuss here. Several approximation techniques have been developed for LDA, including mean field

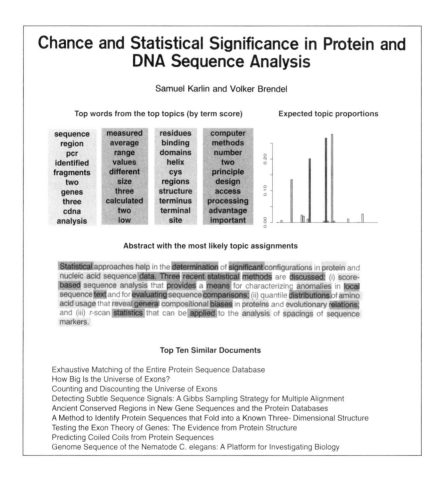

FIGURE 4.4 (SEE COLOR INSERT FOLLOWING PAGE 130.): The analysis of a document from *Science*. Document similarity was computed using Eq. (4.4); topic words were computed using Eq. (4.3).

variational inference (10), collapsed variational inference (36), expectation propagation (26), and Gibbs sampling (33). Each has advantages and disadvantages: choosing an approximate inference algorithm amounts to trading off speed, complexity, accuracy, and conceptual simplicity. A thorough comparison of these techniques is not our goal here; we use the mean field variational approach throughout this chapter.

4.3.1   Mean Field Variational Inference

The basic idea behind variational inference is to approximate an intractable posterior distribution over hidden variables, such as Eq. (4.2), with a simpler distribution containing free *variational parameters*. These parameters are then fit so that the approximation is close to the true posterior.

The LDA posterior is intractable to compute exactly because the hidden variables (i.e., the components of the hidden topic structure) are dependent when conditioned on data. Specifically, this dependence yields difficulty in computing the denominator in Eq. (4.2) because one must sum over all configurations of the interdependent N topic assignment variables $z_{1:N}$.

In contrast to the true posterior, the mean field variational distribution for LDA is one where the variables are *independent* of each other, with each governed by a different variational parameter:

$$q(\vec{\theta}_{1:D}, z_{1:D,1:N}, \vec{\beta}_{1:K}) = \prod_{k=1}^{K} q(\vec{\beta}_k \mid \vec{\lambda}_k) \prod_{d=1}^{D} \left(q(\vec{\theta}_{dd} \mid \vec{\gamma}_d) \prod_{n=1}^{N} q(z_{d,n} \mid \vec{\phi}_{d,n}) \right)$$

(4.5)

Each hidden variable is described by a distribution over its type: the topics $\vec{\beta}_{1:K}$ are each described by a V-Dirichlet distribution $\vec{\lambda}_k$; the topic proportions $\vec{\theta}_{1:D}$ are each described by a K-Dirichlet distribution $\vec{\gamma}_d$; and the topic assignment $z_{d,n}$ is described by a K-multinomial distribution $\vec{\phi}_{d,n}$. We emphasize that in the variational distribution these variables are independent; in the true posterior they are coupled through the observed documents.

With the variational distribution in hand, we fit its variational parameters to minimize the Kullback-Leibler (KL) to the true posterior:

$$\arg\min_{\vec{\gamma}_{1:D}, \vec{\lambda}_{1:K}, \vec{\phi}_{1:D,1:N}} \mathrm{KL}(q(\vec{\theta}_{1:D}, z_{1:D,1:N}, \vec{\beta}_{1:K}) \| p(\vec{\theta}_{1:D}, z_{1:D,1:N}, \vec{\beta}_{1:K} \mid w_{1:D,1:N}))$$

The objective cannot be computed exactly, but it can be computed up to a constant that does not depend on the variational parameters. (In fact, this constant is the log likelihood of the data under the model.)

Specifically, the objective function is

$$\mathcal{L} = \sum_{k=1}^{K} \mathrm{E}[\log p(\vec{\beta}_k \,|\, \eta)] + \sum_{d=1}^{D} \mathrm{E}[\log p(\vec{\theta}_d \,|\, \vec{\alpha})] + \sum_{d=1}^{D} \sum_{n=1}^{N} \mathrm{E}[\log p(Z_{d,n} \,|\, \vec{\theta}_d)]$$

$$+ \sum_{d=1}^{D} \sum_{n=1}^{N} \mathrm{E}[\log p(w_{d,n} \,|\, Z_{d,n}, \vec{\beta}_{1:K})] + \mathrm{H}(q),$$

(4.6)

where H denotes the entropy and all expectations are taken with respect to the variational distribution in Eq. (4.5). See (10) for details on how to compute this function. Optimization proceeds by coordinate ascent, iteratively optimizing each variational parameter to increase the objective.

Mean field variational inference for LDA is discussed in detail in (10), and good introductions to variational methods include (21) and (37). Here, we will focus on the variational inference algorithm for the LDA model and try to provide more intuition for how it learns topics from otherwise unstructured text.

One iteration of the mean field variational inference algorithm performs the coordinate ascent updates in Figure 4.5, and these updates are repeated until the objective function converges. Each update has a close relationship to the *true posterior* of each hidden random variable conditioned on the other hidden and observed random variables.

Consider the variational Dirichlet parameter for the kth topic. The true posterior Dirichlet parameter for a term given all of the topic assignments and words is a Dirichlet with parameters $\eta + n_{k,w}$, where $n_{k,w}$ denotes the number of times word w is assigned to topic k. (This follows from the conjugacy of the Dirichlet and multinomial. See (17) for a good introduction to this concept.) The update in Eq. (4.8) is nearly this expression, but with $n_{k,w}$ replaced by its expectation under the variational distribution. The independence of the hidden variables in the variational distribution guarantees that such an expectation will not depend on the parameter being updated. The variational update for the topic proportions in Eq. (4.9) is analogous.

The variational update for the distribution of $z_{d,n}$ follows a similar formula. Consider the true posterior of $z_{d,n}$, given the other relevant hidden variables and observed word $w_{d,n}$,

$$p(z_{d,n} = k \,|\, \vec{\theta}_d, w_{d,n}, \vec{\beta}_{1:K}) \propto \exp\{\log \theta_{d,k} + \log \beta_{k,w_{d,n}}\}. \qquad (4.7)$$

The update in Eq. (4.10) is this distribution, with the term inside the exponent replaced by its expectation under the variational distribution. Note that under the variational Dirichlet distribution, $\mathrm{E}[\log \beta_{k,w}] = \Psi(\lambda_{k,w}) - \Psi(\sum_v \lambda_{k,v})$, and $\mathrm{E}[\log \theta_{d,k}]$ is similarly computed.

This general approach to mean-field variational methods—update each variational parameter with the parameter given by the expectation of the true

---

One iteration of mean field variational inference for LDA

1. For each topic k and term v:

$$\lambda_{k,v}^{(t+1)} = \eta + \sum_{d=1}^{D} \sum_{n=1}^{N} 1(w_{d,n} = v)\phi_{n,k}^{(t)}. \tag{4.8}$$

2. For each document d:

   (a) Update γ_d:

$$\gamma_{d,k}^{(t+1)} = \alpha_k + \sum_{n=1}^{N} \phi_{d,n,k}^{(t)}. \tag{4.9}$$

   (b) For each word n, update $\vec{\phi}_{d,n}$:

$$\phi_{d,n,k}^{(t+1)} \propto \exp\left\{ \Psi(\gamma_{d,k}^{(t+1)}) + \Psi(\lambda_{k,w_n}^{(t+1)}) - \Psi(\sum_{v=1}^{V} \lambda_{k,v}^{(t+1)}) \right\}, \tag{4.10}$$

   where Ψ is the digamma function, the first derivative of the $\log \Gamma$ function.

FIGURE 4.5: One iteration of mean field variational inference for LDA. This algorithm is repeated until the objective function in Eq. (4.6) converges.

posterior under the variational distribution—is applicable when the conditional distribution of each variable is in the exponential family. This has been described by several authors (5; 41; 7) and is the backbone of the VIBES framework (40).

Finally, we note that the quantities needed to explore and decompose the corpus from Section 4.2.2 are readily computed from the variational distribution. The per-term topic probabilities are

$$\widehat{\beta}_{k,v} = \frac{\lambda_{k,v}}{\sum_{v'=1}^{V} \lambda_{k,v'}}. \tag{4.11}$$

The per-document topic proportions are

$$\widehat{\theta}_{d,k} = \frac{\gamma_{d,k}}{\sum_{k'=1}^{K} \gamma_{d,k'}}. \tag{4.12}$$

The per-word topic assignment expectation is

$$\widehat{z}_{d,n,k} = \phi_{d,n,k}. \tag{4.13}$$

4.3.2 Practical Considerations

Here, we discuss some of the practical considerations in implementing the algorithm of Figure 4.5.

Precomputation. The computational bottleneck of the algorithm is computing the Ψ function, which should be precomputed as much as possible. We typically store $E[\log \beta_{k,w}]$ and $E[\log \theta_{d,k}]$, only recomputing them when their underlying variational parameters change.

Nested computation. In practice, we infer the per-document parameters until convergence for each document before updating the topic estimates. This amounts to repeating steps 2(a) and 2(b) of the algorithm for each document before updating the topics themselves in step 1. For each per-document variational update, we initialize $\gamma_{d,k} = 1/K$.

Repeated updates for ϕ. Note that Eq. (4.10) is identical for each occurrence of the term w_n. Thus, we need not treat multiple instances of the same word in the same document separately. The update for each instance of the word is identical, and we need only compute it once for each unique term in each document. The update in Eq. (4.9) can thus be written as

$$\gamma_{d,k}^{(t+1)} = \alpha_k + \sum_{v=1}^{V} n_{d,v} \phi_{d,v}^{(t)} \tag{4.14}$$

where $n_{d,v}$ is the number of occurrences of term v in document d.

This is a computational advantage of the mean field variational inference algorithm over other approaches, allowing us to analyze very large document collections.

Initialization and restarts. Since this algorithm finds a local maximum of the variational objective function, initializing the topics is important. We find that an effective initialization technique is to randomly choose a small number (e.g., 1–5) of "seed" documents, create a distribution over words by smoothing their aggregated word counts over the whole vocabulary, and from these counts compute a first value for $E[\log \beta_{k,w}]$. The inference algorithm may be restarted multiple times, with different seed sets, to find a good local maximum.

Choosing the vocabulary. It is often computationally expensive to use the entire vocabulary. Choosing the top V words by TFIDF is an effective way to prune the vocabulary. This naturally prunes out stop words and other terms that provide little thematic content to the documents. In the *Science* analysis above we chose the top 10,000 terms this way.

Choosing the number of topics. Choosing the number of topics is a persistent problem in topic modeling and other latent variable analysis. In some cases, the number of topics is part of the problem formulation and specified by an outside source. In other cases, a natural approach is to use cross validation on the error of the task at hand (e.g., information retrieval, text classification). When the goal is qualitative, such as corpus exploration, one can use cross validation on predictive likelihood, essentially choosing the number of topics that provides the best language model. An alternative is to take a nonparametric Bayesian approach. Hierarchical Dirichlet processes can be used to develop a topic model in which the number of topics is automatically selected and may grow as new data is observed (35).

4.4   Dynamic Topic Models and Correlated Topic Models

In this section, we will describe two extensions to LDA: the correlated topic model and the dynamic topic model. Each embellishes LDA to relax one of its implicit assumptions. In addition to describing topic models that are more powerful than LDA, our goal is give the reader an idea of the practice of topic modeling. Deciding on an appropriate model of a corpus depends both on what kind of structure is hidden in the data and what kind of structure the practitioner cares to examine. While LDA may be appropriate for learning a fixed set of topics, other applications of topic modeling may call for discovering the connections between topics or modeling topics as changing through time.

4.4.1   The Correlated Topic Model

One limitation of LDA is that it fails to directly model correlation between the occurrence of topics. In many—indeed most—text corpora, it is natural to expect that the occurrences of the underlying latent topics will be highly correlated. In the *Science* corpus, for example, an article about genetics may be likely to also be about health and disease, but unlikely to also be about x-ray astronomy.

In LDA, this modeling limitation stems from the independence assumptions implicit in the Dirichlet distribution of the topic proportions. Specifically, under a Dirichlet, the components of the proportions vector are nearly independent, which leads to the strong assumption that the presence of one topic is not correlated with the presence of another. (We say "nearly independent" because the components exhibit slight negative correlation because of the constraint that they have to sum to one.)

In the correlated topic model (CTM), we model the topic proportions with an alternative, more flexible distribution that allows for covariance structure among the components (9). This gives a more realistic model of latent topic structure where the presence of one latent topic may be correlated with the presence of another. The CTM better fits the data, and provides a rich way of visualizing and exploring text collections.

The key to the CTM is the logistic normal distribution (2). The logistic normal is a distribution on the simplex that allows for a general pattern of variability between the components. It achieves this by mapping a multivariate random variable from $\mathbf{R}^d$ to the d-simplex.

In particular, the logistic normal distribution takes a draw from a multivariate Gaussian, exponentiates it, and maps it to the simplex via normalization. The covariance of the Gaussian leads to correlations between components of the resulting simplicial random variable. The logistic normal was originally studied in the context of analyzing observed data such as the proportions of minerals in geological samples. In the CTM, it is used in a hierarchical model where it describes the hidden composition of topics associated with each document.

Let $\{\mu, \Sigma\}$ be a K-dimensional mean and covariance matrix, and let topics $\beta_{1:K}$ be K multinomials over a fixed word vocabulary, as above. The CTM assumes that an N-word document arises from the following generative process:

1. Draw $\eta \,|\, \{\mu, \Sigma\} \sim \mathcal{N}(\mu, \Sigma)$.

2. For $n \in \{1, \ldots, N\}$:

    (a) Draw topic assignment $Z_n \,|\, \eta$ from $\mathrm{Mult}(f(\eta))$.
    (b) Draw word $W_n \,|\, \{z_n, \beta_{1:K}\}$ from $\mathrm{Mult}(\beta_{z_n})$.

The function that maps the real-vector η to the simplex is

$$f(\eta_i) = \frac{\exp\{\eta_i\}}{\sum_j \exp\{\eta_j\}}. \qquad (4.15)$$

Note that this process is identical to the generative process of LDA from Section 4.2 except that the topic proportions are drawn from a logistic normal rather than a Dirichlet. The model is shown as a directed graphical model in Figure 4.6.

The CTM is more expressive than LDA because the strong independence assumption imposed by the Dirichlet in LDA is not realistic when analyzing real document collections. Quantitative results illustrate that the CTM better fits held out data than LDA (9). Moreover, this higher order structure given by the covariance can be used as an exploratory tool for better understanding and navigating a large corpus. Figure 4.7 illustrates the topics and their connections found by analyzing the same *Science* corpus as for Figure 4.1. This gives a richer way of visualizing and browsing the latent semantic structure inherent in the corpus.

However, the added flexibility of the CTM comes at a computational cost. Mean field variational inference for the CTM is not as fast or straightforward as the algorithm in Figure 4.5. In particular, the update for the variational distribution of the topic proportions must be fit by gradient-based optimization. See (9) for details.

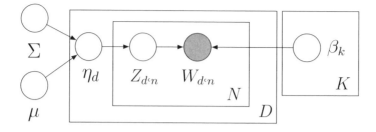

FIGURE 4.6: The graphical model for the correlated topic model in Section 4.4.1.

4.4.2 The Dynamic Topic Model

LDA and the CTM assume that words are *exchangeable* within each document, i.e., their order does not affect their probability under the model. This assumption is a simplification that it is consistent with the goal of identifying the semantic themes within each document.

But LDA and the CTM further assume that documents are exchangeable within the corpus, and, for many corpora, this assumption is inappropriate. Scholarly journals, email, news articles, and search query logs all reflect evolving content. For example, the *Science* articles "The Brain of Professor Laborde" and "Reshaping the Cortical Motor Map by Unmasking Latent Intracortical Connections" may both concern aspects of neuroscience, but the field of neuroscience looked much different in 1903 than it did in 1991. The topics of a document collection evolve over time. In this section, we describe how to explicitly model and uncover the dynamics of the underlying topics.

The *dynamic topic model* (DTM) captures the evolution of topics in a sequentially organized corpus of documents. In the DTM, we divide the data by time slice, e.g., by year. We model the documents of each slice with a K-component topic model, where the topics associated with slice t evolve from the topics associated with slice $t - 1$.

Again, we avail ourselves of the logistic normal distribution, this time using it to capture uncertainty about the time-series topics. We model sequences of simplicial random variables by chaining Gaussian distributions in a dynamic model and mapping the emitted values to the simplex. This is an extension of the logistic normal to time-series simplex data (39).

For a K-component model with V terms, let $\vec{\pi}_{t,k}$ denote a multivariate Gaussian random variable for topic k in slice t. For each topic, we chain $\{\vec{\pi}_{1,k}, \ldots, \vec{\pi}_{T,k}\}$ in a state space model that evolves with Gaussian noise:

$$\vec{\pi}_{t,k} \mid \vec{\pi}_{t-1,k} \sim \mathcal{N}(\vec{\pi}_{t-1,k}, \sigma^2 I). \tag{4.16}$$

When drawing words from these topics, we map the natural parameters back to the simplex with the function f from Eq. (4.15). Note that the time-series

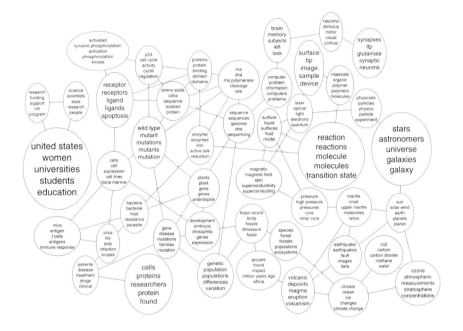

FIGURE 4.7: A portion of the topic graph learned from the 16,351 OCR articles from Science (1990-1999). Each topic node is labeled with its five most probable phrases and has font proportional to its popularity in the corpus. (Phrases are found by permutation test.) The full model can be browsed with pointers to the original articles at http://www.cs.cmu.edu/ lemur/science/ and on STATLIB. (The algorithm for constructing this graph from the co-variance matrix of the logistic normal is given in (9).)

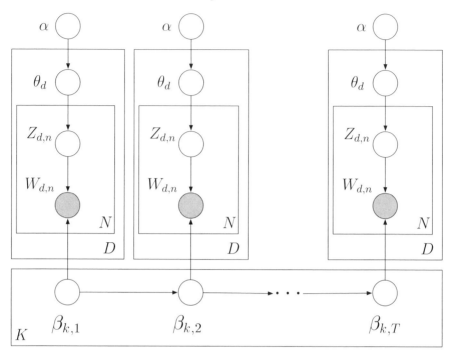

FIGURE 4.8: A graphical model representation of a dynamic topic model (for three time slices). Each topic's parameters $\beta_{t,k}$ evolve over time.

topics use a diagonal covariance matrix. Modeling the full $V \times V$ covariance matrix is a computational expense that is not necessary for our goals.

By chaining each topic to its predecessor and successor, we have sequentially tied a collection of topic models. The generative process for slice t of a sequential corpus is

1. Draw topics $\vec{\pi}_t \mid \vec{\pi}_{t-1} \sim \mathcal{N}(\vec{\pi}_{t-1}, \sigma^2 I)$
2. For each document:
   (a) Draw $\theta_d \sim \text{Dir}(\vec{\alpha})$
   (b) For each word:
       i. Draw $Z \sim \text{Mult}(\theta_d)$
       ii. Draw $W_{t,d,n} \sim \text{Mult}(f(\vec{\pi}_{t,z}))$.

This is illustrated as a graphical model in Figure 4.8. Notice that each time slice is a separate LDA model, where the kth topic at slice t has smoothly evolved from the kth topic at slice $t - 1$.

Again, we can approximate the posterior over the topic decomposition with variational methods (see (8) for details). Here, we focus on the new views of the collection that the hidden structure of the DTM gives.

At the topic level, each topic is now a sequence of distributions over terms. Thus, for each topic and year, we can score the terms with Eq. (4.3) and visualize the topic as a whole with its top words over time. This gives a global sense of how the important words of a topic have changed through the span of the collection. For individual terms of interest, we can examine their score over time within each topic. We can also examine the overall popularity of each topic from year to year by computing the expected number of words that were assigned to it.

As an example, we used the DTM model to analyze the entire archive of *Science* from 1880–2002. This corpus comprises 140,000 documents. We used a vocabulary of 28,637 terms chosen by taking the union of the top 1000 terms by TFIDF for each year. Figure 4.9 illustrates the top words of two of the topics taken every ten years, the scores of several of the most prevalent words taken every year, the relative popularity of the two topics, and selected articles that contain that topic. For sequential corpora such as *Science*, the DTM provides much richer exploratory tools than LDA or the CTM.

Finally, we note that the document similarity metric in Eq. (4.4) has interesting properties in the context of the DTM. The metric is defined in terms of the topic proportions for each document. For two documents in different years, these proportions refer to two different slices of the K topics, but the two sets of topics are linked together by the sequential model. Consequently, the metric provides a *time corrected* notion of document similarity. Two articles about biology might be deemed similar even if one uses the vocabulary of 1910 and the other of 2002.

Figure 4.10 illustrates the top ten most similar articles to the 1994 *Science* article "Automatic Analysis, Theme Generation, and Summarization of Machine-Readable Texts." This article is about ways of summarizing and organizing large archives to manage the modern information explosion. As expected, among the top ten most similar documents are articles from the same era about many of the same topics. Other articles, however, such as "Simple and Rapid Method for the Coding of Punched Cards," (1962) are also about organizing document information on punch cards. This uses a different language from the query article, but is arguably similar in that it is about storing and organizing documents with the precursor to modern computers. Even more striking among the top ten is "The Storing of Pamphlets" (1899). This article addresses the information explosion problem—now considered quaint—at the turn of the century.

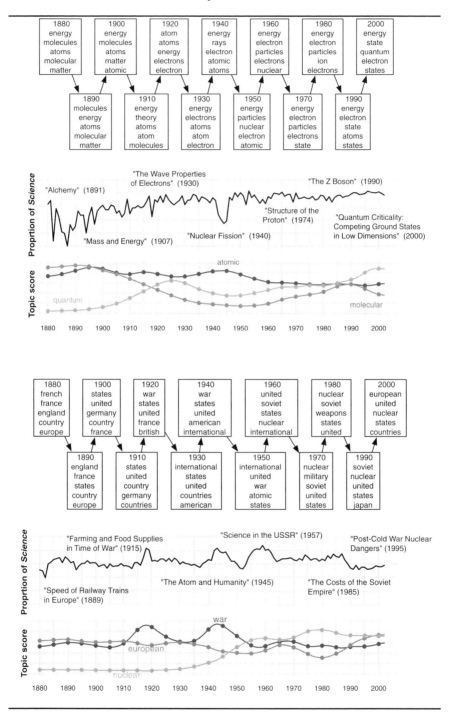

FIGURE 4.9: Two topics from a dynamic topic model fit to the *Science* archive (1880–2002).

Query	Automatic Analysis, Theme Generation, and Summarization of Machine-Readable Texts (1994)
1	Global Text Matching for Information Retrieval (1991)
2	Automatic Text Analysis (1970)
3	Language-Independent Categorization of Text (1995)
4	Developments in Automatic Text Retrieval (1991)
5	Simple and Rapid Method for the Coding of Punched Cards (1962)
6	Data Processing by Optical Coincidence (1961)
7	Pattern-Analyzing Memory (1976)
8	The Storing of Pamphlets (1899)
9	A Punched-Card Technique for Computing Means (1946)
10	Database Systems (1982)

FIGURE 4.10: The top ten most similar articles to the query in *Science* (1880–2002), scored by Eq. (4.4) using the posterior distribution from the dynamic topic model.

4.5 Discussion

We have described and discussed latent Dirichlet allocation and its application to decomposing and exploring a large collection of documents. We have also described two extensions: one allowing correlated occurrence of topics and one allowing topics to evolve through time. We have seen how topic modeling can provide a useful view of a large collection in terms of the collection as a whole, the individual documents, and the relationships between the documents.

There are several advantages of the generative probabilistic approach to topic modeling, as opposed to a non-probabilistic method like LSI (12) or non-negative matrix factorization (23). First, generative models are easily applied to new data. This is essential for applications to tasks like information retrieval or classification. Second, generative models are *modular*; they can easily be used as a component in more complicated topic models. For example, LDA has been used in models of authorship (42), syntax (19), and meeting discourse (29). Finally, generative models are *general* in the sense that the observation emission probabilities need not be discrete. Instead of words, LDA-like models have been used to analyze images (15; 32; 6; 4), population genetics data (28), survey data (13), and social networks data (1).

We conclude with a word of caution. The topics and topical decomposition found with LDA and other topic models are not "definitive." Fitting a topic model to a collection will yield patterns within the corpus whether or not they are "naturally" there. (And starting the procedure from a different place will yield different patterns!)

Rather, topic models are a useful exploratory tool. The topics provide a summary of the corpus that is impossible to obtain by hand; the per-document decomposition and similarity metrics provide a lens through which to browse and understand the documents. A topic model analysis may yield connections between and within documents that are not obvious to the naked eye, and find co-occurrences of terms that one would not expect a priori.

References

[1] E. Airoldi, D. Blei, S. Fienberg, and E. Xing. Combining stochastic block models and mixed membership for statistical network analysis. In *Statistical Network Analysis: Models, Issues and New Directions*, Lecture Notes in Computer Science, pages 57–74. Springer-Verlag, 2007.

[2] J. Aitchison. The statistical analysis of compositional data. *Journal of the Royal Statistical Society, Series B*, 44(2):139–177, 1982.

[3] R. Baeza-Yates and B. Ribeiro-Neto. *Modern Information Retrieval*. ACM Press, New York, 1999.

[4] K. Barnard, P. Duygulu, N. de Freitas, D. Forsyth, D. Blei, and M. Jordan. Matching words and pictures. *Journal of Machine Learning Research*, 3:1107–1135, 2003.

[5] M Beal. *Variational algorithms for approximate Bayesian inference*. PhD thesis, Gatsby Computational Neuroscience Unit, University College London, 2003.

[6] D. Blei and M. Jordan. Modeling annotated data. In *Proceedings of the 26th annual International ACM SIGIR Conference on Research and Development in Information Retrieval*, pages 127–134. ACM Press, 2003.

[7] D. Blei and M. Jordan. Variational inference for Dirichlet process mixtures. *Journal of Bayesian Analysis*, 1(1):121–144, 2005.

[8] D. Blei and J. Lafferty. Dynamic topic models. In *Proceedings of the 23rd International Conference on Machine Learning*, pages 113–120, 2006.

[9] D. Blei and J. Lafferty. A correlated topic model of *Science*. *Annals of Applied Statistics*, 1(1):17–35, 2007.

[10] D. Blei, A. Ng, and M. Jordan. Latent Dirichlet allocation. *Journal of Machine Learning Research*, 3:993–1022, January 2003.

[11] W. Buntine and A. Jakulin. Applying discrete PCA in data analysis. In *Proceedings of the 20th Conference on Uncertainty in Artificial Intelligence*, pages 59–66. AUAI Press, 2004.

[12] S. Deerwester, S. Dumais, T. Landauer, G. Furnas, and R. Harshman. Indexing by latent semantic analysis. *Journal of the American Society of Information Science*, 41(6):391–407, 1990.

[13] E. Erosheva, S. Fienberg, and C. Joutard. Describing disability through individual-level mixture models for multivariate binary data. *Annals of Applied Statistics*, 2007.

[14] E. Erosheva, S. Fienberg, and J. Lafferty. Mixed-membership models of scientific publications. *Proceedings of the National Academy of Science*, 97(22):11885–11892, 2004.

[15] L. Fei-Fei and P. Perona. A Bayesian hierarchical model for learning natural scene categories. *IEEE Computer Vision and Pattern Recognition*, pages 524–531, 2005.

[16] C. Fraley and A. Raftery. Model-based clustering, discriminant analysis, and density estimation. *Journal of the American Statistical Association*, 97(458):611–631, 2002.

[17] A. Gelman, J. Carlin, H. Stern, and D. Rubin. *Bayesian Data Analysis*. Chapman & Hall, London, 1995.

[18] T. Griffiths and M. Steyvers. Finding scientific topics. *Proceedings of the National Academy of Science*, 2004.

[19] T. Griffiths, M. Steyvers, D. Blei, and J. Tenenbaum. Integrating topics and syntax. In Lawrence K. Saul, Yair Weiss, and Léon Bottou, editors, *Advances in Neural Information Processing Systems 17*, pages 537–544, Cambridge, MA, 2005. MIT Press.

[20] T. Hofmann. Probabilistic latent semantic indexing. *Research and Development in Information Retrieval*, pages 50–57, 1999.

[21] M. Jordan, Z. Ghahramani, T. Jaakkola, and L. Saul. Introduction to variational methods for graphical models. *Machine Learning*, 37:183–233, 1999.

[22] R. Kalman. A new approach to linear filtering and prediction problems: a new approach to linear filtering and prediction problems. *Transaction of the AMSE: Journal of Basic Engineering*, 82:35–45, 1960.

[23] D. Lee and H. Seung. Learning the parts of objects by non-negative matrix factorization. *Nature*, 401(6755):788–791, October 1999.

[24] B. Mau, M. Newton, and B. Larget. Bayesian phylogenies via Markov Chain Monte Carlo methods. *Biometrics*, 55:1–12, 1999.

[25] G. McLachlan and D. Peel. *Finite mixture models*. Wiley-Interscience, 2000.

[26] T. Minka and J. Lafferty. Expectation-propagation for the generative aspect model. In *Uncertainty in Artificial Intelligence (UAI)*, 2002.

[27] K. Nigam, A. McCallum, S. Thrun, and T. Mitchell. Text classification from labeled and unlabeled documents using EM. *Machine Learning*, 39(2/3):103–134, 2000.

[28] J. Pritchard, M. Stephens, and P. Donnelly. Inference of population structure using multilocus genotype data. *Genetics*, 155:945–959, June 2000.

[29] M. Purver, K. Kording, T. Griffiths, and J. Tenenbaum. Unsupervised topic modelling for multi-party spoken discourse. In *ACL*, 2006.

[30] L. R. Rabiner. A tutorial on hidden Markov models and selected applications in speech recognition. *Proceedings of the IEEE*, 77:257–286, 1989.

[31] M. Rosen-Zvi, T. Griffiths, M. Steyvers, and P. Smith. The author-topic model for authors and documents. In *Proceedings of the 20th Conference on Uncertainty in Artificial Intelligence*, pages 487–494. AUAI Press, 2004.

[32] B. Russell, A. Efros, J. Sivic, W. Freeman, and A. Zisserman. Using multiple segmentations to discover objects and their extent in image collections. In *IEEE Conference on Computer Vision and Pattern Recognition*, pages 1605–1614, 2006.

[33] M. Steyvers and T. Griffiths. Probabilistic topic models. In T. Landauer, D. McNamara, S. Dennis, and W. Kintsch, editors, *Latent Semantic Analysis: A Road to Meaning*. Laurence Erlbaum, 2006.

[34] Z. Tang and J. MacLennan. *Data Mining with SQL Server 2005*. Wiley, 2005.

[35] Y. Teh, M. Jordan, M. Beal, and D. Blei. Hierarchical Dirichlet processes. *Journal of the American Statistical Association*, 101(476):1566–1581, 2007.

[36] Y. Teh, D. Newman, and M. Welling. A collapsed variational Bayesian inference algorithm for latent Dirichlet allocation. In *Neural Information Processing Systems*, 2006.

[37] M. Wainwright and M. Jordan. A variational principle for graphical models. In *New Directions in Statistical Signal Processing*, chapter 11. MIT Press, 2005.

[38] X. Wei and B. Croft. LDA-based document models for ad-hoc retrieval. In *SIGIR*, 2006.

[39] M. West and J. Harrison. *Bayesian Forecasting and Dynamic Models*. Springer, 1997.

[40] J. Winn and C. Bishop. Variational message passing. *Journal of Machine Learning Research*, 6:661–694, 2005.

[41] E. Xing, M. Jordan, and S. Russell. A generalized mean field algorithm for variational inference in exponential families. In *Proceedings of the 19th Conference on Uncertainty in Artificial Intelligence*, 2003.

[42] A. McCallum, X. Wang, and A. Corrada-Emmanuel. Topic and role discovery in social networks. *Journals of Artificial Intelligence*, 30:249–272.

Chapter 5

Nonnegative Matrix and Tensor Factorization for Discussion Tracking

Brett W. Bader, Michael W. Berry, and Amy N. Langville

5.1   Introduction

After the filing for Chapter 11 bankruptcy by Enron in December of 2001, an unprecedented amount of information (over 1.5 million electronic mail messages, phone tapes, internal documents) was released into the public domain. Such information served the needs of the Federal Energy Regulatory Commission (FERC) in its investigation against Enron. The emails originally posted on the FERC web site (18) had various integrity problems which required some cleaning as well as the removal of sensitive (private) and irrelevant information. Dr. William Cohen and his research group at Carnegie Mellon University have addressed many of these problems in their release of the Enron Email Sets. The version of the Enron Email Sets[1] dated March 2, 2004 contains $517,431$ email messages of 150 Enron email accounts covering a period from December 1979 through February 2004 with the majority of messages spanning the three years: 1999, 2000, and 2001.

The emails in this corpus reflect the day-to-day activities of what was the seventh largest company in the United States at that time. There were, however, certain topics of discussion uniquely linked to Enron activities (5). Enron's development of the Dabhol Power Company (DPC) in the Indian

---

[1]http://www-2.cs.cmu.edu/~enron

state of Maharashtra (involving years of logistical and political problems) was one such topic. The deregulation of the California energy market and the subsequent rolling blackouts during the summer of 2000 was another topic. The infamous practices of greed, overspeculation, and deceptive accounting, which led to the collapse of Enron in the fourth quarter of 2001, are also documented in the emails. The corpus not only facilitates the study of employee communications within a sizeable network, but it also offers a more detailed view of how large multinational corporations operate on a daily basis.

5.1.1   Extracting Discussions

The goal of this study is to extract meaningful threads of discussion from subsets of the Enron Email Set. The underlying idea is as follows. Suppose we extract a collection of q emails from n authors over a period of p days (or other unit of time). In aggregate, there are a collection of m terms parsed from the q emails. From this data, suppose we create an $m \times n \times p$ term-author-day array[2] $\mathcal{X}$. We then decompose $\mathcal{X}$ using a nonnegative tensor factorization based on PARAFAC to track discussions over time. With some effort, the three-way term-author-day array can be expanded to a four-way term-author-recipient-day array $\mathcal{Y}$ whereby the recipients of the emails (which may or may not be from the list n authors) are also identified. A subsequent nonnegative tensor factorization of $\mathcal{Y}$ would facilitate the tracking of topics through time among different social groups.

In the next section, we provide background information (and related work) on tensor decompositions. Section 5.2 explains the notations used to define these decompositions and algorithms that are given in Section 5.3. Details of the specific Enron subset used in this study are provided in Section 5.4, followed by observations and results obtained from the application of PARAFAC to the subset in Section 9.6. Section 5.6 discusses a visualization approach for identifying clusters in the nonnegative factorizations, which is applied here to the nonnegative matrix factorization. We conclude with a brief discussion of future work in the use of nonnegative tensor factorization for topic/discussion tracking in Section 5.7.

5.1.2   Related Work

For the past forty years, tensor decompositions (38; 19; 11) have been used extensively in a variety of domains, from chemometrics (35) to signal processing (34). PARAFAC is a three-way decomposition that was proposed by Harshman (19) using the name PARAllel FACtors or PARAFAC, while

---

[2]Note that the array $\mathcal{X}$ is generally sparse due to the word distribution used by each author over time.

Carroll and Chang (11) published the same mathematical model under the name Canonical Decomposition or CANDECOMP. A comprehensive review by Kolda and Bader (22) summarizes these tensor decompositions and provides references for a wide variety of applications using them.

In the context of text analysis and mining, Acar et al. (1) used various tensor decompositions of (user × key word × time) data to separate different streams of conversation in chatroom data. Several web search applications involving tensors relied on query terms or anchor text to provide a third dimension. Sun et al. (36) have used a three-way Tucker decomposition (38) to analyze (user × query term × web page) data for personalized web search. Kolda et al. (23) and Kolda and Bader (21) have used PARAFAC on a (web page × web page × anchor text) sparse, three-way tensor representing the web graph with anchor-text-labeled edges to get hub/authority rankings of pages related to (identified) topics.

Regarding use of nonnegative PARAFAC, Mørup et al. (27) have studied its use for EEG-related applications. They used the associated multiplicative update rule for a least squares and Kulbach-Leibler (KL) divergence implementation of nonnegative PARAFAC, which they called NMWF-LS and NMWF-KL, respectively. FitzGerald et al. (15) and Mørup et al. (26) both used nonnegative PARAFAC for sound source separation and automatic music transcription of stereo signals.

Bader, Berry, and Browne (5) described the first use of a nonnegative PARAFAC algorithm to extract and detect meaningful discussions from email messages. They encoded one year of messages from the Enron Email Set into a sparse term-author-month array and found that the nonnegative decomposition was more easily interpretable through its preservation of data nonnegativity in the results. They showed that Gantt-like charts can be constructed/used to assess the duration, order, and dependencies of focused discussions against the progression of time. This study expands upon that work and demonstrates the first application of a four-way term-author-recipient-day array for the tracking of targeted threads of discussion through time.

5.2   Notation

Three-way and higher multidimensional arrays or tensors are denoted by boldface Euler script letters, e.g., $\boldsymbol{\mathcal{X}}$. An element is denoted by the requisite number of subscripts. For example, element (i, j, k, l) of a fourth-order tensor $\boldsymbol{\mathcal{X}}$ is denoted by x_{ijkl}.

The symbol ∘ denotes the tensor outer product,

$$A_1 \circ B_1 = \begin{pmatrix} A_{11}B_{11} & \cdots & A_{11}B_{m1} \\ \vdots & \ddots & \vdots \\ A_{m1}B_{11} & \cdots & A_{m1}B_{m1} \end{pmatrix}.$$

The symbol $*$ denotes the Hadamard (i.e., elementwise) matrix product,

$$A * B = \begin{pmatrix} A_{11}B_{11} & \cdots & A_{1n}B_{1n} \\ \vdots & \ddots & \vdots \\ A_{m1}B_{m1} & \cdots & A_{mn}B_{mn} \end{pmatrix}.$$

And the symbol ⊙ denotes the Khatri-Rao product (columnwise Kronecker) (35),

$$A \odot B = \begin{pmatrix} A_1 \otimes B_1 & \cdots & A_n \otimes B_n \end{pmatrix},$$

where the symbol $\otimes$ denotes the Kronecker product.

The concept of *matricizing* or *unfolding* is simply a rearrangement of the entries of $\mathcal{X}$ into a matrix. We will follow the notation used in (35), but alternate notations exist. For a four-way array $\mathcal{X}$ of size $m \times n \times p \times q$, the notation $X^{(m \times npq)}$ represents a matrix of size $m \times npq$ in which the n-index runs the fastest over the columns and p the slowest. Many other permutations, such as $X^{(q \times mnp)}$, are possible by changing the row index and the fastest-to-slowest column indices.

The norm of a tensor, $\| \mathcal{X} \|$, is the square root of the sum of squares of all its elements, which is the same as the Frobenius norm of any of the various matricized arrays.

5.3   Tensor Decompositions and Algorithms

While the original PARAFAC algorithm was presented for three-way arrays, it generalizes to higher-order arrays (22). Earlier text analysis work using PARAFAC in (5) focused on the three-way case, but here we present the four-way case because our application also pertains to four-way data.

Suppose we are given a tensor $\mathcal{X}$ of size $m \times n \times p \times q$ and a desired approximation rank r. The goal is to decompose $\mathcal{X}$ as a sum of vector outer products as shown in Figure 5.1 for the three-way case. It is convenient to group all r vectors together in factor matrices A, B, C, and D, each having r columns. The following mathematical expressions of this model use different

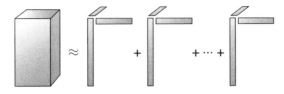

FIGURE 5.1: PARAFAC provides a three-way decomposition with some similarity to the singular value decomposition.

notations but are equivalent:

$$x_{ijkl} \approx \sum_{t=1}^{r} A_{it} B_{jt} C_{kt} D_{lt},$$

$$\mathcal{X} \approx \sum_{t=1}^{r} A_t \circ B_t \circ C_t \circ D_t, \qquad (5.1)$$

$$X^{(m \times npq)} \approx A(D \odot C \odot B)^T.$$

Without loss of generality, we typically normalize all columns of the factor matrices to have unit length and store the accumulated weight (i.e., like a singular value) in a vector λ:

$$\mathcal{X} \approx \sum_{t=1}^{r} \lambda_t (A_t \circ B_t \circ C_t \circ D_t).$$

It is common practice to order the final solution so that $\lambda_1 \geq \lambda_2 \geq \cdots \geq \lambda_r$. In the discussion that follows, we describe a general algorithm for a four-way model without λ because this normalization can be performed in a post-processing step.

Our goal is to find the best fitting matrices $A, B, C,$ and D in the minimization problem:

$$\min_{A,B,C,D} \left\| \mathcal{X} - \sum_{t=1}^{r} A_t \circ B_t \circ C_t \circ D_t \right\|^2. \qquad (5.2)$$

The factor matrices are not required to be orthogonal and, in fact, are usually not in most practical applications. Under mild conditions, PARAFAC provides a unique solution that is invariant to factor rotation (19).

Given a value $r > 0$ (loosely corresponding to the number of distinct topics or conversations in our data), PARAFAC finds matrices $A \in \mathbb{R}^{m \times r}$, $B \in \mathbb{R}^{n \times r}$, $C \in \mathbb{R}^{p \times r}$, and $D \in \mathbb{R}^{q \times r}$ to yield Equation (5.1). Each group $\{A_j, B_j, C_j, D_j\}$, for $j = 1, \ldots, r$, defines scores for a set of terms, authors, recipients, and time for a particular conversation in our email collection; the value λ_r after normalization defines the weight of the conversation. (Without loss of generality, we assume the columns of our matrices are normalized to have unit length.) The scales in D indicate the activity of each conversation topic over time.

5.3.1 PARAFAC-ALS

A common approach to solving Equation (5.2) is an alternating least squares (ALS) algorithm (19; 13; 37), due to its simplicity and ability to handle constraints. At each inner iteration, we compute an entire factor matrix while holding all the others fixed.

Starting with random initializations for A, B, C, and D, we update these quantities in an alternating fashion using the method of normal equations. The minimization problem involving A in Equation (5.2) can be rewritten in *matrix* form as a least squares problem (13):

$$\min_A \left\| X^{(m \times npq)} - AZ \right\|^2, \tag{5.3}$$

where $Z = (D \odot C \odot B)^T$.

The least squares solution for Equation (5.3) involves the pseudo-inverse of Z:

$$A = X^{(m \times npq)} Z^\dagger.$$

Conveniently, the pseudo-inverse of Z may be computed in a special way that avoids computing $Z^T Z$ with an explicit Z (35), so the solution to Equation (5.3) is given by:

$$A = X^{(m \times np)}(D \odot C \odot B)(B^T B * C^T C * D^T D)^{-1}.$$

Furthermore, if $\mathcal{X}$ is sparse, then the product $X^{(m \times npq)}(D \odot C \odot B)$ may be computed efficiently (3) without explicitly forming $D \odot C \odot B$. Thus, computing A essentially reduces to several matrix inner products, sparse tensor-matrix multiplication of B, C, and D into $\mathcal{X}$, and inverting an $R \times R$ matrix.

Analogous least-squares steps may be used to update B, C, and D.

5.3.2 Nonnegative Tensor Factorization

When analyzing nonnegative data, such as scaled term frequencies, it is desirable for the decompositions to retain the nonnegative characteristics of the original data and thereby facilitate easier interpretation (24). Just as with matrix factorization, it is possible to impose nonnegativity constraints on tensor factorizations.

Several authors have considered nonnegative tensor factorizations (NTF), and the resulting methods can be categorized into four classes of algorithms:

1. Least squares updates where all negative values are truncated to zero (10),

2. Nonnegative least squares (10; 16),

3. Paatero's penalty function approach (29; 28), and

4. Lee-and-Seung-style (24) multiplicative updates (39; 32; 20).

The first class is not recommended because one does not obtain least squares estimates, meaning that the residual error may increase. Hence, when employing such a technique in an iterative, multi-way algorithm such as PARAFAC-ALS, the algorithm may actually diverge (10). The three remaining classes of algorithms have better convergence properties, and nonnegative least-squares approaches solve a bound-constrained linear least squares problem. Paatero's PMF3 algorithm (28) uses a logarithmic penalty function and solves for all modes simultaneously using a Gauss-Newton approach, which enjoys fast convergence but is slower on larger problems. The multiplicative update is appealing because it is simple and fast to program, scales well with very large datasets, but it can be slow to converge.

With the exception of Paatero's PMF3, each approach harkens back to PARAFAC-ALS except that the factor matrices are updated differently. Each method generally relies on the fact that the residual norm of the various matrix formulations of the PARAFAC model are equal:

$$||X^{(m \times npq)} - A(D \odot C \odot B)^T||_F =$$
$$||X^{(n \times pqm)} - B(A \odot D \odot C)^T||_F =$$
$$||X^{(p \times qmn)} - C(B \odot A \odot D)^T||_F =$$
$$||X^{(q \times mnp)} - D(C \odot B \odot A)^T||_F.$$

Each of these matrix systems may be treated as a separate nonnegative factorization problem using the techniques mentioned previously and solved in an alternating fashion.

For example, Friedlander and Hatz (16) solve each subproblem as a bound constrained linear least-squares problem. They impose sparseness constraints by regularizing the nonnegative tensor factorization with an l_1-norm penalty function. While this function is nondifferentiable, it effectively removes small values yet keeps large entries. While the solution of the standard problem is unbounded (due to the indeterminacy of scale), regularizing the problem has the added benefit of keeping the solution bounded.

Alternatively, Welling and Weber (39), and subsequently others (32; 20; 15; 27), update A using the multiplicative update introduced in (24) while holding B, C, and D fixed, and so on:

$$A_{i\rho} \leftarrow A_{i\rho} \frac{(X^{(m \times npq)} Z)_{i\rho}}{(AZ^T Z)_{i\rho} + \epsilon}, \ \ Z = (D \odot C \odot B)$$

$$B_{j\rho} \leftarrow B_{j\rho} \frac{(X^{(n \times pqm)} Z)_{j\rho}}{(BZ^T Z)_{j\rho} + \epsilon}, \ \ Z = (A \odot D \odot C)$$

$$C_{k\rho} \leftarrow C_{k\rho} \frac{(X^{(p \times qmn)} Z)_{k\rho}}{(CZ^T Z)_{k\rho} + \epsilon}, \ \ Z = (B \odot A \odot D)$$

$$D_{l\rho} \leftarrow D_{l\rho} \frac{(X^{(q \times mnp)} Z)_{l\rho}}{(CZ^T Z)_{l\rho} + \epsilon}, \ \ Z = (C \odot B \odot A).$$

Here ϵ is a small number like 10^{-9} that adds stability to the calculation and guards against introducing a negative number from numerical underflow. Because our data is large, this is the approach that we use.

As was mentioned previously, $\mathcal{X}$ is sparse, which facilitates a simpler computation in the procedure above. The matrix Z from each step should not be formed explicitly because it would be a large, dense matrix. Instead, the product of a matricized $\mathcal{X}$ with Z should be computed specially, exploiting the inherent Kronecker product structure in Z so that only the required elements in Z need to be computed and multiplied with the nonzero elements of $\mathcal{X}$. See (3) for details.

5.4   Enron Subset

The original collection of Enron emails used in this study (and in the NTF discussed in (5)) is available online (12). Although this collection comprises 517,431 emails extracted from 150 different mail directories, we use the Enron email subset (or graph) prepared by Priebe et al. (30) that consists of messages among 184 Enron email addresses plus thirteen more that have been identified in (6) as interesting. We considered messages only in 2001, which resulted in a total of 53,733 messages over 12 months (messages were sent on a total of 357 days).

As discussed in (5), the lack of information on the former Enron employees has hampered the performance evaluation of any model of the Enron Email Set. Having access to a corporate directory or organizational chart of Enron at the time of these emails (at least for the year 2001) would greatly help test the validity of results (via PARAFAC or any other model). Other researchers using the Enron Email Set have had this same problem. Hopefully, in time, more historical information will be available. Illustrations of the true/false positive rates of NTF-based classification on a different dataset are discussed in (5).

The Priebe dataset (30) provided partial information on the 184 employees of the small Enron network, which appears to be based largely on information collected by Shetty and Adibi (33). Most of the employees' position and business unit data is provided. Additional employee information was collected from the email messages themselves and from relevant information posted on the FERC website (14). To further help our assessment of results, we searched for corroborating information of the preexisting data or for new identification information, such as title, business unit, or manager. Table 5.1 lists eleven of the most notable authors (and their titles) whose emails have been tracked (5).

TABLE 5.1: Eleven of the 197 email authors represented in the term-author-time array $\mathcal{X}$.

Name	Email Account (@enron.com)	Title
Richard Sanders	b..sanders	VP Enron Wholesale Services
Greg Whalley	greg.whalley	President
Jeff Dasovich	jeff.dasovich	Employee Government Relationship Executive
Jeffery Skilling	jeff.skilling	CEO
Steven Kean	j..kean	VP and Chief of Staff
John Lavorato	john.lavorato	CEO Enron America
Kenneth Lay	kenneth.lay	CEO
Louise Kitchen	louise.kitchen	President Enron Online
Mark Haedicke	mark.haedicke	Managing Director Legal Department
Richard Shapiro	richard.shapiro	VP Regulatory Affairs
Vince Kaminski	vince.kaminski	Manager Risk Management Head, Enron Energy Services

Aliasing of email addresses was used by some of the 197 authors in the year 2001), namely different email accounts of the form employee_id@enron.com were used by the same employee. For example, sample aliases of Vince Kaminski, one of the eleven notable authors in Table 5.1, include j.kaminski, j..kaminski, and vince.kaminski.

5.4.1 Term Weighting Techniques

In this study, we considered two datasets: three-way term-author-day and four-way term-author-recipient-day data. The three-way data correspond to a sparse array $\mathcal{X}$ of size $69157 \times 197 \times 357$ with $1,770,233$ nonzeros. The

$69,157$ terms were parsed from the $53,733$ messages using a master dictionary of $121,393$ terms created by the General Text Parser (GTP) software environment (in C++) maintained at the University of Tennessee (17). This larger set of terms was previously obtained when GTP was used to parse $289,695$ of the $517,431$ emails defining the Cohen distribution at CMU (see Section 7.1). To be accepted into the dictionary, a term had to occur in more than one email and more than 10 times among the $289,695$ emails.

The four-way data correspond to a sparse array $\mathcal{Y}$ of size $39573 \times 197 \times 197 \times 357$ with $639,179$ nonzeros. The $39,573$ terms were parsed from the email messages in the same manner as for the three-way data. There are fewer terms because we are restricting the set of messages to be only those between the same 197 individuals. In the three-way set, there are more messages because many are sent to individuals outside of the set of 197.

We scaled the nonzero entries of $\mathcal{X}$ and $\mathcal{Y}$ according to a weighted frequency:

$$x_{ijk} = w_{ijk} g_i a_j,$$
$$y_{ijkl} = w_{ijkl} g_i a_j r_k,$$

where w_{ijkl} is the local weight for term i sent to recipient k by author j in day l, g_i is the global weight for term i, a_j is an author normalization factor, and r_k is a recipient normalization factor. While some scaling and normalization are necessary to properly balance the arrays, many schemes are possible.

For the three-way data, we used the scaling from a previous study in (5) for consistency. Let f_{ijk} be the number of times term i is written by author j in day k, and define $h_{ij} = \frac{\sum_k f_{ijk}}{\sum_{jk} f_{ijk}}$. The specific components of each nonzero are listed below:

Log local weight	$w_{ijk} = \log(1 + f_{ijk})$
Entropy global weight	$g_i = 1 + \sum_{j=1}^{n} \dfrac{h_{ij} \log h_{ij}}{\log n}$
Author normalization	$a_j = \dfrac{1}{\sqrt{\sum_{i,k} (w_{ijk} g_i)}}$

For the four-way data, we followed a different scheme. Let f_{ijkl} be the number of times term i is sent to recipient k by author j in day l. Define the entropy of term i by

$$e_i = -\sum_{j,k,l} f_{ijkl} \log f_{ijkl}.$$

The specific components of each nonzero are listed below:

Log local weight	$w_{ijkl} = \log(1 + f_{ijkl})$
Entropy global weight	$g_i = 1 - \frac{e_i}{\max_i e_i}$
Author normalization	$a_j = \dfrac{1}{\sqrt{\sum\limits_{i,k} (w_{ijkl} g_i)^2}}$
Recipient normalization	$r_k = \dfrac{1}{\sqrt{\sum\limits_{i,k} (w_{ijkl} g_i a_j)^2}}$

These weights are adapted from the well-known log-entropy weighting scheme (8) used on term-by-document matrices. The log local weight scales the raw term frequencies to diminish the importance of high frequency terms. The entropy global weight attempts to emulate an entropy calculation of the terms over all messages in the collection to help discriminate important terms from frequent, less important terms. The author and recipient normalizations help to correct imbalances in the number of messages sent from and received by each individual. Without some type of normalization, discussions involving prolific authors and/or popular recipients would tend to dominate the results.

Scaling in different ways can influence the analysis. Our scaling of the four-way data in $\mathcal{Y}$ does a decent job of balancing authors, recipients, and time. We find single spikes and some multiple spike groups, plus multiple authors communicating with multiple recipients in several cases. Other schemes may be used to focus more on single authors, recipients, or days.

5.5   Observations and Results

In this section, we summarize our findings of applying NTF on the three- and four-way versions of the Enron email collection. Our algorithms were written in MATLAB, using sparse extensions of the Tensor Toolbox (2; 3; 4). All tests were performed on a dual 3GHz Pentium Xeon desktop computer with 2GB of RAM.

5.5.1   Nonnegative Tensor Decomposition

We computed a 25-component ($r = 25$) nonnegative decomposition of the term-author-day array $\mathcal{X}$. One iteration took about 26 seconds, and the average run required about 17 iterations to satisfy a tolerance of 10^{-4} in the relative change of fit. We chose the smallest minimizer from among ten runs from random starting points, and the relative norm of the difference was 0.9561.

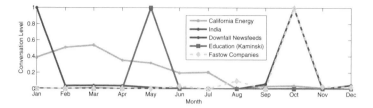

FIGURE 5.2 (SEE COLOR INSERT FOLLOWING PAGE 130.):
Five discussion topics identified in the three-way analysis over months.

We also computed a 25-component $(r = 25)$ nonnegative decomposition of the term-author-recipient-day array $\mathcal{Y}$. One iteration required just under 16 seconds, and between 8 and 12 iterations would satisfy a tolerance of 10^{-4} in the relative change of fit. We chose the smallest minimizer from among ten runs from random starting points, and the relative norm of the difference was 0.9716.

5.5.2   Analysis of Three-Way Tensor

PARAFAC can be used to identify and track discussions over time in each triad $\{A_j, B_j, C_j\}$, for $j = 1, \ldots, r$. A discussion or thread is associated with the topic and primary participants identified in the columns of A and B, respectively, and the corresponding column of C provides a profile over time, showing the relative activity of that discussion over 12 months or over 357 days.[3] As demonstrated in (5), discussions can be visualized as a histogram (or Gantt chart) of the monthly activity for each discussion identified by the classical and nonnegative PARAFAC models, respectively. Here, we comment on both the monthly and daily discussions that were uncovered by both models.

Qualitatively, the results of the nonnegative decomposition and the standard three-way PARAFAC were very similar. The major difference lies in the ability to interpret the results. In the 25 discussion groups tracked by PARAFAC, only six of the groups had any discernible meaning based on known Enron activities (25). In comparison, the nonnegative PARAFAC model revealed eight group discussions that could be interpreted. Figure 5.2 shows the temporal activity of some of these discussions.

The topics generated by the nonnegative PARAFAC model certainly reflected known events of the year 2001. In the first quarter of that year, Enron was still dealing with the fallout of the 2000 California energy crisis. Discussions about the Federal and California state governments' investigation of the California situation were observed as well as Enron's attempted development

---

[3]Eight days of the year 2001 involved no discussions for the 197 author subset used.

of the Dabhol Power Company (DPC) in the Indian State of Maharashtra. Whereas the company's efforts in India had been ongoing for several years, emails of the first six months of 2001 reflected several of the day-to-day dealings with that situation.

By October of 2001, Enron was in serious financial trouble. A merger with the Dynegy energy company fell through and forced Enron to file for Chapter 11 bankruptcy. Many of the emails in the months of October and November were newsfeeds from various organizations that were being routed through the company. As it was reported that Chief Financial Officer Andy Fastow was heavily involved with the deceptive accounting practices,[4] it is not surprising that a topic we labelled *Fastow companies* emerged. Predictably, a *college Football* topic emerged in late fall as well. One of the surprise topics uncovered was an education-related topic due in large part to the interests and responsibilities of Vince Kaminski, head of research. Kaminski taught a class at Rice University in Houston in the Spring of 2001, and was the focal point of emails about internships, class assignments, and resume evaluation (5).

Since only eight of the 25 topics had any discernible meaning, it would seem apparent that a significant amount of *noise* or undefined content can still permeate a term-author-month array. In some instances, there are indicators of a possible thread of some kind (not necessarily directly related to Enron), but a closer inspection of those emails reveals no identifiable topic of discussion.

The daily results reported in (5) provided a similar interpretation as the monthly results but at a finer resolution. In general, one observed four different types of discussions: (*i*) discussions centered largely on one or a few days, (*ii*) continual activity, represented as multiple weekly spikes in activity throughout the year, (*iii*) continual activity with lulls, where a period of calm separates bursts of discussion, and (*iv*) a series of weekly spikes of activity usually spanning three or more months.

Of the 25 discussion groups mined with the PARAFAC model, roughly half were of the first type. Examples include a flood of emails about the possible Dynegy/Enron merger (November 11 and 12th), a topic on January 7th in which Enron employees (Kean, Hughes, and Ambler) were discussing India based on an article published by Reuters and another media report, and a discussion centered on the August 27 U.S. Court of Appeals ruling on section 126 of an Environment Protection Agency code.

The nonnegative PARAFAC model identified temporal patterns similar to those of PARAFAC with a majority being a series of weekly activity spikes spanning three or more months. Roughly one third were single spikes patterns, and just two discussions are somewhat bimodal with a lull. A few of the more interesting (single spike) discussion groups extracted by the nonnegative model included a flurry of emails on August 22 in response to an email

---

[4]Setting up bogus companies to improve Enron's bottom line, for example.

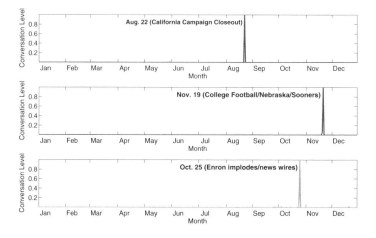

FIGURE 5.3: Three discussion topics identified in the three-way analysis over days.

with subject line *California Campaign Closeout*. In essence, Richard Shapiro praised a subset of employees who worked on California-related projects and many responded to his acknowledgement. A second discussion group identified by terms such as *college football, Nebraska, Sooners, bowl, Cougars,* and *Tennessee* was initiated by M. Motley on November 20. Finally, a third group (involving many news wire stories) described Enron's pending implosion around October 25 and 26. PARAFAC also found this topic but two days earlier—we speculate that the difference is due to the random initialization of both the PARAFAC and nonnegative PARAFAC models. Figure 5.3 shows the temporal activity of these discussions.

5.5.3 Analysis of Four-Way Tensor

When analyzing the four-way term-author-recipient-day array $\mathcal{Y}$, we observed four types of profiles over time: (i) discussions centered largely on one or a few days, resulting in a single spike, (ii) continual activity, represented as multiple weekly spikes throughout the year, (iii) continual activity with lulls, where a period of calm separates bursts of discussion, and (iv) a series of weekly spikes usually spanning three or more months.

In the analysis of the three-way $\mathcal{X}$ data, NTF identified temporal patterns that include these four cases. Roughly one third are single spikes patterns, and just two discussions are of the bimodal type with a lull. Of the 25 groups found in the four-way analysis of $\mathcal{Y}$, roughly half were single spikes. Four were double spikes in time, and nine had sustained activity over many weeks.

Previous research in (5) showed results containing a single spike in time

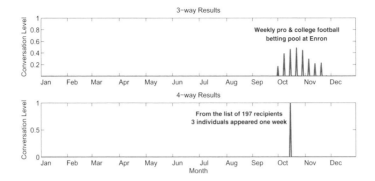

FIGURE 5.4: Weekly betting pool identified in the three-way (top) and four-way (bottom) analyses.

but not any examples that spanned some number of days. Here we present several examples of the latter type and also show what is gained in going from a three-way to four-way analysis.

Figure 5.4 shows a series of email messages announcing the results of a weekly betting pool based on the number of winning teams chosen correctly out of all pro and college football games for the week. Most of the top terms were names, but after a dozen terms more interesting terms, such as *games*, *score*, *picked*, and *prize*, start to appear. Each email lists all of the names entered in that week's pool and their record, which explains why the names appear high in the list of terms for the group.

The unusual feature of this group is that the time profile is so regular. This is because the discussion took place weekly for one day. Results of the betting pool were sent out after the conclusion of all games in the pro and college football schedules.

The four-way analysis identified this discussion but only found a single spike in time. The group showed that the organizer only sent this message to four recipients (out of 197 email addresses) in this case. Presumably the four recipients did not participate in other weeks, and none of the remaining 193 addresses participated in other weeks. If the recipient list were expanded to include others in the betting pool, then the four-way analysis might have picked up other days and recipients as well.

As a second example, Figure 5.5 shows the temporal activity for a discussion involving FERC and its rulings on RTOs. From one of the newsfeeds from `issuealert@scientech.com` on May 4, 2001 there was this description:

> "For background, an RTO is a regional entity that is designed to consolidate control and delivery of electricity across various types of transmission systems within a particular region. The origins of FERC's RTO policy dates back to its December 1999 Order 2000, in which it strongly encouraged all transmission-owning util-

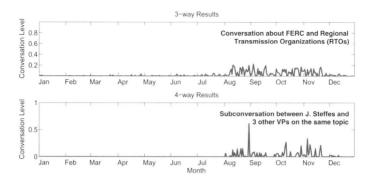

FIGURE 5.5: Long running discussion on FERC's various rulings of RTOs.

ities to submit plans for joining or forming an RTO by Oct. 15, 2000, with actual membership established by December of this year. FERC is now sorting through the applications that it has received, and its approvals or rejections illuminate certain preferences that some members of the commission hold. Over the last year or two, FERC has engaged in an ongoing debate between its preference for transco (for-profit) models for RTOs, as opposed to independent system operators (non-profit). Chairman Curt Heacutebert has been the most vocal supporter of the transco model, while other commissioners such as William Massey have supported ISOs. However, moving forward, it is becoming increasingly clear that FERC also seems to have other set agendas for how it wants the network of RTOs to operate, including the limit of one entity per region."

S. Novosel sent email with subjects like "Subject: FERC Orders on CA and RTO West." A lot of the discussion in this group is reactions and opinions to FERC rulings. The four-way analysis identified this large conversation with many of the same terms, such as RTO, FERC, market, as well as many of the same names. What distinguishes the four-way analysis from the three-way analysis group is that it is a thread of the larger conversation involving primarily the VP's of government affairs, regulatory affairs, chief of staff and Enron wholesale services. As such the time profile of this subconversation nests within the larger conversation identified in the three-way analysis. What is gained from this four-way analysis is the direction of discussion and the recipients in this social network.

The third example in Figure 5.6 is a group identified in the four-way analysis that was not previously identified in any three-way analysis. This email exchange involves the forwarding of the Texas A&M school fight song wav file from E. Bass to four others in the list of 197 recipients. It is reasonable to suggest that perhaps these folks were A&M alumni. Alternatively, the sender

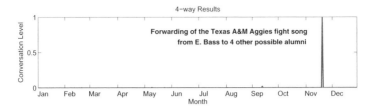

FIGURE 5.6: Forwarding of Texas A&M school fight song.

may be an alum and the four recipients went to a football game and asked "what is everyone singing?" Exposing that type of social interaction is an advantage for four-way analysis over the three-way analysis without recipients.

5.6   Visualizing Results of the NMF Clustering

The previous sections demonstrate the value of three-way and four-way tensor decompositions. Yet it is either very cumbersome or often impossible to visualize these higher-dimensional tensors. Figures 5.4–5.6 are attempts at visualizing the information provided by the tensors, yet they are somewhat limited in scope. As an alternative, in this section, we resort to the standard two-way (or matrix) decomposition to help us visualize some of the patterns uncovered by the three-way and higher decompositions. In general, one can always easily visualize any two dimensions of an n-way tensor decomposition by considering the matrix associated with those dimensions as created by the tensor decomposition. In this spirit, we discuss a tool for visualizing clusters in two-way factors.

It is well known (9) that the nonnegative matrix factorization (NMF) can be used to cluster items in a collection. For instance, if the data matrix is a term-by-document matrix X, which has been factored with the NMF as $X = AB$, then the rows of A can be used to cluster terms, while the columns of B can be used to cluster documents. As a result, terms and documents are, in some sense, clustered independently. There are two main types of clustering: hard clustering and soft clustering. Hard clustering means that items (in this case, terms and documents) can belong to only one cluster, whereas in soft clustering items are allowed to belong to multiple clusters, perhaps with varying weights for these multiple assignments. If hard clustering is employed, then cluster assignment is easy. Term i belongs to cluster j if $A(i,j)$ is the maximum element in the ith row of A. Similarly, document k belongs to cluster l if $B(l,k)$ is the maximum element in the kth column of B.

Once cluster assignments are available (by either hard or soft clustering), a

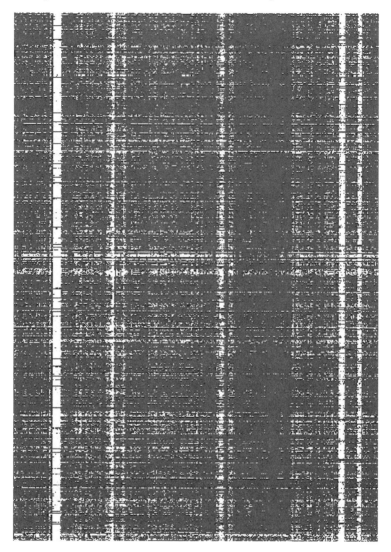

FIGURE 5.7 (SEE COLOR INSERT FOLLOWING PAGE 130.):
Pixel plot of the raw Enron term-by-email matrix.

very useful next step is to display the clustering results visually. We demonstrate the value of this by considering once again the Enron email dataset described in Section 5.4. The raw term-by-email matrix for this dataset appears to have no structure, as shown in the pixel plot of Figure 5.7. Each nonzero entry in the raw matrix is represented by a pixel, and the magnitude of the entry is captured by the intensity of the pixel.

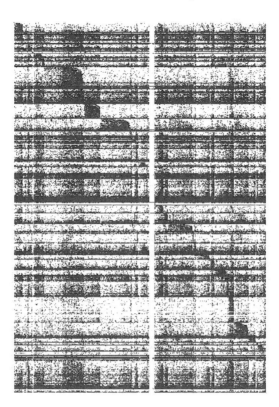

FIGURE 5.8 (SEE COLOR INSERT FOLLOWING PAGE 130.):
Pixel plot of the reordered Enron term-by-email matrix.

Figure 5.8 is simply a reordered version of the raw Enron term-by-email matrix using $r = 50$ (the number of columns of A and rows of B). Both the terms and the documents were reordered according to the hard cluster assignments produced by the NMF. The nice block structure of the reordered matrix reveals the hidden clusters. For instance, a dense block means that a set of documents frequently used the same set of terms. Contrasting Figure 5.7 with Figure 5.8 reveals just how much structure was hidden in the dataset.

While the visualization of Figure 5.8, which was created with the NMF, is valuable to practitioners, an even more valuable tool allows the practitioner to more deeply examine clusters of interest and perhaps attach a meaning to the cluster. This is possible with the help of the vismatrix tool[5] created by David Gleich.

---

[5]http://www.stanford.edu/~dgleich/programs/vismatrix

This tool has a mouseover feature that enables a user to hold the mouse over any pixel in the matrix (reordered or otherwise) and determine which term and which document the pixel corresponds to. Figure 5.9 is a screenshot from the vismatrix tool.

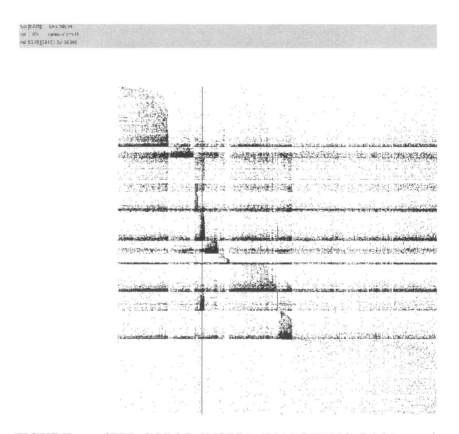

FIGURE 5.9 (SEE COLOR INSERT FOLLOWING PAGE 130.): Pixel plot of the reordered Enron term-by-document matrix with term and document labels.

Notice the upper lefthand corner contains the word `touchdown`, which represents the term (term ID#6635) being pointed to, and the identifier `dean-cinfo84`, which represents the document ID. This document, document 3819, was email message #84 saved by an Enron employee named Dean in his `cinfo` folder. Scrolling over pixels in a dense block causes the term and document labels to change in this area of the vismatrix tool. The human brain can quickly process many terms at once. As a result, the user can attach a judgment to the quality of the clustering and can often attach a label as well. For instance, the cluster over which the yellow crosshairs of Figure 5.9 lie also contains the terms (among others) *football, longhorn, Texas, quarterback, score, redshirt, freshmen, punt,* and *tackle,* prompting a user to potentially label this cluster *Texas Longhorn Football.*

The vismatrix tool also allows a user to quickly scan document labels as well. Thus, hidden patterns that pertain to the documents can be found. For instance, this Enron dataset contains one small cluster of 12 documents using 447 terms. Figure 5.10 is a close-up[6] of this part of the reordered Enron term-by-email matrix.

FIGURE 5.10 (SEE COLOR INSERT FOLLOWING PAGE 130.): Close-up of one section of pixel plot of the reordered Enron term-by-document matrix.

---

[6]The vismatrix tool also contains zoom in and zoom out features.

Using the mouse to scroll over this small dense block reveals that the following terms (among others) are assigned to this small cluster: *fortune, ceo, coo, top, women,* and *powerful.* These terms and abbreviations, in fact, refer to Louise Kitchen (a top-ranking Enron employee responsible for energy trading and Enron Online) who was named one of the 50 most powerful women in business by Fortune Magazine in 2001. Mousing over this same small but dense block, but focusing on the document labels this time reveals that all 12 of these emails have the label `kitchen-1-americaspress#`, meaning that they were all saved in Louise Kitchen's own private `1-americaspress` folder. So what appeared to be a small possibly interesting cluster, after further inspection thanks to the vismatrix tool, is an "ego cluster," and thus perhaps of only marginal interest.

5.7 Future Work

As demonstrated by this study, nonnegative tensor factorization (implemented by PARAFAC) can be used to extract meaningful discussions from email communications. The ability to assess term-to-author (or term-to-email) associations both semantically and temporally via three-way and four-way decompositions is an important advancement in email surveillance research. Previously reported clusters of Enron emails using nonnegative matrix factorization (i.e., two-way decompositions) (7; 9; 31) were unable to extract discussions such as the *Education* thread mentioned in Section 5.5.1 or sequence the discussion of the company's downfall by source (newfeeds versus employee-generated). The optimal segmentation of *time* as a third (or fourth) dimension for email clustering may be problematic. Grouping or clustering emails by month may not be sufficient for tracking event-driven activities and so more research in the cost-benefit tradeoffs of finer time segmentation (e.g., grouping by weeks, days, or even minutes) is certainly needed. Determining the optimal tensor rank r for models such as PARAFAC is certainly another important research topic. Determining an optimal term weighting scheme for multi-way arrays is also an important task that could greatly influence the quality of results—more research on this topic is especially needed. Finally, the visualization of multi-way arrays (tensors) certainly constitutes an important area of software development that could greatly facilitate both the identification and interpretation of communications.

Acknowledgments

This research was sponsored by the United States Department of Energy and by Sandia National Laboratory, a multiprogram laboratory operated by Sandia Corporation, a Lockheed Martin Company, for the United States Department of Energy under contract DE–AC04–94AL85000. The authors would like to thank the anonymous referees for their helpful comments and suggestions on improving the original version.

References

[1] E. Acar, S. A. Çamtepe, M. S. Krishnamoorthy, and Bülent Yener. Modeling and multiway analysis of chatroom tensors. In *ISI 2005: IEEE International Conference on Intelligence and Security Informatics*, volume 3495 of *Lecture Notes in Computer Science*, pages 256–268. Springer-Verlag, 2005.

[2] B. W. Bader and T. G. Kolda. Algorithm 862: MATLAB tensor classes for fast algorithm prototyping. *ACM Transactions on Mathematical Software*, 32(4):635–653, December 2006.

[3] B. W. Bader and T. G. Kolda. Efficient MATLAB computations with sparse and factored tensors. *SIAM Journal on Scientific Computing*, July 2007. Accepted.

[4] B. W. Bader and T. G. Kolda. Matlab tensor toolbox, version 2.2. `http://csmr.ca.sandia.gov/~tgkolda/TensorToolbox/`, January 2007.

[5] B. W. Bader, M. W. Berry, and M. Browne. Discussion Tracking in Enron Email Using PARAFAC. In M.W. Berry and M. Castellanos, editors, *Survey of Text Mining II: Clustering, Classification, and Retrieval*, pages 147–163. Springer-Verlag, London, 2008.

[6] M. W. Berry and M. Browne. Email surveillance using nonnegative matrix factorization. In *Workshop on Link Analysis, Counterterrorism and Security, SIAM Conf. on Data Mining*, Newport Beach, CA, 2005.

[7] M. W. Berry and M. Browne. Email surveillance using nonnegative matrix factorization. *Computational & Mathematical Organization Theory*, 11:249–264, 2005.

[8] M. W. Berry and M. Browne. *Understanding Search Engines: Mathematical Modeling and Text Retrieval*. SIAM, Philadelphia, PA, second edition, 2005.

[9] M. W. Berry, M. Browne, A. N. Langville, V. P. Pauca, and R. J. Plemmons. Algorithms and applications for approximate nonnegative matrix factorization. *Computational Statistics & Data Analysis*, 52(1):155–173, 2007.

[10] R. Bro and S. De Jong. A fast non-negativity-constrained least squares algorithm. *J. Chemometr.*, 11(5):393–401, 1997.

[11] J. D. Carroll and J. J. Chang. Analysis of individual differences in multidimensional scaling via an N-way generalization of 'Eckart-Young' decomposition. *Psychometrika*, 35:283–319, 1970.

[12] W. W. Cohen. Enron email dataset. Webpage. `http://www.cs.cmu.edu/~enron/`.

[13] N. (Klaas) M. Faber, R. Bro, and P. K. Hopke. Recent developments in CANDECOMP/PARAFAC algorithms: a critical review. *Chemometr. Intell. Lab. Syst.*, 65(1):119–137, January 2003.

[14] Federal Energy Regulatory Commision. Ferc: Information released in Enron investigation. `http://www.ferc.gov/industries/electric/indus-act/wec/enron/info-release.asp`.

[15] D. FitzGerald, M. Cranitch, and E. Coyle. Non-negative tensor factorisation for sound source separation. In *ISSC 2005: Proceedings of the Irish Signals and Systems Conference*, 2005.

[16] M. P. Friedlander and K. Hatz. Computing nonnegative tensor factorizations. Technical Report TR-2006-21, Department of Computer Science, University of British Columbia, October 2006.

[17] J. T. Giles, L. Wo, and M. W. Berry. GTP (General Text Parser) Software for Text Mining. In H. Bozdogan, editor, *Statistical Data Mining and Knowledge Discovery*, pages 455–471. CRC Press, Boca Raton, FL, 2003.

[18] T. Grieve. The Decline and Fall of the Enron Empire. *Slate*, October 14 2003. `http://www.salon.com/news/feature/2003/10/14/enron/index\_np.html`.

[19] R. A. Harshman. Foundations of the PARAFAC procedure: models and conditions for an "explanatory" multi-modal factor analysis. *UCLA working papers in phonetics*, 16:1–84, 1970. Available at `http://publish.uwo.ca/~harshman/wpppfac0.pdf`.

[20] T. Hazan, S. Polak, and A. Shashua. Sparse image coding using a 3D non-negative tensor factorization. In *ICCV 2005: 10th IEEE International Conference on Computer Vision*, volume 1, pages 50–57. IEEE Computer Society, 2005.

[21] T. G. Kolda and B. W. Bader. The TOPHITS model for higher-order web link analysis. In *Workshop on Link Analysis, Counterterrorism and Security*, 2006.

[22] T. G. Kolda and B. W. Bader. Tensor decompositions and applications. *SIAM Review*, 2008. to appear.

[23] T. G. Kolda, B. W. Bader, and J. P. Kenny. Higher-order web link analysis using multilinear algebra. In *ICDM 2005: Proceedings of the 5th IEEE International Conference on Data Mining*, pages 242–249. IEEE Computer Society, 2005.

[24] D. D. Lee and H. S. Seung. Learning the parts of objects by non-negative matrix factorization. *Nature*, 401:788–791, 21 October 1999.

[25] B. Mclean and P. Elkind. *The Smartest Guys in the Room: The Amazing Rise and Scandalous Fall of Enron*. Portfolio, 2003.

[26] M. Mørup, M. N. Schmidt, and L. K. Hansen. Shift invariant sparse coding of image and music data. Technical report, Technical University of Denmark, 2007.

[27] M. Mørup, L. Hansen, J. Parnas, and S. M. Arnfred. Decomposing the time-frequency representation of EEG using nonnegative matrix and multi-way factorization. Available at `http://www2.imm.dtu.dk/pubdb/views/edoc_download.php/4144/pdf/imm4144.pdf`, 2006.

[28] P. Paatero. A weighted non-negative least squares algorithm for three-way "PARAFAC" factor analysis. *Chemometr. Intell. Lab. Syst.*, 38(2):223–242, October 1997.

[29] P. Paatero and U. Tapper. Positive matrix factorization: A non-negative factor model with optimal utilization of error estimates of data values. *Environmetrics*, 5(2):111–126, 1994.

[30] C. E. Priebe, J. M. Conroy, D. J. Marchette, and Y. Park. Enron data set. Webpage, February 2006. `http://cis.jhu.edu/~parky/Enron/enron.html`.

[31] F. Shahnaz, M. W. Berry, V. P. Pauca, and R. J. Plemmons. Document clustering using nonnegative matrix factorization. *Information Processing & Management*, 42(2):373–386, 2006.

[32] A. Shashua and T. Hazan. Non-negative tensor factorization with applications to statistics and computer vision. In *ICML 2005: Machine Learning, Proceedings of the Twenty-second International Conference*, 2005.

[33] J. Shetty and J. Adibi. Ex employee status report. Online, 2005. `http:www.isi.edu/~adibi/Enron/Enron_Employee_Status.xls`.

[34] N. D. Sidiropoulos, G. B. Giannakis, and R. Bro. Blind PARAFAC receivers for DS-CDMA systems. *IEEE Transactions on Signal Processing*, 48(3):810–823, 2000.

[35] A. Smilde, R. Bro, and P. Geladi. *Multi-Way Analysis: Applications in the Chemical Sciences.* Wiley, West Sussex, England, 2004.

[36] J.-T. Sun, H.-J. Zeng, H. Liu, Y. Lu, and Z. Chen. CubeSVD: a novel approach to personalized Web search. In *WWW 2005: Proceedings of the 14th international conference on World Wide Web*, pages 382–390. ACM Press, New York, 2005.

[37] G. Tomasi and R. Bro. PARAFAC and missing values. *Chemometr. Intell. Lab. Syst.*, 75(2):163–180, February 2005.

[38] L. R. Tucker. Some mathematical notes on three-mode factor analysis. *Psychometrika*, 31:279–311, 1966.

[39] M. Welling and M. Weber. Positive tensor factorization. *Pattern Recogn. Lett.*, 22(12):1255–1261, 2001.

Chapter 6

Text Clustering with Mixture of von Mises-Fisher Distributions

Arindam Banerjee, Inderjit Dhillon, Joydeep Ghosh, and Suvrit Sra

6.1 Introduction

There is a long-standing folklore in the information retrieval community that a vector space representation of text data has directional properties, i.e., the direction of the vector is much more important than its magnitude. This belief has led to practices such as using the cosine between two vectors for measuring similarity between the corresponding text documents, and to the scaling of vectors to unit L_2 norm (41; 40; 20).

In this chapter, we describe a probabilistic generative model (44; 25) based on directional distributions (30) for modeling text data.[1] Specifically, we suggest that a set of text documents that form multiple topics can be well modeled by a mixture of von Mises-Fisher (vMF) distributions, with each component corresponding to a topic. Generative models often provide greater insights into the anatomy of the data as compared to discriminative approaches. Moreover, domain knowledge can be easily incorporated into generative models; for example, in this chapter the directional nature of the data is reflected in our choice of vMF distributions as the mixture components.

---

[1]This chapter treats L_2 normalized data and directional data as synonymous.

We derive two clustering algorithms based on Expectation Maximization (EM) for estimating the parameters of the mixture model from first principles. Our algorithms involve estimating a *concentration* parameter, κ, for each component of the mixture model. The ability to adapt κ on a per-component basis leads to substantial performance improvements over existing generative approaches to modeling directional data. We show a connection between the proposed methods and a class of existing algorithms for clustering high-dimensional directional data. In particular, our generative model has the same relation to spherical kmeans (`spkmeans`) (20) as a model based on a mixture of identity covariance Gaussians has to classical `kmeans` that uses squared Euclidean distances (9). We also present detailed experimental comparisons of the proposed algorithms with `spkmeans` and one of its variants. Our formulation uncovers the theoretical justification behind the use of the cosine similarity measure that has largely been *ad hoc*, i.e., based on empirical or intuitive justification, so far.

While this chapter focuses on text analysis, we note that many other important domains such as bioinformatics and collaborative filtering involve directional data as well. Thus, the scope and applications of the approaches taken in this chapter are much broader and not limited to text alone.

The remainder of the chapter is organized as follows. In Section 6.2, we discuss related work on mixture models, text clustering, and vMF distributions. We review the multivariate vMF distribution in Section 6.3. In Section 6.4 we introduce a generative model using a mixture of vMF distributions. We then derive the maximum likelihood parameter estimates of this model by employing an EM framework. Section 6.5 highlights our new method of approximating κ and also presents a mathematical analysis of hard assignments. Sections 6.4 and 6.5 form the basis for two clustering algorithms using soft and hard-assignments, respectively, and these algorithms are described in Section 6.6. Detailed experimental results and comparisons with other algorithms are offered in Section 6.7. A discussion on the behavior of our algorithms and a connection with simulated annealing follows in Section 6.8, and we conclude in Section 6.9.

Notation. Bold faced variables, e.g., $\mathbf{x}, \mu$ represent vectors; the norm $\| \cdot \|$ denotes the L_2 norm; sets are represented by script-style upper-case letters, e.g., $\mathcal{X}$, $\mathcal{Z}$. The set of reals is denoted by $\mathbb{R}$, while $\mathbb{S}^{d-1}$ denotes the $(d-1)$-dimensional sphere embedded in $\mathbb{R}^d$. Probability density functions are denoted by lower case letters such as f, p, q, and the probability of a set of events is denoted by P.

6.2   Related Work

There has been an enormous amount of work on clustering a wide variety of datasets across multiple disciplines over the past fifty years (26). The methods presented in this chapter are tailored for high-dimensional data with directional characteristics, rather than for arbitrary datasets. In the learning community, perhaps the most widely studied high-dimensional directional data stem from text documents represented by vector space models. Much of the work in this domain uses discriminative approaches (48; 54). For example, hierarchical agglomerative methods based on cosine, Jaccard or Dice coefficients were dominant for text clustering till the mid-1990s (39). Over the past few years several new approaches, ranging from spectral partitioning (27; 54), to the use of generative models from the exponential family, e.g., mixture of multinomials or Bernoulli distributions (35) etc., have emerged. A fairly extensive list of references on generative approaches to text clustering can be found in (55).

Of particular relevance to this work is the `spkmeans` algorithm (20), which adapts the `kmeans` algorithm to normalized data by using the cosine similarity for cluster allocation, and also by re-normalizing the cluster means to unit length. The `spkmeans` algorithm is superior to regular `kmeans` for high-dimensional text data, and competitive or superior in both performance and speed to a wide range of other existing alternatives for text clustering (49). It also provides better characterization of clusters in terms of their top representative or discriminative terms.

The vMF distribution is known in the literature on directional statistics (30), and the maximum likelihood estimates (MLE) of the parameters have been given for a single distribution. Recently Piater (37) obtained parameter estimates for a mixture for circular, i.e., 2-dimensional vMFs. In an Appendix to his thesis, Piater starts on an EM formulation for 2-D vMFs but cites the difficulty of parameter estimation (especially κ) and eventually avoids doing EM in favor of another numerical gradient descent based scheme. Mooney et al. (33) use a mixture of two circular von Mises distributions to estimate the parameters using a quasi-Newton procedure. Wallace and Dowe (51) perform mixture modeling for circular von Mises distributions and have produced a software called Snob that implements their ideas. McLachlan and Peel (31) discuss mixture analysis of directional data and mention the possibility of using Fisher distributions (3-dimensional vMFs), but instead use 3-dimensional Kent distributions (30). They also mention work related to the clustering of directional data, but all the efforts included by them are restricted to 2-D or 3-D vMFs. Indeed, (31) also draws attention to the difficulty of parameter estimation even for 3-D vMFs.

The connection between a generative model involving vMF distributions with constant κ and the `spkmeans` algorithm was first observed by (6). A variant that could adapt in an on-line fashion leading to balanced cluster-ing solutions was developed by (7). Balancing was encouraged by taking a frequency-sensitive competitive learning approach in which the concentra-tion of a mixture component was made inversely proportional to the number of data points already allocated to it. Another online competitive learning scheme using vMF distributions for minimizing a KL-divergence based distor-tion was proposed by (43). Note that the full EM solution was not obtained or employed in either of these works. Recently a detailed empirical study of several generative models for document clustering, including a simple movMF model that constrains the concentration κ to be the same for all mixture com-ponents during any iteration, was presented by (56). Even with this restric-tion, this model was superior to both hard and soft versions of multivariate Bernoulli and multinomial models. In recent years, the movMF model has been successfully applied to text mining and anomaly detection applications for the NASA Aviation Safety Reporting System (ASRS) (47; 46).

Recently, (10) discussed the modeling of high dimensional directional data using mixtures of Watson distributions, mainly to handle axial symmetries in the data. The authors of (10) followed the parameter estimation techniques developed in this chapter to obtain numerical estimates for the concentration parameter κ for Watson distributions. Additionally, alternate parameter esti-mates along with a connection of mixture of Watson based models to *diametric clustering* (19) were developed in (45). For text data, mixtures of Watson dis-tributions usually perform inferior to moVMF based models, though for gene expression data they could be potentially better.

6.3   Preliminaries

In this section, we review the von Mises-Fisher distribution and maximum likelihood estimation of its parameters from independent samples.

6.3.1   The von Mises-Fisher (vMF) Distribution

A d-dimensional unit random vector $\mathbf{x}$ (i.e., $\mathbf{x} \in \mathbb{R}^d$ and $\|\mathbf{x}\| = 1$, or equiva-lently $\mathbf{x} \in \mathbb{S}^{d-1}$) is said to have d-variate von Mises-Fisher (vMF) distribution if its probability density function is given by

$$f(\mathbf{x}|\mu, \kappa) = c_d(\kappa)e^{\kappa\mu^T\mathbf{x}} , \tag{6.1}$$

where $\|\mu\| = 1$, $\kappa \geq 0$ and $d \geq 2$. The normalizing constant $c_d(\kappa)$ is given by

$$c_d(\kappa) = \frac{\kappa^{d/2-1}}{(2\pi)^{d/2}I_{d/2-1}(\kappa)} , \tag{6.2}$$

where $I_p(\cdot)$ represents the modified Bessel function of the first kind and order p, and is defined as (1)

$$I_p(\kappa) = \sum_{k \geq 0} \frac{1}{\Gamma(p+k+1)k!} \left(\frac{\kappa}{2}\right)^{2k+p},$$

where $\Gamma(\cdot)$ is the well-known Gamma function.

The density $f(\mathbf{x}|\mu, \kappa)$ is parameterized by the mean direction μ, and the *concentration* parameter κ, so-called because it characterizes how strongly the unit vectors drawn according to $f(\mathbf{x}|\mu, \kappa)$ are concentrated about the mean direction μ. Larger values of κ imply stronger concentration about the mean direction. In particular when $\kappa = 0$, $f(\mathbf{x}|\mu, \kappa)$ reduces to the uniform density on $\mathbb{S}^{d-1}$, and as $\kappa \to \infty$, $f(\mathbf{x}|\mu, \kappa)$ tends to a point density. The interested reader is referred to (30), (24), or (21) for details on vMF distributions.

The vMF distribution is one of the simplest parametric distributions for directional data, and has properties analogous to those of the multivariate Gaussian distribution for data in $\mathbb{R}^d$. For example, the maximum entropy density on $\mathbb{S}^{d-1}$ subject to the constraint that $E[\mathbf{x}]$ is fixed is a vMF density (see (38, pp. 172–174) and (29) for details).

6.3.2 Maximum Likelihood Estimates

In this section we look briefly at maximum likelihood estimates for the parameters of a single vMF distribution. The detailed derivations can be found in (5). Let $\mathcal{X}$ be a finite set of sample unit vectors drawn independently following $f(\mathbf{x}|\mu, \kappa)$ (6.1), i.e.,

$$\mathcal{X} = \{\mathbf{x}_i \in \mathbb{S}^{d-1} \mid \mathbf{x}_i \text{ drawn following } f(\mathbf{x}|\mu, \kappa) \text{ for } 1 \leq i \leq n\}.$$

Given $\mathcal{X}$ we want to find maximum likelihood estimates for the parameters μ and κ of the distribution $f(\mathbf{x}|\mu, \kappa)$. Assuming the $\mathbf{x}_i$ to be independent and identically distributed, we can write the log-likelihood of $\mathcal{X}$ as

$$\ln P(\mathcal{X}|\mu, \kappa) = n \ln c_d(\kappa) + \kappa \mu^T \mathbf{r}, \tag{6.3}$$

where $\mathbf{r} = \sum_i \mathbf{x}_i$. To obtain the maximum likelihood estimates of μ and κ, we have to maximize (6.3) subject to the constraints $\mu^T \mu = 1$ and $\kappa \geq 0$. A simple calculation (5) shows that the MLE solutions $\widehat{\mu}$ and $\widehat{\kappa}$ may be obtained from the following equations:

$$\widehat{\mu} = \frac{\mathbf{r}}{\|\mathbf{r}\|} = \frac{\sum_{i=1}^n \mathbf{x}_i}{\|\sum_{i=1}^n \mathbf{x}_i\|}, \tag{6.4}$$

$$\text{and} \qquad \frac{I_{d/2}(\widehat{\kappa})}{I_{d/2-1}(\widehat{\kappa})} = \frac{\|\mathbf{r}\|}{n} = \bar{r}. \tag{6.5}$$

Since computing $\widehat{\kappa}$ involves an implicit equation (6.5) that is a ratio of Bessel functions, it is not possible to obtain an analytic solution, and we have to resort to numerical or asymptotic methods to obtain an approximation (see Section 6.5).

6.4   EM on a Mixture of vMFs (moVMF)

We now consider a mixture of k vMF (moVMF) distributions that serves as a generative model for directional data, and obtain the update equations for estimating the mixture-density parameters from a given dataset using the Expectation Maximization (EM) framework. Let $f_h(\mathbf{x}|\theta_h)$ denote a vMF distribution with parameters $\theta_h = (\mu_h, \kappa_h)$ for $1 \leq h \leq k$. Then a mixture of these k vMF distributions has a density given by

$$f(\mathbf{x}|\Theta) = \sum_{h=1}^{k} \alpha_h f_h(\mathbf{x}|\theta_h), \qquad (6.6)$$

where $\Theta = \{\alpha_1, \cdots, \alpha_k, \theta_1, \cdots, \theta_k\}$ and the α_h are non-negative and sum to one. To sample a point from this mixture density we choose the h-th vMF randomly with probability α_h, and then sample a point (on $\mathbb{S}^{d-1}$) following $f_h(\mathbf{x}|\theta_h)$. Let $\mathcal{X} = \{\mathbf{x}_1, \cdots, \mathbf{x}_n\}$ be a dataset of n independently sampled points that follow (6.6). Let $\mathcal{Z} = \{\mathbf{z}_1, \cdots, \mathbf{z}_n\}$ be the corresponding set of hidden random variables that indicate the particular vMF distribution from which the points are sampled. In particular, $\mathbf{z}_i = h$ if $\mathbf{x}_i$ is sampled from $f_h(\mathbf{x}|\theta_h)$. Assuming that the values in the set $\mathcal{Z}$ are known, the log-likelihood of the observed data is given by

$$\ln P(\mathcal{X}, \mathcal{Z}|\Theta) = \sum_{i=1}^{n} \ln \left(\alpha_{\mathbf{z}_i} f_{\mathbf{z}_i}(\mathbf{x}_i|\theta_{\mathbf{z}_i}) \right). \qquad (6.7)$$

Obtaining maximum likelihood estimates for the parameters would have been easy were the $\mathbf{z}_i$ truly known. Unfortunately that is not the case, and (6.7) is really a random variable dependent on the distribution of $\mathcal{Z}$—this random variable is usually called the *complete data log-likelihood*. For a given $(\mathcal{X}, \Theta)$, it is possible to estimate the most likely conditional distribution of $\mathcal{Z}|(\mathcal{X}, \Theta)$, and this estimation forms the E-step in an EM framework. Using an EM approach for maximizing the expectation of (6.7) with the constraints $\mu_h^T \mu_h = 1$ and

$\kappa_h \geq 0$, we obtain

$$\alpha_h = \frac{1}{n} \sum_{i=1}^{n} p(h|\mathbf{x}_i, \Theta),$$
(6.8)

$$\mathbf{r}_h = \sum_{i=1}^{n} \mathbf{x}_i p(h|\mathbf{x}_i, \Theta),$$
(6.9)

$$\widehat{\mu}_h = \frac{\mathbf{r}_h}{\|\mathbf{r}_h\|},$$
(6.10)

$$\frac{I_{d/2}(\widehat{\kappa}_h)}{I_{d/2-1}(\widehat{\kappa}_h)} = \frac{\|\mathbf{r}_h\|}{\sum_{i=1}^{n} p(h|\mathbf{x}_i, \Theta)}.$$
(6.11)

Observe that (6.10) and (6.11) are intuitive generalizations of (6.4) and (6.5) respectively, and they correspond to an M-step in an EM framework. Given these parameter updates, we now look at schemes for updating the distributions of $\mathcal{Z}|(\mathcal{X}, \Theta)$ (i.e., an E-step) to maximize the likelihood of the data given the parameters estimates above.

From the standard EM framework, the distribution of the hidden variables (34; 11) is given by

$$p(h|\mathbf{x}_i, \Theta) = \frac{\alpha_h \, f_h(\mathbf{x}_i|\Theta)}{\sum_{l=1}^{k} \alpha_l \, f_l(\mathbf{x}_i|\Theta)}.$$
(6.12)

It can be shown (15) that the *incomplete data log-likelihood*, $\ln p(\mathcal{X}|\Theta)$, is non-decreasing at each iteration of the parameter and distribution updates. Iteration over these two updates provides the foundation for our `soft-moVMF` algorithm given in Section 6.6.

Our second update scheme is based on the widely used hard-assignment heuristic for unsupervised learning. In this case, the distribution of the hidden variables is given by

$$q(h|\mathbf{x}_i, \Theta) = \begin{cases} 1, & \text{if } h = \operatorname*{argmax}_{h'} \ p(h'|\mathbf{x}_i, \Theta), \\ 0, & \text{otherwise.} \end{cases}$$
(6.13)

It can be shown (5) that the above hard-assignment rule actually maximizes a non-trivial lower bound on the incomplete data log-likelihood. Iteration over the M-step and the hard-assignment rule leads to the `hard-moVMF` algorithm given in Section 6.6.

6.5 Handling High-Dimensional Text Datasets

Although the mixture model outlined in Section 6.4 appears to be straightforward, there is one critical issue that needs to be addressed before one can apply the model to real life text datasets: How to efficiently and accurately compute $\kappa_h, h = 1, \ldots, k$ from (6.11) for high-dimensional data? The problem of estimating κ_h is analyzed in Section 6.5.1 and experimentally studied in Section 6.5.2.

6.5.1   Approximating κ

Recall that due to the lack of an analytical solution, it is not possible to directly estimate the κ values (see (6.5) and (6.11)). One may employ a nonlinear root-finder for estimating κ, but for high dimensional data, problems of overflows and numerical instabilities plague such root-finders. Therefore, an asymptotic approximation of κ is the best choice for estimating κ. Such approaches also have the benefit of taking constant computation time as opposed to any iterative method.

Mardia and Jupp (30) provide approximations for estimating κ for a single component (6.5) for two limiting cases (Approximations (10.3.7) and (10.3.10) of (30, pp. 198)):

$$\widehat{\kappa} \approx \frac{d-1}{2(1-\bar{r})} \qquad\qquad \text{valid for large } \bar{r}, \qquad (6.14)$$

$$\widehat{\kappa} \approx d\bar{r}\left(1 + \frac{d}{d+2}\bar{r}^2 + \frac{d^2(d+8)}{(d+2)^2(d+4)}\bar{r}^4\right) \qquad \text{valid for small } \bar{r}, \qquad (6.15)$$

where $\bar{r}$ is given by (6.5).

These approximations assume that $\kappa \gg d$, which is typically not valid for high dimensional data (see the discussion in Section 6.8 for an intuition). Furthermore, the $\bar{r}$ values corresponding to the text datasets considered in this chapter are in the mid-range rather than in the two extreme ranges of $\bar{r}$ that are catered to by the above approximations. We obtain a more accurate approximation for κ as described below. With $A_d(\kappa) = \frac{I_{d/2}(\kappa)}{I_{d/2-1}(\kappa)}$, observe that $A_d(\kappa)$ is a ratio of Bessel functions that differ in their order by just one. Fortunately there exists a continued fraction representation of $A_d(\kappa)$ (52) given by

$$A_d(\kappa) = \frac{I_{d/2}(\kappa)}{I_{d/2-1}(\kappa)} = \cfrac{1}{\cfrac{d}{\kappa} + \cfrac{1}{\cfrac{d+2}{\kappa} + \cdots}} . \qquad (6.16)$$

Letting $A_d(\kappa) = \bar{r}$, we can write (6.16) approximately as

$$\frac{1}{\bar{r}} \approx \frac{d}{\kappa} + \bar{r} ,$$

which yields

$$\kappa \approx \frac{d\bar{r}}{1 - \bar{r}^2} .$$

We empirically found (see Section 6.5.2 below) that the quality of the above approximation can be improved by adding a correction term of $-\bar{r}^3/(1 - \bar{r}^2)$ to it. Thus, we finally get

$$\hat{\kappa} = \frac{\bar{r}d - \bar{r}^3}{1 - \bar{r}^2} . \tag{6.17}$$

Recently Tanabe et al. (50) used some inequalities regarding the Bessel function ratio $A_d(\kappa)$ (3) to bound the solution to $A_d(\kappa) = \bar{r}$ as

$$\frac{\bar{r}(d-2)}{1 - \bar{r}^2} \leq \hat{\kappa} \leq \frac{\bar{r}d}{1 - \bar{r}^2}.$$

Our solution (6.17) lies within these bounds, thus leading to a better theoretical justification in retrospect.

The approximation in (6.17) could perhaps be made even more accurate by adding other correction terms that are functions of $\bar{r}$ and d. However, we remark that if one wants a more accurate approximation, it is easier to use (6.17) as a starting point and then perform Newton-Raphson iterations for solving $A_d(\hat{\kappa}) - \bar{r} = 0$, since it is easy to evaluate $A'_d(\kappa) = 1 - A_d(\kappa)^2 - \frac{d-1}{\kappa} A_d(\kappa)$. However, for high-dimensional data, accurately computing $A_d(\kappa)$ can be quite slow compared to efficiently approximating $\hat{\kappa}$ using (6.17), and a very high accuracy for κ is not that critical. For other approximations of κ and some related issues, the reader is referred to (21; 5).

We now show some numerical results to assess the quality of our approximation in comparison to (6.14) and (6.15). First note that a particular value of $\bar{r}$ may correspond to many different combinations of κ and d values. Then, one needs to evaluate the accuracy of the approximations over the parts of the d-κ plane that are expected to be encountered in the target application domains. Section 6.5.2 below provides such an assessment by comparing performances over different slices of the d-κ plane and over a range of $\bar{r}$ values. Below we simply compare the accuracies at a set of points on this plane via Table 6.1 which shows the actual numerical values of κ that the three approximations (6.14), (6.15), and (6.17) yielded at these points. The $\bar{r}$ values shown in the table were computed using (6.5).

TABLE 6.1: Approximations $\hat{\kappa}$ for a sampling of κ and d values.

$(d, \bar{r}, \kappa)$	$\hat{\kappa}$ in (6.14)	$\hat{\kappa}$ in (6.15)	$\hat{\kappa}$ in (6.17)
$(10, 0.633668, 10)$	12.3	9.4	**10.2**
$(100, 0.46945, 60)$	93.3	59.4	**60.1**
$(500, 0.46859, 300)$	469.5	296.8	**300.1**
$(1000, 0.554386, 800)$	1120.9	776.8	**800.1**

6.5.2   Experimental Study of the Approximation

In this section we provide a brief experimental study to assess the quality of our approximation of the concentration parameter κ. Recall that our approximation (6.17) attempts to solve the implicit non-linear equation

$$\frac{I_{d/2}(\kappa)}{I_{d/2-1}(\kappa)} = \bar{r}. \tag{6.18}$$

We note that for large values of $\bar{r}$ ($\bar{r}$ close to 1), approximation (6.14) is reasonable; for small values of $\bar{r}$ (usually for $\bar{r} < 0.2$) estimate (6.15) is quite good; whereas (6.17) yields good approximations for most values of $\bar{r}$.

Since a particular value of $\bar{r}$ may correspond to many different combinations of κ and d values, to assess the quality of various approximations, we need to evaluate their performance across the (κ, d) plane. However, such an assessment is difficult to illustrate through 2-dimensional plots. To supplement Table 6.1, which showed how the three approximations behave on a sampling of points from the (κ, d) plane, in this section we present experimental results on some slices of this plane, where we either keep d fixed and vary κ, or we keep κ fixed and vary d. For all our evaluations, the $\bar{r}$ values were computed using (6.18).

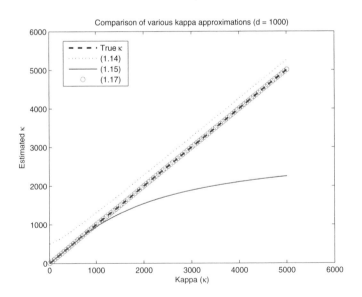

FIGURE 6.1: Comparison of true and approximated κ values, with $d = 1000$.

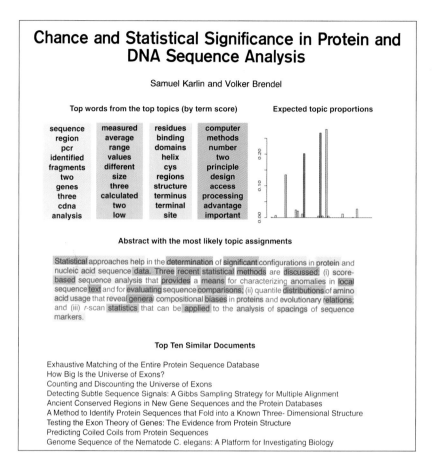

Chance and Statistical Significance in Protein and DNA Sequence Analysis

Samuel Karlin and Volker Brendel

Top words from the top topics (by term score)

sequence	measured	residues	computer
region	average	binding	methods
pcr	range	domains	number
identified	values	helix	two
fragments	different	cys	principle
two	size	regions	design
genes	three	structure	access
three	calculated	terminus	processing
cdna	two	terminal	advantage
analysis	low	site	important

Expected topic proportions

Abstract with the most likely topic assignments

Statistical approaches help in the determination of significant configurations in protein and nucleic acid sequence data. Three recent statistical methods are discussed: (i) score-based sequence analysis that provides a means for characterizing anomalies in local sequence text and for evaluating sequence comparisons; (ii) quantile distributions of amino acid usage that reveal general compositional biases in proteins and evolutionary relations; and (iii) r-scan statistics that can be applied to the analysis of spacings of sequence markers.

Top Ten Similar Documents

Exhaustive Matching of the Entire Protein Sequence Database
How Big Is the Universe of Exons?
Counting and Discounting the Universe of Exons
Detecting Subtle Sequence Signals: A Gibbs Sampling Strategy for Multiple Alignment
Ancient Conserved Regions in New Gene Sequences and the Protein Databases
A Method to Identify Protein Sequences that Fold into a Known Three- Dimensional Structure
Testing the Exon Theory of Genes: The Evidence from Protein Structure
Predicting Coiled Coils from Protein Sequences
Genome Sequence of the Nematode C. elegans: A Platform for Investigating Biology

FIGURE 4.4: The analysis of a document from *Science*. Document similarity was computed using Eq. 4.4; topic words were computed using Eq. 4.3.

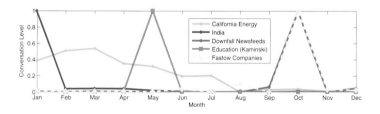

FIGURE 5.2: Five discussion topics identified in the three-way analysis over months.

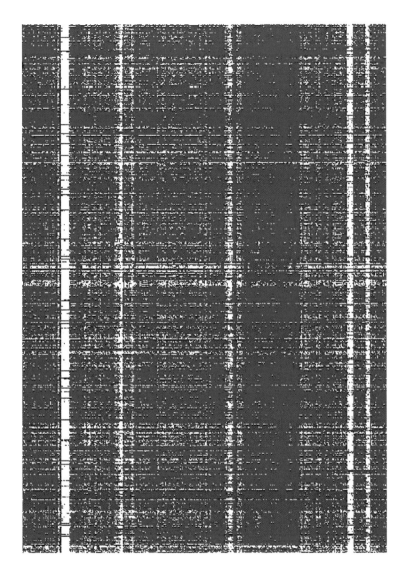

FIGURE 5.7: Pixel plot of the raw Enron term-by-email matrix.

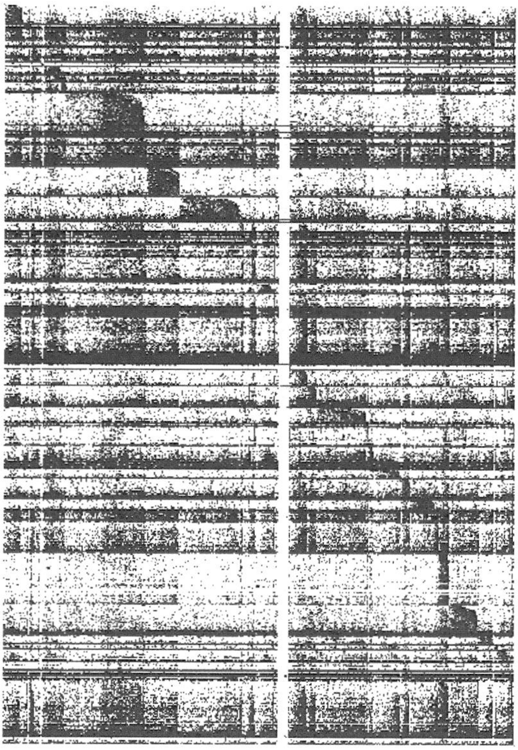

FIGURE 5.8: Pixel plot of the reordered Enron term-by-email matrix.

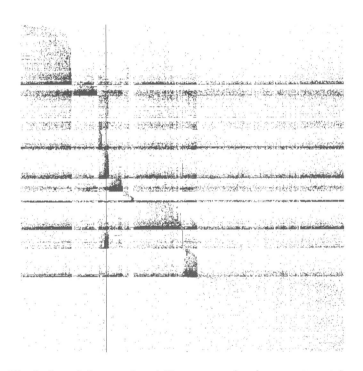

FIGURE 5.9: Pixel plot of the reordered Enron term-by-document matrix with term and document labels.

FIGURE 5.10: Close-up of one section of pixel plot of the reordered Enron term-by-document matrix.

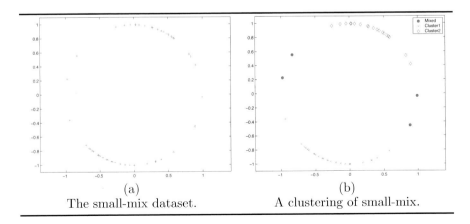

(a)
The small-mix dataset.

(b)
A clustering of small-mix.

FIGURE 6.4: Small-mix dataset and its clustering by `soft-moVMF`.

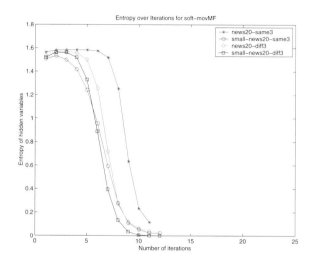

FIGURE 6.8: Variation of entropy of hidden variables with number of iterations (`soft-movMF`).

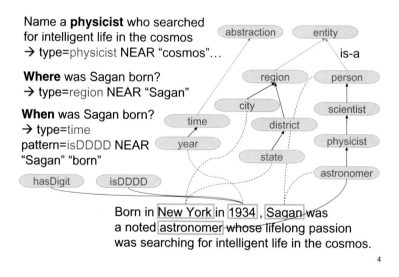

FIGURE 10.1: Document as a linear sequence of tokens, some connected to a type hierarchy. Some sample queries and their approximate translation to a semi-structured form are shown.

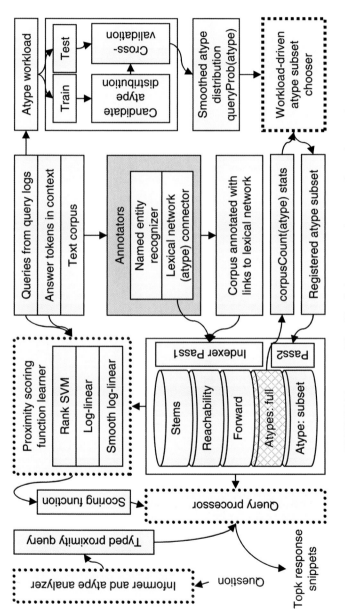

FIGURE 10.2: The IR4QA system that we describe in this paper.

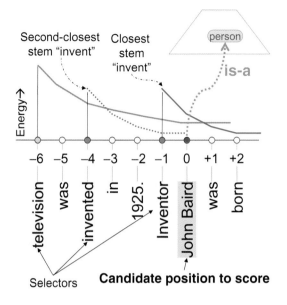

FIGURE 10.13: Setting up the proximity scoring problem.

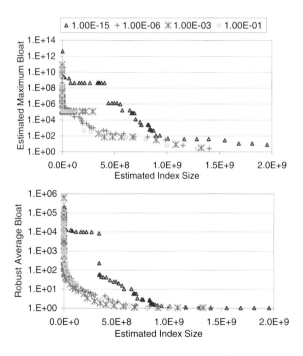

FIGURE 10.28: Estimated space-time tradeoffs produced by **Atype-SubsetChooser**. The y-axis uses a log scale. Note that the curve for $\ell = 10^{-3}$ (suggested by Figure 10.19) has the lowest average bloat.

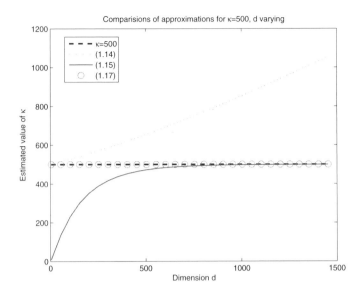

FIGURE 6.2: Comparison of approximations for varying d, $\kappa = 500$.

We begin by holding d fixed at 1000, and allow κ to vary from 10 to 5010. Figure 6.1 shows the values of computed $\widehat{\kappa}$ (estimation of κ) using the three approximations. From this figure one can see that (6.14) overestimates the true κ, while (6.15) underestimates it. However, our approximation (6.17) is very close to the true κ values.

Next we illustrate the quality of approximation when κ is held fixed and d is allowed to vary. Figure 6.2 illustrates how the various approximations behave as the dimensionality d is varied from $d = 4$ till $d = 1454$. The concentration parameter κ was set at 500 for this experiment. We see that (6.15) catches up with the true value of κ after approximately $d \geq 2\kappa$ (because the associated $\bar{r}$ values become small), whereas (6.17) remains accurate throughout.

Since all the approximations depend on $\bar{r}$ (which implicitly depends on κ and d), it is illustrative to also plot the approximation errors as $\bar{r}$ is allowed to vary. Figure 6.3 shows how the three approximations perform as $\bar{r}$ ranges from 0.05 to 0.95. Let $f(d, \bar{r})$, $g(d, \bar{r})$, and $h(d, \bar{r})$ represent the approximations to κ using (6.14), (6.15), and (6.17), respectively. Figure 6.3 displays $|A_d(f(d, \bar{r})) - \bar{r}|$, $|A_d(g(d, \bar{r})) - \bar{r}|$, and $|A_d(h(d, \bar{r})) - \bar{r}|$ for the varying $\bar{r}$ values. Note that the y-axis is on a log-scale to appreciate the differences between the three approximations. We see that up to $\bar{r} \approx 0.18$ (dashed line on the plot), the approximation yielded by (6.15) has lower error. Thereafter, approximation (6.17) becomes better.

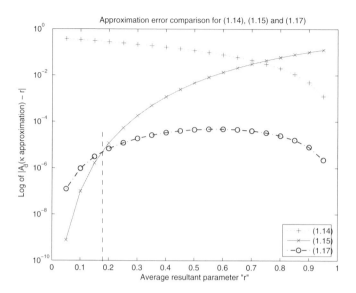

FIGURE 6.3: Comparison of approximations for varying $\bar{r}$ (with $d = 1000$).

6.6   Algorithms

Mixture models based on vMF distributions naturally lead to two algorithms for clustering directional data. The algorithms are centered on soft and hard-assignment schemes and are titled `soft-moVMF` and `hard-moVMF` respectively. The `soft-moVMF` algorithm (Algorithm 5) estimates the parameters of the mixture model exactly following the derivations in Section 6.4 using EM. Hence, it assigns soft (or probabilistic) labels to each point that are given by the posterior probabilities of the components of the mixture conditioned on the point. On termination, the algorithm gives the parameters $\Theta = \{\alpha_h, \mu_h, \kappa_h\}_{h=1}^{k}$ of the k vMF distributions that model the dataset $\mathcal{X}$, as well as the *soft-clustering*, i.e., the posterior probabilities $p(h|\mathbf{x}_i, \Theta)$, for all h and i.

The `hard-moVMF` algorithm (Algorithm 6) estimates the parameters of the mixture model using a hard assignment, or, *winner takes all* strategy. In other words, we do the assignment of the points based on a derived posterior distribution given by (6.13). After the hard assignments in every iteration, each point *belongs* to a single cluster. As before, the updates of the component parameters are done using the posteriors of the components, given the points. The crucial difference in this case is that the posterior probabilities are allowed to take only binary (0/1) values. Upon termination, Algorithm 6 yields a hard

---

Algorithm 5 `soft-moVMF`

Require: Set $\mathcal{X}$ of data points on $\mathbb{S}^{d-1}$
Ensure: A soft clustering of $\mathcal{X}$ over a mixture of k vMF distributions
  Initialize all $\alpha_h, \mu_h, \kappa_h, \ h = 1, \cdots, k$
  repeat
    {The E (Expectation) step of EM}
    for $i = 1$ to n **do**
      for $h = 1$ to k **do**
        $f_h(\mathbf{x}_i|\theta_h) \leftarrow c_d(\kappa_h)e^{\kappa_h \mu_h^T \mathbf{x}_i}$
      for $h = 1$ to k **do**
        $p(h|\mathbf{x}_i, \Theta) \leftarrow \dfrac{\alpha_h f_h(\mathbf{x}_i|\theta_h)}{\sum_{l=1}^{k} \alpha_l f_l(\mathbf{x}_i|\theta_l)}$
    {The M (Maximization) step of EM}
    for $h = 1$ to k **do**
      $\alpha_h \leftarrow \frac{1}{n}\sum_{i=1}^{n} p(h|\mathbf{x}_i, \Theta)$
      $\mu_h \leftarrow \sum_{i=1}^{n} \mathbf{x}_i p(h|\mathbf{x}_i, \Theta)$
      $\bar{r} \leftarrow \|\mu_h\|/(n\alpha_h)$
      $\mu_h \leftarrow \mu_h/\|\mu_h\|$
      $\kappa_h \leftarrow \frac{\bar{r}d - \bar{r}^3}{1 - \bar{r}^2}$
  until *convergence*

---

clustering of the data and the parameters $\Theta = \{\alpha_h, \mu_h, \kappa_h\}_{h=1}^{k}$ of the k vMFs that model the input dataset $\mathcal{X}$.

Finally, we show that by enforcing certain restrictive assumptions on the generative model, the `spkmeans` algorithm (Algorithm 7) can be viewed as a special case of both the `soft-moVMF` and `hard-moVMF` algorithms. In a mixture of vMF model, assume that the priors of all the components are equal, i.e., $\alpha_h = 1/k, \forall h$, and that all the components have (equal) infinite concentration parameters, i.e., $\kappa_h = \kappa \to \infty, \forall h$. Under these assumptions the E-step in the `soft-moVMF` algorithm reduces to assigning a point to its *nearest* cluster, where nearness is computed as a cosine similarity between the point and the cluster representative, i.e., a point $\mathbf{x}_i$ will be assigned to cluster $h^* = \text{argmax}_h \ \mathbf{x}_i^T \mu_h$, since

$$p(h^*|\mathbf{x}_i, \Theta) = \lim_{\kappa \to \infty} \frac{e^{\kappa \ \mathbf{x}_i^T \mu_{h^*}}}{\sum_{h=1}^{k} e^{\kappa \ \mathbf{x}_i^T \mu_h}} = 1,$$

and $p(h|\mathbf{x}_i, \Theta) \to 0$, as $\kappa \to \infty$ for all $h \neq h^*$.

To show that `spkmeans` can also be seen as a special case of the `hard-moVMF`, in addition to assuming the priors of the components to be equal, we further assume that the concentration parameters of all the components are equal, i.e., $\kappa_h = \kappa$ for all h. With these assumptions on the model, the estimation of the common concentration parameter becomes unessential since the hard assignment will depend only on the value of the cosine similarity $\mathbf{x}_i^T \mu_h$, and `hard-moVMF` reduces to `spkmeans`.

Algorithm 6 `hard-moVMF`

Require: Set $\mathcal{X}$ of data points on $\mathbb{S}^{d-1}$
Ensure: A disjoint k-partitioning of $\mathcal{X}$
   Initialize all $\alpha_h, \mu_h, \kappa_h, \; h = 1, \cdots, k$
   repeat
     {The Hardened E (Expectation) step of EM}
     for $i = 1$ to n **do**
       for $h = 1$ to k **do**
         $f_h(\mathbf{x}_i|\theta_h) \leftarrow c_d(\kappa_h)e^{\kappa_h \mu_h^T \mathbf{x}_i}$

$$q(h|\mathbf{x}_i, \Theta) \leftarrow \begin{cases} 1, & \text{if } h = \arg\max_{h'} \alpha_{h'} \; f_{h'}(\mathbf{x}_i|\theta_{h'}) \\ 0, & \text{otherwise.} \end{cases}$$

     {The M (Maximization) step of EM}
     for $h = 1$ to k **do**
       $\alpha_h \leftarrow \frac{1}{n}\sum_{i=1}^{n} q(h|\mathbf{x}_i, \Theta)$
       $\mu_h \leftarrow \sum_{i=1}^{n} \mathbf{x}_i q(h|\mathbf{x}_i, \Theta)$
       $\bar{r} \leftarrow \|\mu_h\|/(n\alpha_h)$
       $\mu_h \leftarrow \mu_h/\|\mu_h\|$
       $\kappa_h \leftarrow \frac{\bar{r}d - \bar{r}^3}{1 - \bar{r}^2}$
   until *convergence.*

In addition to the above mentioned algorithms, we report experimental results on another algorithm `fskmeans` (6) that belongs to the same class in the sense that, like `spkmeans`, it can be derived from the mixture of vMF models with some restrictive assumptions. In `fskmeans`, the centroids of the mixture components are estimated as in `hard-movMF`. The κ value for a component is *explicitly set* to be inversely proportional to the number of points in the cluster corresponding to that component. This explicit choice simulates a frequency sensitive competitive learning that implicitly prevents the formation of null clusters, a well-known problem in regular kmeans (14).

6.7   Experimental Results

We now offer some experimental validation to assess the quality of clustering results achieved by our algorithms. We compare the following four algorithms on several datasets.

1. Spherical KMeans (20)—`spkmeans`.

2. Frequency Sensitive Spherical KMeans (6)—`fskmeans`.

3. moVMF based clustering using hard assignments—`hard-moVMF`.

Algorithm 7 `spkmeans`

Require: Set $\mathcal{X}$ of data points on $\mathbb{S}^{d-1}$
Ensure: A disjoint k-partitioning $\{\mathcal{X}_h\}_{h=1}^k$ of $\mathcal{X}$
  Initialize μ_h, $h = 1, \cdots, k$
  repeat
    {The E (Expectation) step of EM}
    Set $\mathcal{X}_h \leftarrow \emptyset$, $h = 1, \cdots, k$
    for $i = 1$ to n **do**
      $\mathcal{X}_h \leftarrow \mathcal{X}_h \cup \{\mathbf{x}_i\}$ where $h = \underset{h'}{\arg\max}\ \mathbf{x}_i^T \mu_{h'}$
    {The M (Maximization) step of EM}
    for $h = 1$ to k **do**
      $\mu_h \leftarrow \dfrac{\sum_{\mathbf{x} \in \mathcal{X}_h} \mathbf{x}}{\|\sum_{\mathbf{x} \in \mathcal{X}_h} \mathbf{x}\|}$
  until *convergence.*

---

4. moVMF based clustering using soft assignments—`soft-moVMF`.

It has already been established that `kmeans` using Euclidean distance performs much worse than `spkmeans` for text data (49), so we do not consider it here. Generative model based algorithms that use mixtures of Bernoulli or multinomial distributions, which have been shown to perform well for text datasets, have also not been included in the experiments. This exclusion is done as a recent empirical study over 15 text datasets showed that simple versions of vMF mixture models (with κ constant for all clusters) outperform the multinomial model except for only one dataset (Classic3), and the Bernoulli model was inferior for all datasets (56). Further, for certain datasets, we compare clustering performance with latent Dirichlet allocation (LDA) (12) and exponential family approximation of Dirichlet compounded multinomial (EDCM) models (23).

6.7.1 Datasets

The datasets that we used for empirical validation and comparison of our algorithms were carefully selected to represent some typical clustering problems. We also created various subsets of some of the datasets for gaining greater insight into the nature of clusters discovered or to model some particular clustering scenario (e.g., balanced clusters, skewed clusters, overlapping clusters, etc.). We drew our data from five sources: Simulated, Classic3, Yahoo News, 20 Newsgroups, and Slashdot. For all the text document datasets, the toolkit MC (17) was used for creating a high-dimensional vector space model that each of the four algorithms utilized. MATLAB code was used to render the input as a vector space for the simulated datasets.

- **Simulated.** We use simulated data to verify that the discrepancy between computed values of the parameters and their true values is small. Our simulated data serves the principal purpose of validating the "correctness" of our implementations. We used a slight modification of the algorithm given by (53) to generate a set of data points following a given vMF distribution. We describe herein two synthetic datasets. The first dataset **small-mix** is 2-dimensional and is used to illustrate soft-clustering. The second dataset **big-mix** is a high-dimensional dataset that could serve as a model for real world text datasets. Let the triple (n, d, k) denote the number of sample points, the dimensionality of a sample point, and the number of clusters respectively.

  1. **small-mix:** This data has $(n, d, k) = (50, 2, 2)$. The mean direction of each component is a random unit vector. Each component has $\kappa = 4$.

  2. **big-mix:** data has $(n, d, k) = (5000, 1000, 4)$. The mean direction of each component is a random unit vector, and the κ values of the components are 650.98, 266.83, 267.83, and 612.88. The mixing weights for each component are 0.251, 0.238, 0.252, and 0.259.

- **Classic3.** This is a well known collection of documents. It is an easy dataset to cluster since it contains documents from three well-separated sources. Moreover, the intrinsic clusters are largely balanced.

  1. **Classic3** is a corpus containining 3893 documents, among which 1400 CRANFIELD documents are from aeronautical system papers, 1033 MEDLINE documents are from medical journals, and 1460 CISI documents are from information retrieval papers. The particular vector space model used had a total of 4666 features (words). Thus each document, after normalization, is represented as a unit vector in a 4666-dimensional space.

  2. **Classic300** is a subset of the Classic3 collection and has 300 documents. From each category of Classic3, we picked 100 documents at random to form this particular dataset. The dimensionality of the data was 5471.[2]

  3. **Classic400** is a subset of Classic3 that has 400 documents. This dataset has 100 randomly chosen documents from the MEDLINE and CISI categories and 200 randomly chosen documents from the CRANFIELD category. This dataset is specifically designed to create unbalanced clusters in an otherwise easily separable and balanced dataset. The dimensionality of the data was 6205.

---

[2]Note that the dimensionality in Classic300 is larger than that of Classic3. Although the same options were used in the MC toolkit for word pruning, due to very different word distributions, fewer words got pruned for Classic300 in the 'too common' or 'too rare' categories.

- **Yahoo News (K-series).** This compilation has 2340 Yahoo news articles from 20 different categories. The underlying clusters in this dataset are highly skewed in terms of the number of documents per cluster, with sizes ranging from 9 to 494. The skewness presents additional challenges to clustering algorithms.

- **20 Newsgroup.** The 20 Newsgroup dataset is a widely used compilation of documents (28). We tested our algorithms on not only the original dataset, but on a variety of subsets with differing characteristics to explore and understand the behavior of our algorithms.

  1. **News20** is a standard dataset that comprises 19,997 messages, gathered from 20 different USENET newsgroups. One thousand messages are drawn from the first 19 newsgroups, and 997 from the twentieth. The headers for each of the messages are then removed to avoid biasing the results. The particular vector space model used had 25924 words. News20 embodies the features characteristic of a typical text dataset—high-dimensionality, sparsity, and significantly overlapping clusters.

  2. **Small-news20** is formed by selecting 2000 messages from the original News20 dataset. We randomly selected 100 messages from each category in the original dataset. Hence this dataset has balanced classes (though there may be overlap). The dimensionality of the data was 13406.

  3. **Same-100/1000** is a collection of 100/1000 messages from 3 very similar newsgroups: comp.graphics, comp.os.ms-windows, comp.windows.x.

  4. **Similar-100/1000** is a collection of 100/1000 messages from 3 somewhat similar newsgroups: talk.politics.{guns,mideast,misc}.

  5. **Different-100/1000** is a collection of 100/1000 messages from 3 very different newsgroups: alt.atheism, rec.sport.baseball, sci.space.

- **Slash-dot.** We harvested news articles from the Slashdot website and created 2 datasets. For each category in these datasets, we collected 1000 articles primarily tagged with the category label, and then removed articles that were posted to multiple categories.

  1. **Slash-7** contains 6714 news articles posted to 7 Slashdot categories: Business, Education, Entertainment, Games, Music, Science, and Internet.

  2. **Slash-6** contains 5182 articles posted to the 6 categories: Biotech, Microsoft, Privacy, Google, Security, Space.

6.7.2   Methodology

Performance of the algorithms on all the datasets has been analyzed using *mutual information* (MI) between the cluster and class labels. MI quantifies the amount of statistical similarity between the cluster and class labels (16). If X is a random variable for the cluster assignments and Y is a random variable for the pre-existing labels on the same data, then their MI is given by $I(X;Y) = E[\ln \frac{p(X,Y)}{p(X)p(Y)}]$ where the expectation is computed over the joint distribution of (X,Y) estimated from a particular clustering of the dataset under consideration. To facilitate computing MI, for `soft-moVMF` we "harden" the clustering produced by labeling a point with the cluster label for which it has the highest value of posterior probability (ties broken arbitrarily). Note that variants of MI have been used to evaluate clustering algorithms by several researchers. The authors of (32) used a related concept called variation of information to compare clusterings. An MDL-based formulation that uses the MI between cluster assignments and class labels was proposed by (22).

All results reported herein have been averaged over 10 runs. All algorithms were started with the same random initialization to ensure fairness of comparison. Each run was started with a *different* random initialization. However, no algorithm was restarted within a given run and all of them were allowed to run to completion. Since the standard deviations of MI were reasonably small for all algorithms, to reduce clutter, we have chosen to omit a display of error bars in our plots. Also, for practical reasons, the estimate of κ was upper bounded by a large number (10^4, in this case) in order to prevent numeric overflows. For example, during the iterations, if a cluster has only one point, the estimate of κ will be infinity (a divide by zero error). Upper bounding the estimate of κ is similar in flavor to ensuring the non-singularity of the estimated covariance of a multivariate Gaussian in a mixture of Gaussians.

6.7.3   Simulated Datasets

First, to build some intuition and confidence in the working of our vMF based algorithms we exhibit relevant details of `soft-moVMF`'s behavior on the small-mix dataset shown in Figure 6.4(a).

The clustering produced by our soft cluster assignment algorithm is shown in Figure 6.4(b). The four points (taken clockwise) marked with solid circles have cluster labels $(0.15, 0.85)$, $(0.77, 0.23)$, $(.82, .18)$, and $(.11, .89)$, where a cluster label $(p, 1 - p)$ for a point means that the point has probability p of belonging to Cluster 1 and probability $1 - p$ of belonging to Cluster 2. All other points are categorized to belong to a single cluster by ignoring small (less than 0.10) probability values.

The confusion matrix, obtained by "hardening" the clustering produced by `soft-moVMF` for the small-mix dataset, is $\begin{bmatrix} 26 & 1 \\ 0 & 23 \end{bmatrix}$. As is evident from this confusion matrix, the clustering performed by `soft-moVMF` is excellent,

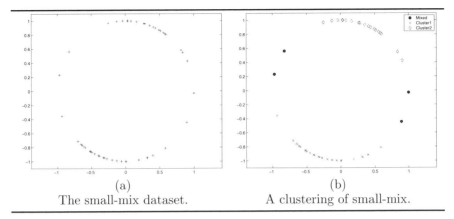

(a)
The small-mix dataset.

(b)
A clustering of small-mix.

FIGURE 6.4 (SEE COLOR INSERT FOLLOWING PAGE 130.):
Small-mix dataset and its clustering by `soft-moVMF`.

though not surprising, since small-mix is a dataset with well-separated clusters. Further testimony to `soft-moVMF`'s performance is served by Table 6.2,
which shows the discrepancy between true and estimated parameters for the
small-mix collection.

TABLE 6.2:   True and estimated parameters for small-mix
using `soft-moVMF`.

Cluster	μ	$\widehat{\mu}$	κ	$\widehat{\kappa}$	α	$\widehat{\alpha}$
1	(-0.251, -0.968)	(-0.279, -0.960)	4	3.78	0.48	0.46
2	(0.399, 0.917)	(0.370, 0.929)	4	3.53	0.52	0.54

In the table μ, κ, α represent the true parameters and $\widehat{\mu}, \widehat{\kappa}, \widehat{\alpha}$ represent the
estimated parameters. We can see that even in the presence of a limited
number of data points in the small-mix dataset (50 points), the estimated
parameters approximate the true parameters quite well.

Before moving onto real datasets let us briefly look at the behavior of the
algorithms on the larger dataset big-mix. On calculating MI as described
previously we found that all the algorithms performed similarly with MI values
close to one. We attribute this good performance of all the algorithms to the
availability of a sufficient number of data points and similar sized clusters.
For reference Table 6.3 offers numerical evidence about the performance of
`soft-moVMF` on the big-mix dataset.

TABLE 6.3:   Performance of `soft-moVMF` on big-mix dataset.

$\min \mu^T \widehat{\mu}$	$\mathrm{avg}\, \mu^T \widehat{\mu}$	$\max \frac{\lvert \kappa - \widehat{\kappa} \rvert}{\lvert \kappa \rvert}$	$\mathrm{avg}\, \frac{\lvert \kappa - \widehat{\kappa} \rvert}{\lvert \kappa \rvert}$	$\max \frac{\lvert \alpha - \widehat{\alpha} \rvert}{\lvert \alpha \rvert}$	$\mathrm{avg}\, \frac{\lvert \alpha - \widehat{\alpha} \rvert}{\lvert \alpha \rvert}$
0.994	0.998	0.006	0.004	0.002	0.001

6.7.4   Classic3 Family of Datasets

Table 6.4 shows typical confusion matrices obtained for the full Classic3 dataset. We observe that the performance of all the algorithms is quite similar and there is no added advantage yielded by using the general moVMF model as compared to the other algorithms. This observation can be explained by noting that the clusters of Classic3 are well separated and have a sufficient number of documents. For this clustering `hard-moVMF` yielded κ values of $(732.13, 809.53, 1000.04)$, while `soft-moVMF` reported κ values of $(731.55, 808.21, 1002.95)$.

TABLE 6.4:   Comparative confusion matrices for 3 clusters of Classic3 (rows represent clusters).

fskmeans			spkmeans			hard-moVMF			soft-moVMF		
med	cisi	cran	med	cisi	cran	med	cisi	cran	med	cisi	cran
1019	0	0	**1019**	0	0	**1018**	0	0	**1019**	0	1
1	6	**1386**	1	6	**1386**	2	6	**1387**	1	4	**1384**
13	**1454**	12	13	**1454**	12	13	**1454**	11	13	**1456**	13

Table 6.5 shows the confusion matrices obtained for the Classic300 dataset. Even though Classic300 is well separated, the small number of documents per cluster makes the problem somewhat difficult for `fskmeans` and `spkmeans`, while `hard-moVMF` has a much better performance due to its model flexibility. The `soft-moVMF` algorithm performs appreciably better than the other three algorithms.

It seems that the low number of documents does not pose a problem for `soft-moVMF` and it ends up getting an almost perfect clustering for this dataset. Thus in this case, despite the low number of points per cluster, the superior modeling power of our moVMF based algorithms prevents them from getting trapped in inferior local-minima as compared to the other algorithms—resulting in a better clustering.

The confusion matrices obtained for the Classic400 dataset are displayed in Table 6.6. The behavior of the algorithms for this dataset is quite interesting. As before, due to the small number of documents per cluster, `fskmeans` and `spkmeans` give a rather mixed confusion matrix. The `hard-moVMF` algorithm gets a significant part of the bigger cluster correctly and achieves some amount of separation between the two smaller clusters. The `soft-moVMF` algorithm exhibits a somewhat intriguing behavior. It splits the bigger cluster into two,

TABLE 6.5:   Comparative confusion matrices for 3 clusters of Classic300.

fskmeans			spkmeans			hard-moVMF			soft-moVMF		
med	cisi	cran	med	cisi	cran	med	cisi	cran	med	cisi	cran
29	**38**	22	29	**38**	22	3	**72**	1	0	**98**	0
31	27	**38**	31	27	**38**	**62**	28	17	**99**	2	0
40	35	**40**	**40**	35	**40**	35	0	**82**	1	0	**100**

TABLE 6.6:   Comparative confusion matrices for 3 clusters of Classic400.

fskmeans			spkmeans			hard-moVMF			soft-moVMF		
med	cisi	cran	med	cisi	cran	med	cisi	cran	med	cisi	cran
27	16	**55**	27	17	**54**	**56**	28	20	0	0	**91**
51	**83**	12	**51**	**82**	12	44	**72**	14	**82**	**99**	2
23	1	**132**	23	1	**133**	1	0	**165**	19	1	**106**

relatively pure segments, and merges the smaller two into one cluster. When 4 clusters are requested from `soft-moVMF`, it returns 4 very pure clusters (not shown in the confusion matrices), two of which are almost equal sized segments of the bigger cluster.

An insight into the working of the algorithms is provided by considering their clustering performance when they are requested to produce greater than the "natural" number of clusters. In Table 6.7 we show the confusion matrices resulting from 5 clusters of the Classic3 corpus. The matrices suggest that the moVMF algorithms have a tendency of trying to maintain larger clusters intact as long as possible, and breaking them into reasonably pure and comparably sized parts when they absolutely must. This behavior of our moVMF algorithms coupled with the observations in Table 6.6 suggest a clustering method in which one could generate a slightly higher number of clusters than required, and then agglomerate them appropriately.

TABLE 6.7:   Comparative confusion matrices for 5 clusters of Classic3.

fskmeans			spkmeans			hard-moVMF			soft-moVMF		
med	cisi	cran	med	cisi	cran	med	cisi	cran	med	cisi	cran
2	4	**312**	2	4	**323**	3	5	**292**	0	1	**1107**
8	**520**	10	8	**512**	9	**511**	1	0	5	**1455**	14
5	**936**	6	5	**944**	6	**514**	1	0	**526**	2	1
1018	0	1	**1018**	0	1	0	2	**1093**	**501**	0	0
0	0	**1069**	0	0	**1059**	5	**1451**	13	1	2	**276**

The MI plots for the various Classic3 datasets are given in Figures 6.5(a)-(c). For the full Classic3 dataset (Figure 6.5(a)), all the algorithms perform almost

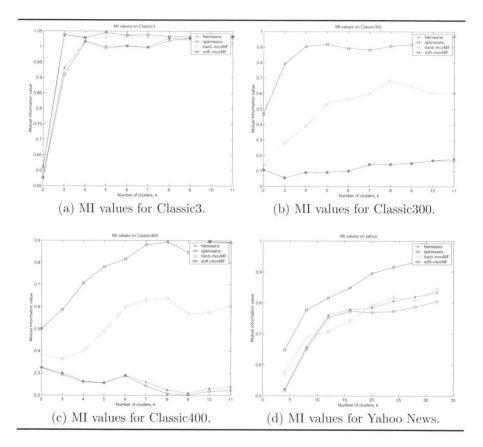

(a) MI values for Classic3.

(b) MI values for Classic300.

(c) MI values for Classic400.

(d) MI values for Yahoo News.

FIGURE 6.5: Comparison of the algorithms for the Classic3 datasets and the Yahoo News dataset.

similarly at the true number of clusters. However, as the number of clusters increases, `soft-moVMF` seems to outperform the others by a significant margin. For Classic300 (Figure 6.5(b)) and Classic400 (Figure 6.5(c)), `soft-moVMF` seems to significantly outperform the other algorithms. In fact, for these two datasets, `soft-moVMF` performs substantially better than the other three, even at the correct number of clusters. Among the other three, `hard-moVMF` seems to perform better than `spkmeans` and `fskmeans` across the range of clusters.

6.7.5   Yahoo News Dataset

The Yahoo News dataset is a relatively difficult dataset for clustering since it has a fair amount of overlap among its clusters and the number of points per cluster is low. In addition, the clusters are highly skewed in terms of their comparative sizes.

Results for the different algorithms can be seen in Figure 6.5(d). Over the entire range, `soft-moVMF` consistently performs better than the other algorithms. Even at the correct number of clusters $k = 20$, it performs significantly better than the other algorithms.

6.7.6   20 Newsgroup Family of Datasets

Now we discuss clustering performance of the four algorithms on the 20 Newsgroup datasets. Figure 6.6(a) shows the MI plots for the full News20 dataset. All the algorithms perform similarly until the true number of clusters after which `soft-moVMF` and `spkmeans` perform better than the others. We do not notice any interesting differences between the four algorithms from this Figure.

Figure 6.6(b) shows MI plots for the Small-News20 dataset and the results are of course different. Since the number of documents per cluster is small (100), as before `spkmeans` and `fskmeans` do not perform that well, even at the true number of clusters, whereas `soft-moVMF` performs considerably better than the others over the entire range. Again, `hard-moVMF` exhibits good MI values until the true number of clusters, after which it falls sharply. On the other hand, for the datasets that have a reasonably large number of documents per cluster, another kind of behavior is usually observed. All the algorithms perform quite similarly until the true number of clusters, after which `soft-moVMF` performs significantly better than the other three. This behavior can be observed in Figures 6.6(d), 6.6(f), and 6.7(b). We note that the other three algorithms perform quite similarly over the entire range of clusters. We also observe that for an easy dataset like Different-1000, the MI values peak at the true number of clusters, whereas for a more difficult dataset such as Similar-1000 the MI values increase as the clusters get further refined. This behavior is expected since the clusters in Similar-1000 have much greater overlap than those in Different-1000.

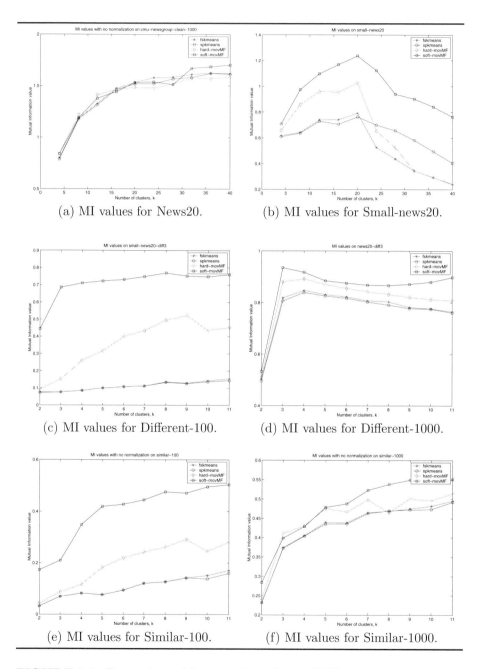

(a) MI values for News20.

(b) MI values for Small-news20.

(c) MI values for Different-100.

(d) MI values for Different-1000.

(e) MI values for Similar-100.

(f) MI values for Similar-1000.

FIGURE 6.6: Comparison of the algorithms for the 20 Newsgroup and some subsets.

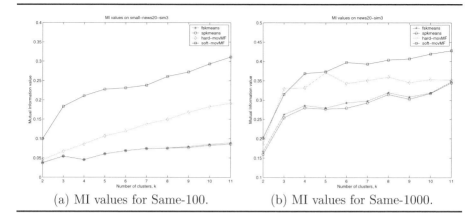

(a) MI values for Same-100.   (b) MI values for Same-1000.

FIGURE 6.7: Comparison of the algorithms for more subsets of 20 News-group data.

6.7.7 Slashdot Datasets

The Slashdot dataset was created to test the performance of the moVMF model on a typical web application. To gain a better understanding of the relative performance of the model compared to other state-of-the-art models for text clustering and topic modeling, moVMF was compared with latent Dirichlet allocation (LDA) (12) and the exponential family approximation of the Dirichlet compounded multinomial (EDCM) model (23). Table 6.8 shows the comparative performance in terms of cluster quality measured by normalized mutual information (NMI), and in terms of running time. Overall, moVMF gives significantly better clustering results, while the running time is an order of magnitude less compared to the other algorithms. Similar results on other benchmark datasets have been reported by (4).

TABLE 6.8: Performance comparison of algorithms averaged over 5 runs.

	NMI			Run Time (sec)		
Dataset	moVMF	EDCM	LDA	vMF	EDCM	LDA
slash-7	**0.39**	0.22	0.31	15	40	47
slash-6	**0.65**	0.36	0.46	6	26	36

Table 6.9 shows the qualitative performance of moVMF model on the Slash-7 dataset in terms of the top keywords associated with five of the clusters. The "topics" associated with each cluster is of comparable quality to that

generated by Bayesian topic models such as LDA (4).

TABLE 6.9:   Five of the topics obtained by running batch vMF on slash-7.

music	web	scientists	internet	games
apple	google	nasa	broadband	gaming
itunes	search	space	domain	game
riaa	yahoo	researchers	net	nintendo
ipod	site	science	network	sony
wikipedia	online	years	verisign	xbox
digital	sites	earth	bittorrent	gamers
napster	ebay	found	icann	wii
file	amazon	brain	service	console
drm	engine	university	access	video

6.8   Discussion

The mixture of vMF distributions gives a parametric model-based generalization of the widely used cosine similarity measure. As discussed in Section 6.6, the spherical kmeans algorithm that uses cosine similarity arises as a special case of EM on mixture of vMFs when, among other things, the concentration κ of all the distributions is held constant. Interestingly, an alternative and more formal connection can be made from an information geometry viewpoint (2). More precisely, consider a dataset that has been sampled following a vMF distribution with a given κ, say $\kappa = 1$. Assuming the Fisher-Information matrix is identity, the Fisher kernel similarity (25) corresponding to the vMF distribution is given by

$$K(\mathbf{x}_i, \mathbf{x}_j) = (\nabla_\mu \ln f(\mathbf{x}_i|\mu))^T (\nabla_\mu \ln f(\mathbf{x}_j|\mu)) \quad (\text{see } (6.1))$$
$$= (\nabla_\mu(\mu^T \mathbf{x}_i))^T (\nabla_\mu(\mu^T \mathbf{x}_j)) = \mathbf{x}_i^T \mathbf{x}_j,$$

which is exactly the cosine similarity. This provides a theoretical justification for a long-practiced approach in the information retrieval community.

In terms of performance, the magnitude of improvement shown by the soft-movMF algorithm for the difficult clustering tasks was surprising, especially since for low-dimensional non-directional data, the improvements using a soft, EM-based kmeans or fuzzy kmeans over the standard hard-assignment based versions are often quite minimal. In particular, a couple of issues appear intriguing: (i) why is soft-movMF performing substantially better than `hard-movMF`, even though the final probability values obtained by `soft-movMF` are actually very close to 0 and 1; and (ii) why is `soft-movMF`, which needs to estimate more parameters, doing better even when there are insufficient number of points relative to the dimensionality of the space.

It turns out that both these issues can be understood by taking a closer look at how `soft-moVMF` converges. In all our experiments, we initialized κ to 10, and the initial centroids to small random perturbations of the global centroid. Hence, for `soft-movMF`, the initial posterior membership distributions of the data points are almost uniform and the Shannon entropy of the hidden random variables is very high. The change of this entropy over iterations for the News20 subsets is presented in Figure 6.8. The behavior is similar for all the other datasets that we studied. Unlike kmeans-based algorithms where most of the relocation happens in the first two or three iterations with only minor adjustments later on, in `soft-movMF` the data points are non-committal in the first few iterations, and the entropy remains very high (the maximum possible entropy for 3 clusters can be $\log_2 3 = 1.585$). The cluster patterns are discovered only after several iterations, and the entropy drops drastically within a small number of iterations after that. When the algorithm converges, the entropy is practically zero and all points are effectively hard-assigned to their respective clusters. Note that this behavior is strikingly similar to (locally adaptive) annealing approaches where κ can be considered as the inverse of the temperature parameter. The drastic drop in entropy after a few iterations is the typical critical temperature behavior observed in annealing.

As text data has only non-negative features values, all the data points lie in the first orthant of the d-dimensional hypersphere and, hence, are naturally very concentrated. Thus, the final κ values on convergence are very high, reflecting the concentration in the data, and implying a low final temperature from the annealing perspective. Then, initializing κ to a low value, or equivalently a high temperature, is a good idea because in that case when `soft-movMF` is running, the κ values will keep on increasing over successive iterations to get to its final large values, giving the effect of a decreasing temperature in the process, without any explicit deterministic annealing strategy. Also different mixture components can take different values of κ, as automatically determined by the EM updates, and need not be controlled by any external heuristic. The cost of the added flexibility in `soft-moVMF` over `spkmeans` is the extra computation in estimating the κ values. Thus the `soft-movMF` algorithm provides a trade-off between modeling power and computational demands, but one that, judging from the empirical results, seems quite worthwhile. The `hard-movMF` algorithm, instead of using the more general vMF model, suffers because of hard-assignments from the very beginning. The `fskmeans` and `spkmeans` do not do well for difficult datasets due to their hard assignment scheme as well as their significantly less modeling capabilities.

Finally, a word on model selection, since choosing the number of clusters remains one of the widely debated topics in clustering (31). A new objec-

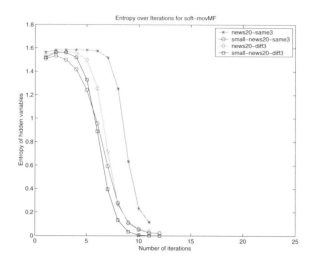

FIGURE 6.8 (SEE COLOR INSERT FOLLOWING PAGE 130.): Variation of entropy of hidden variables with number of iterations (`soft-movMF`).

tive criterion for evaluation and model-selection for clustering algorithms was proposed in (8): how well does the clustering algorithm perform as a prediction algorithm. The prediction accuracy of the clustering is measured by the PAC-MDL bound (13; 8) that upper-bounds the error-rate of predictions on the test-set. The way to use it for model-selection is quite straightforward: among a range of number of clusters, choose the one that achieves the minimum bound on the test-set error-rate. Experiments on model selection applied to several clustering algorithms were reported by (8). Interestingly, the movMF-based algorithms almost always obtained the 'right number of clusters'—in this case, the underlying labels in the dataset were actually known and the number of labels were considered to be the right number of clusters. It is important to note that this form of model-selection only works in a semi-supervised setting where a little amount of labeled data is available for model selection.

6.9   Conclusions and Future Work

From the experimental results, it seems that high-dimensional text data have properties that match well with the modeling assumptions of the vMF mixture model. This motivates further study of such models. For example, one can consider a hybrid algorithm that employs `soft-moVMF` for the first few (more important) iterations, and then switches to `hard-moVMF` for speed, and measure the speed-quality tradeoff that this hybrid approach provides. Another possible extension would be to consider an online version of the EM-based algorithms as discussed in this paper, developed along the lines of (34). Online algorithms are particularly attractive for dealing with streaming data when memory is limited, and for modeling mildly non-stationary data sources. We could also adapt a local search strategy such as the one in (18), for incremental EM to yield better local minima for both hard and soft-assignments.

The vMF distribution that we considered in the proposed techniques is one of the simplest parametric distributions for directional data. The iso-density lines of the vMF distribution are circles on the hypersphere, i.e., all points on the surface of the hypersphere at a constant angle from the mean direction. In some applications, more general iso-density contours may be desirable. There are more general models on the unit sphere, such as the Bingham distribution, the Kent distribution, the Watson distribution (already discussed in the previous section), the Fisher-Bingham distribution, the Pearson type VII distributions (42; 30), etc., that can potentially be more applicable in the general setting. For example, the Fisher-Bingham distributions have added modeling power since there are $O(d^2)$ parameters for each distribution. However, the parameter estimation problem, especially in high-dimensions, can be significantly more difficult for such models, as more parameters need to be estimated from the data. One definitely needs substantially more data to get reliable estimates of the parameters. Further, for some cases, e.g., the Kent distribution, it can be difficult to solve the estimation problem in more than 3-dimensions (36). Hence these more complex models may not be viable for many high-dimensional problems. Nevertheless, the tradeoff between model complexity (in terms of the number of parameters and their estimation) and sample complexity needs to be studied in more detail in the context of directional data.

Acknowledgments

The authors would like to thank Sugato Basu and Jiye Yu for experiments with the Slashdot datasets. This research was supported in part by the Digital Technology Center Data Mining Consortium (DDMC) at the University of Minnesota, Twin Cities.

References

[1] M. Abramowitz and I. A. Stegun, editors. *Handbook of Mathematical Functions*. Dover Publ. Inc., New York, 1974.

[2] S. I. Amari. Information geometry of the EM and em algorithms for neural networks. *Neural Networks*, 8(9):1379–1408, 1995.

[3] D. E. Amos. Computation of modified Bessel functions and their ratios. *Mathematics of Computation*, 28(125):235–251, 1974.

[4] A. Banerjee and S. Basu. Topic models over text streams: A study of batch and online unsupervised learning. In *Proceedings of the 7th SIAM International Conference on Data Mining*, 2007.

[5] A. Banerjee, I. Dhillon, J. Ghosh, and S. Sra. Clustering on the unit hypersphere using von Mises-Fisher distributions. *Journal of Machine Learning Research*, 6:1345–1382, 2005.

[6] A. Banerjee and J. Ghosh. Frequency sensitive competitive learning for clustering on high-dimensional hyperspheres. In *Proceedings International Joint Conference on Neural Networks*, pages 1590–1595, May 2002.

[7] A. Banerjee and J. Ghosh. Frequency Sensitive Competitive Learning for Scalable Balanced Clustering on High-dimensional Hyperspheres. *IEEE Transactions on Neural Networks*, 15(3):702–719, May 2004.

[8] A. Banerjee and J. Langford. An objective evaluation criterion for clustering. In *Proc. 10th International Conference on Knowledge Discovery and Data Mining (KDD)*, pages 515–520, 2004.

[9] A. Banerjee, S. Merugu, I. Dhillon, and J. Ghosh. Clustering with Bregman divergences. *Journal of Machine Learning Research*, 6:1705–1749, 2005.

[10] A. Bijral, M. Breitenbach, and G. Z. Grudic. Mixture of Watson Distributions: A Generative Model for Hyperspherical Embeddings. In *AISTATS*, 2007.

[11] J. Bilmes. A Gentle Tutorial on the EM Algorithm and its Application to Parameter Estimation for Gaussian Mixture and Hidden Markov Models. Technical Report ICSI-TR-97-021, University of Berkeley, 1997.

[12] D. M. Blei, A. Y. Ng, and M. I. Jordan. Latent Dirichlet allocation. *Journal of Machine Learning Research*, 3:993–1022, 2003.

[13] A. Blum and J. Langford. PAC-MDL bounds. In *Proc. 16th Annual Conference on Learning Theory (COLT)*, 2003.

[14] P. S. Bradley, K. P. Bennett, and A. Demiriz. Constrained k-means clustering. Technical report, Microsoft Research, May 2000.

[15] M. Collins. The EM algorithm. In fulfillment of Written Preliminary Exam II requirement, September 1997.

[16] T. M. Cover and J. A. Thomas. *Elements of Information Theory*. Wiley-Interscience, 1991.

[17] I. S. Dhillon, J. Fan, and Y. Guan. Efficient clustering of very large document collections. In V. Kumar R. Grossman, C. Kamath and R. Namburu, editors, *Data Mining for Scientific and Engineering Applications*. Kluwer Academic Publishers, 2001.

[18] I. S. Dhillon, Y. Guan, and J. Kogan. Iterative clustering of high dimensional text data augmented by local search. In *Proceedings of The 2002 IEEE International Conference on Data Mining*, 2002.

[19] I. S. Dhillon, E. M. Marcotte, and U. Roshan. Diametrical clustering for identifying anti-correlated gene clusters. *Bioinformatics*, 19(13):1612–1619, 2003.

[20] I. S. Dhillon and D. S. Modha. Concept decompositions for large sparse text data using clustering. *Machine Learning*, 42(1):143–175, 2001.

[21] I. S. Dhillon and S. Sra. Modeling data using directional distributions. Technical Report TR-03-06, Department of Computer Sciences, University of Texas at Austin, Austin, TX, 2003.

[22] B. E. Dom. An information-theoretic external cluster-validity measure. Technical Report RJ 10219, IBM Research Report, 2001.

[23] C. Elkan. Clustering documents with an exponential-family approximation of the Dirichlet compund multinomial distribution. In *Proceedings of the 23rd International Conference on Machine Learning*, 2006.

[24] N. I. Fisher. *Statistical Analysis of Circular Data*. Cambridge University Press, 1996.

[25] T. Jaakkola and D. Haussler. Exploiting generative models in discriminative classifiers. In M. S. Kearns, S. A. Solla, and D. D. Cohn, editors, *Advances in Neural Information Processing Systems*, volume 11, pages 487–493. MIT Press, 1999.

[26] A. K. Jain and R. C. Dubes. *Algorithms for Clustering Data*. Prentice Hall, New Jersey, 1988.

[27] R. Kannan, S. Vempala, and A. Vetta. On clusterings—good, bad and spectral. In *41st Annual IEEE Symposium Foundations of Computer Science*, pages 367–377, 2000.

[28] K Lang. News Weeder: Learning to filter netnews. In *Proceedings 12th International Conference on Machine Learning*, pages 331–339, San Francisco, 1995.

[29] K. V. Mardia. *Statistical Distributions in Scientific Work*, volume 3, chapter "Characteristics of directional distributions," pages 365–385. Reidel, Dordrecht, 1975.

[30] K. V. Mardia and P. Jupp. *Directional Statistics*. John Wiley and Sons Ltd., 2nd edition, 2000.

[31] G. J. McLachlan and D. Peel. *Finite Mixture Models*. Wiley series in Probability and Mathematical Statistics: Applied Probability and Statistics Section. John Wiley & Sons, 2000.

[32] M. Meilă. Comparing clusterings by the variation of information. In *Proceedings of the 16th Annual Conference on Learning Theory*, 2003.

[33] J. A. Mooney, P. J. Helms, and I. T. Jolliffe. Fitting mixtures of von Mises distributions: a case study involving sudden infant death syndrome. *Computational Statistics & Data Analysis*, 41:505–513, 2003.

[34] R. M. Neal and G. E. Hinton. A view of the EM algorithm that justifies incremental, sparse, and other variants. In M. I. Jordan, editor, *Learning in Graphical Models*, pages 355–368. MIT Press, 1998.

[35] K. Nigam, A. K. Mccallum, S. Thrun, and T. Mitchell. Text classification from labeled and unlabeled documents using EM. *Machine Learning*, 39(2/3):103–134, 2000.

[36] D. Peel, W. J. Whiten, and G. J. McLachlan. Fitting mixtures of Kent distributions to aid in joint set identification. *Journal of American Statistical Association*, 96:56–63, 2001.

[37] J. H. Piater. *Visual Feature Learning*. PhD thesis, University of Massachussets, June 2001.

[38] C. R. Rao. *Linear Statistical Inference and its Applications*. Wiley, New York, 2nd edition, 1973.

[39] E. Rasmussen. Clustering algorithms. In W. Frakes and R. Baeza-Yates, editors, *Information Retrieval: Data Structures and Algorithms*, pages 419–442. Prentice Hall, New Jersey, 1992.

[40] G. Salton and C. Buckley. Term-weighting approaches in automatic text retrieval. *Information Processing & Management*, 4(5):513–523, 1988.

[41] G. Salton and M. J. McGill. *Introduction to Modern Retrieval*. McGraw-Hill Book Company, 1983.

[42] K. Shimizu and K. Iida. Pearson type VII distributions on spheres. *Communications in Statistics: Theory & Methods*, 31(4):513–526, 2002.

[43] J. Sinkkonen and S. Kaski. Clustering based on conditional distributions in an auxiliary space. *Neural Computation*, 14:217–239, 2001.

[44] P. Smyth. Clustering sequences with hidden Markov models. In M. C. Mozer, M. I. Jordan, and T. Petsche, editors, *Advances in Neural Information Processing*, volume 9, pages 648–654. MIT Press, 1997.

[45] S. Sra. *Matrix Nearness Problems in Data Mining*. PhD thesis, The University of Texas at Austin, August 2007.

[46] A. N. Srivastava and R. Akella. Enabling the discovery of recurring anomalies in aerospace system problem reports using high-dimensional clustering techniques. In *Proceedings of the IEEE Aerospace Conference*, 2006.

[47] A. N. Srivastava and B. Zane-Ulman. Discovering hidden anomalies in text reports regarding complex space systems. In *IEEE Aerospace Conference*, 2005.

[48] M. Steinbach, G. Karypis, and V. Kumar. A comparison of document clustering techniques. In *KDD Workshop on Text Mining*, 2000.

[49] A. Strehl, J. Ghosh, and R. Mooney. Impact of similarity measures on web-page clustering. In *Proc 7th Natl Conf on Artificial Intelligence : Workshop of AI for Web Search (AAAI 2000)*, pages 58–64. AAAI, July 2000.

[50] A. Tanabe, K. Fukumizu, S. Oba, T. Takenouchi, and S. Ishii. Parameter estimation for von Mises-Fisher distributions. *Computational Statistics*, 22(1):145–157, 2007.

[51] C. S. Wallace and D. L. Dowe. MML clustering of multi-state, Poisson, von Mises circular and Gaussian distributions. *Statistics and Computing*, 10(1):73–83, January 2000.

[52] G. N. Watson. *A Treatise on the Theory of Bessel Functions*. Cambridge University Press, 2nd edition, 1995.

[53] A. T. A. Wood. Simulation of the von-Mises Distribution. *Communications of Statistics, Simulation and Computation*, 23:157–164, 1994.

[54] Y. Zhao and G. Karypis. Empirical and theoretical comparisons of selected criterion functions for document clustering. *Machine Learning*, 55(3):311–331, June 2004.

[55] S. Zhong and J. Ghosh. A unified framework for model-based clustering. *Journal of Machine Learning Research*, 4:1001–1037, November 2003.

[56] S. Zhong and J. Ghosh. A comparative study of generative models for document clustering. In *Workshop on Clustering High Dimensional Data: Third SIAM Conference on Data Mining*, April 2003.

Chapter 7

Constrained Partitional Clustering of Text Data: An Overview

Sugato Basu and Ian Davidson

7.1   Introduction

Clustering is ubiquitously used in data mining as a method of discovering novel and actionable subsets within a set of data. Given a set of data X, the typical aim of partitional clustering is to form a k-block set partition Π_k of the data. The process of clustering is important since, being completely unsupervised, it allows the addition of structure to previously unstructured items such as free-form text documents. For example, Cohn et al. (12) discuss a problem faced by Yahoo!, namely that one is given very large corpora of text documents/papers/articles and asked to create a useful taxonomy so that similar documents are closer in the taxonomy. Once the taxonomy is formed, the documents can be efficiently browsed and accessed. Unconstrained clustering is ideal for this initial situation, since in this case little domain expertise exists to begin with. However, as data mining progresses into more demanding areas, the chance of finding actionable patterns consistent with background knowledge and expectation is limited.

Clustering with constraints or semi-supervised clustering is an emerging area of great importance to data mining that allows the incorporation of background domain expertise. Work so far has incorporated this knowledge into clustering in the form of instance level constraints. The two types of constraints introduced by Wagstaff (46) are must-link denoted by $c_=(x,y)$ and cannot-link denoted by $c_{\neq}(x,y)$, meaning that two instance x and y must be in the same cluster or cannot be in the same cluster respectively. Must-link and cannot-link constraints, though apparently simple, share interesting properties. Must-link constraints are an example of an equivalence relation and hence are symmetrical, reflexive and transitive; this means that $c_=(x,y)$ and $c_=(y,z) \Rightarrow c_=(x,z)$ such that x,y,z form a connected component, i.e., each is connected to the other via an explicit or implied must-link constraint. Similarly, multiple connected components of must-link constraints can give rise to entailed cannot-link constraints, between pairs of instances in different components.

Though apparently simple, must-link and cannot-link constraints are powerful. In sufficient numbers they can shatter the training set X and specify any set partition of X. These constraints can be used to improve clustering in different ways, which are outlined in the next section. Let us consider some real-world examples where constraints are useful in text clustering.

Content Management: In content-management tasks (routinely performed by companies like Google, Interwoven or Verity), the goal is to automatically categorize large amounts (often in the order of millions) of text documents into groups or clusters. In this case, constraints can be obtained from multiple auxiliary sources, e.g., the co-occurrence of two documents in a directory can be used to infer a must-link constraint between the documents, two documents in different categories of the Open Directory Project[1] hierarchy can be considered as cannot-linked, etc. Using these constraints from the auxiliary data sources, one can customize the clustering output for the particular task, e.g., make a document hierarchy that is close to the input directory structure in which the documents are placed.

Web mining: Constrained clustering is quite useful in post processing search results, as performed by companies like Vivisimo.[2] Here, the goal is to automatically cluster the results of ambiguous search-engine queries like "jaguar" into clusters of URLs that refer to concepts like "Jaguar cars," "Jaguar animal" or "Jaguar Mac OS". In this case, constraints can be mined from query sessions in web logs – one can get valuable information regarding which websites are visited together, by analyzing co-occurrence of url's within the same user session. Clustering using this auxiliary data can help in biasing the search result clustering towards the preferences of the user.

---

[1] www.dmoz.org

[2] www.vivisimo.com

7.2 Uses of Constraints

The typical supervised learning situations involves having a label associated with each instance. The semi-supervised learning situation is when only a small subset of instances have labels. If the available labeled data represent all the relevant categories, then semi-supervised classification algorithms can be readily used for data categorization. For details see the various algorithms in the surveys (42; 49). However in many domains, knowledge of the relevant categories is incomplete. Moreover, pairwise constraints are often a more naturally available form of supervision than labels in certain clustering tasks. Moreover, in an interactive learning setting, a user who is not a domain expert can sometimes provide feedback in the form of must-link and cannot-link constraints (12; 14) more easily than class labels, since providing constraints does not require the user to have significant prior knowledge about the categories in the dataset.

Constraints have typically been used in clustering algorithms in two ways. Constraints can be used to modify the cluster assignment stage of the cluster algorithm, to enforce satisfaction of the constraints as much as possible. Alternatively, the distance function of the clustering algorithm can also be trained either before or after the clustering actually occurs using the constraints. In all of these cases, constraints can also be used in the initialization phase, where the initial clusters are formed such that must-linked instances are in the same clusters and cannot-linked instances are in different clusters. Based on this categorization, existing methods for constrained clustering can be put into two general approaches that we call *constraint-based* and *distance-based* methods.

7.2.1 Constraint-Based Methods

In constraint-based approaches, the clustering algorithm itself is modified so that the available labels or constraints are used to bias the search for an appropriate clustering of the data. The pairwise constraints specify whether two instances should be in the same cluster (must-link) or in different clusters (cannot-link). Constraint-based clustering has been done using several techniques:

- modifying the clustering objective function so that it includes a term for satisfying specified constraints (17)

- clustering using side-information from conditional distributions in an auxiliary space (44)

- enforcing constraints to be satisfied during the cluster assignment in the clustering process (47)

- initializing clusters and inferring clustering constraints based on neighborhoods derived from labeled examples (5).

Constraint-based clustering techniques have been an active topic of research, where recent techniques include variational techniques (28) or sampling methods (36) for constrained clustering using a graphical model, and feasibility studies for clustering under different types of constraints (16). There have typically been two types of constraint-based approaches: (1) ones with strict enforcement, which find the best feasible clustering respecting all the given constraints (47; 15), and (2) ones with partial enforcement, which find the best clustering while maximally respecting constraints (6; 43; 16; 28). Figure 7.2 shows an example of a clustering which respects all the given constraints in Figure 7.1. Details of these algorithms are outlined in later sections.

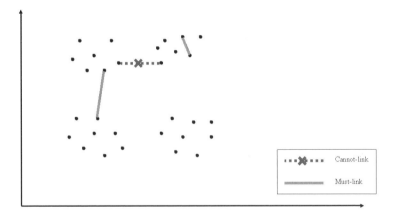

FIGURE 7.1: Input instances and constraints.

7.2.2 Distance-Based Methods

In distance-based approaches, an existing clustering algorithm that uses a distance measure is employed. However, rather than use a given distance metric, the distance measure is first trained to "satisfy" the given constraints. In this context, satisfying the constraints means that must-linked (similar) instances are close together and cannot-linked (different) instances are far apart in the learned distance space. Several distance measures have been used for distance-based constrained clustering:

- string-edit distance trained using EM (8),

- Jensen-Shannon divergence trained using gradient descent (12),

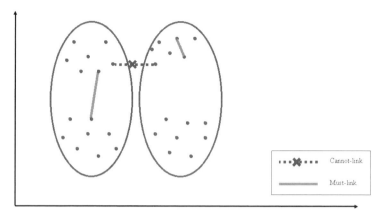

FIGURE 7.2: Constraint-based clustering.

- Euclidean distance modified by a shortest-path algorithm (31) and

- Mahalanobis distances trained using convex optimization (4; 48)

Several clustering algorithms using trained distance measures have been employed for constrained clustering, including single-link (8) and complete-link (31) agglomerative clustering, EM (12; 4), and KMeans (4; 48). Recent techniques in distance-metric learning for clustering include learning a margin-based clustering distance measure using boosting (27), and learning a distance metric transformation that is globally non-linear but locally linear (11). Figure 7.4 shows an example of learning a distance function from the constraints given in Figure 7.3 and then clustering. Notice that in Figure 7.4 the input data space has been stretched in the horizontal dimension and compressed in the vertical dimension, to draw the must-linked instances closer and put the cannot-linked instances farther apart. Section 7.5 outlines methods of learning distance functions from constraints.

There have been some algorithms that try to both enforce constraints and learn distance functions from constraints — details of these algorithms will be presented in Section 7.6.

7.3   Text Clustering

In this section, we outline some of the specific steps of pre-processing and distance function selection that are necessary for both unsupervised and constrained text clustering.

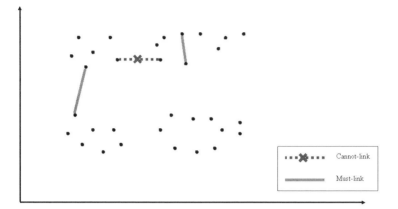

FIGURE 7.3: Input instances and constraints.

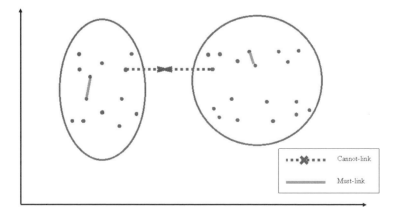

FIGURE 7.4: Distance-based clustering.

7.3.1 Pre-Processing

Most of the clustering algorithms discussed in this chapter use the standard vector space model for text, where a text document is represented as a sparse high-dimensional vector of weighted term counts (41). The creation of the vector space model can be divided into two stages. At first, the content-bearing terms (which are typically words or short phrases) are extracted from the document text and the weight of each term in the document vector is set to the count of the corresponding term in the document. In the second stage, the terms are suitably weighted according to information retrieval principles to increase the weights of important terms.

Some terms in a document do not describe any important content, e.g., common words like "the," "is" – these words are called stop-words. While processing a document to count the number of occurrences of each term and create the term count vector in the first phase, these stop-words are usually filtered from the document and not included in the vector. Note that this vector is often more than 99% sparse, since the dimensionality of the vector is equal to the number of terms in the whole document collection and most documents just have a small subset of these terms.

In the second phase, the term-frequencies or counts of the terms are multiplied by the inverse document frequency of a term in the document collection. This is done so that terms that are common to most documents in a document collection (e.g., "god" is a common term in a collection of articles posted to newsgroups like `alt.atheism` or `soc.religion.christian`) are given lesser weight, since they are not very content-bearing in the context of the collection. This method of term weighting, called "Term Frequency and Inverse Document Frequency" (TFIDF), is a popular method of pre-processing documents in the information retrieval community (1).

The TFIDF weighting procedure we use is as follows. If f_{ij} is the frequency of the ith term in the jth document, then the corresponding term frequency (TF) tf_{ij} is f_{ij} (sometimes normalized) across the entire document corpus:

$$tf_{ij} = f_{ij}$$

The inverse document frequency (IDF) idf_i of the ith term is defined as:

$$idf_i = \log_2(N/df_i)$$

where N is the total number of documents in the corpus and df_i is the total number of documents containing the ith term. The overall TFIDF score w_{ij} of the ith term in the jth document is therefore:

$$w_{ij} = tf_{ij} idf_i = f_{ij} \log_2(N/df_i)$$

After TFIDF processing, terms which have a very low (occurring in less than 5 documents) and very high frequency (occurring in more than 95% of the documents) are sometimes removed from the documents (19) in further filtering steps. Some other specific pre-processing steps are also occasionally performed based on the types of the documents, e.g., headers and email signatures are removed for newsgroup articles, HTML tags are removed for webpages, etc.

7.3.2   Distance Measures

High dimensional spaces like text have good directional properties, which has made directional distance measures like cosine distance (1 - cosine similarity) between the vector representations of text data a popular measure of distance in the information retrieval community (1). Other distance measures, e.g., probabilistic document overlap (26), have also been used successfully for text clustering. Some practitioners use SquaredEuclidean distance for text clustering, after all data instance vectors have been normalized to have unit length according to the L_2 norm. This normalization makes the SquaredEuclidean distance between two instances proportional to the cosine distance between them, as illustrated by the following relation:

$$SquaredEuclideanDist(x_1, x_2) = \|x_1 - x_2\|^2 = \|x_1\|^2 + \|x_2\|^2 - 2\|x_1\|\|x_2\|$$
$$= 2(1 - x_1^T x_2) = 2 \times CosineDist(x_1, x_2),$$

since $\|x_i\| = 1 \forall i$. This prior normalization of the instances is crucial so that subsequent clustering algorithms can group text documents based on their content words and get good quality, since otherwise clustering text using SquaredEuclidean distance can result in poor quality(25).

Spherical KMeans (SP-KMeans) is a version of KMeans (outlined in the next section) that uses cosine distance as its underlying distance metric. In the SP-KMeans algorithm, standard Euclidean KMeans is applied to data vectors $\{x_i\}_{i=1}^n$ that have been normalized to have unit L_2 norm, so that the data instances lie on a unit sphere (21). Note that there is one additional step in SP-KMeans — in the cluster re-estimation step *the centroid vectors* $\{\mu_j\}_{j=1}^k$ *are also constrained to lie on the unit sphere.* This is the main difference between SP-KMeans and Euclidean KMeans on L_2 normalized document vectors. The SP-KMeans clustering problem can be equivalently formulated as that of maximizing the objective function:

$$\mathcal{J}_{\text{sp-kmeans}} = \sum_{j=1}^k \sum_{x_i \in X_j} x_i^T \mu_j, \tag{7.1}$$

where the centroid μ_j of the jth cluster is the mean of all the instances in that cluster, normalized to have unit L_2 norm. The SP-KMeans algorithm gives a local maximum of this objective function.

In all the algorithms in this chapter that use SquaredEuclidean distance, the data have been pre-normalized to have unit L_2 norm. In practice, KMeans and SP-KMeans clustering involving the text vectors are performed efficiently by using sparse representations of document vectors.

7.4   Partitional Clustering with Constraints

Some of the very first algorithms that made use of constraints were variations of the popular KMeans iterative algorithm. The purpose of the KMeans algorithm is to (locally) minimize the vector quantization error (also known as the distortion) shown in Equation 7.2.

$$VQE = \sum_{j=1}^{k} VQE_j \qquad (7.2)$$

$$VQE_j = \frac{1}{2} \sum_{x_i \in \pi_j} D(\mu_j, x_i)^2 \qquad (7.3)$$

where j indexes over the clusters, and k is the number of clusters (specified as an input parameter), and D is the distance function.

The KMeans algorithm is an iterative algorithm which in every step attempts to further minimize the distortion. Given a set of cluster centroids, the algorithm assigns instances to their **nearest** centroid which of course minimizes the distortion. This is step 1 of the algorithm. Step 2 is to recalculate the cluster centroids so as to minimize the distortion. This can be achieved by taking the first order derivative of the error (Equation 7.3) with respect to the jth centroid and setting it to zero and solving. A solution to the resulting equation gives us the KMeans centroid update rule as shown in Equation 7.5.

$$\frac{d(VQE_j)}{d(\mu_j)} = \frac{d(\sum_{x_i \in \pi_j} D(\mu_j, x_i)^2)}{d(\mu_j)} = 0 \qquad (7.4)$$

$$\Rightarrow \mu_j = \sum_{x_i \in \pi_j} x_i / |\pi_j| \qquad (7.5)$$

Recall that π_j is the set of instances closest to the centroid of the jth cluster. These two steps are used in the standard KMeans algorithm shown in Figure 7.4.

7.4.1   COP-KMeans

The COP-KMeans algorithm shown in Figure 7.4.1 can be seen to be a two part variation of the KMeans algorithm that incorporates conjunctions of constraints. Firstly, the transitive closure over the must-linked instances is computed, so that $c_=(x, y)$ and $c_=(y, z) \Rightarrow c_=(x, z)$ and x, y, z form a connected component. The resultant connected components are replaced by a

Input: A dataset $X = \{x_1, \ldots, x_n\}$ to cluster, k: the number of clusters to find.

Output: A partition of $X, \Pi_k = \{\pi_1, \ldots, \pi_k\}$ into k clusters that is a local optima of the VQE (Equation 7.2).

1. Randomly generate cluster centroids $\mu_1, \ldots, \mu_k$.

2. **loop** until convergence **do**

   (a) **for** $i = 1$ **to** $|X|$ **do**

       (a.1) Assign x_i to the nearest cluster π_j, where nearness is measured in terms of distance from x_i to centroid μ_j.

   (b) Recalculate centroids $\mu_1, \ldots, \mu_k$ according to Equation 7.5

3. Return the final partitions.

FIGURE 7.5: Clustering using KMeans.

super-instance, whose co-ordinates are the average of the connected component's and whose weight is equal to the number of instances within it (lines 1 and 2). Secondly, rather than performing a nearest centroid assignment (step 2a.1) in Figure 7.4), a nearest **feasible** centroid assignment is performed (lines 4a.1), where an assignment is feasible if it does not violate any cannot-link constraints. When performing the nearest feasible centroid assignment step the previous set partition is *forgotten* and the new partition built up incrementally. Therefore, the first instance assigned to a cluster can **never** violate any constraints, even if it is involved in many. Similarly if there is only one constraint, $c_{\neq}(x, y)$, if x is assigned first then y is assigned to its closest feasible centroid and the assignment of x is not revisited. In this way, we can view this algorithm as greedily trying to attempt constructing a feasible clustering with *no* backtracking of previous instance assignments.

Natural variations of trying to satisfy all constraints are: a) attempting to satisfy as many constraints as possible while ignoring noisy or inappropriate constraints and b) having degrees of belief/importance associated with each constraint. Both can be viewed as frameworks that allow trading of satisfying the lesser important constraints.

7.4.2 Algorithms with Penalties – PKM, CVQE

The COP-KMeans algorithm can (see Section 7.4.1) improve the accuracy at predicting an extrinsic label and also shape clusters into desirable forms. However, when constraints are generated from labeled data there is the possibility of class label noise, thereby generating incorrect cannot-link or must-

Input: X: A set of data instances to cluster, $C_=$: set of pairwise must-link constraints, $C_{\neq}$: set of pairwise cannot-link constraints, k: the number of clusters to find. Initially, the weight of each instance is 1.

Output: A partition of X, $\Pi_k = \{\pi_1, \ldots, \pi_k\}$ into k clusters that is a local optima of the VQE (Equation 7.2). and all constraints in $C = C_= \cup C_{\neq}$ are satisfied.

1. Compute the transitive closure of the set $C_=$ to obtain the connected components $CC_1, \ldots, CC_r$.

2. For each i, $1 \le i \le r$, replace all the data instances in CC_i by a single instance with weight $|CC_i|$; the instance's coordinates are obtained by averaging the coordinates of the instances in CC_i.

3. Randomly generate cluster centroids $\mu_1, \ldots, \mu_k$.

4. **loop** until convergence **do**

    (a) **for** $i = 1$ **to** $|X|$ **do**

        (a.1) Assign x_i to the nearest **feasible** cluster π_j, where nearness is measured in terms of distance from x_i to centroid μ_j.

        (a.2) If assignment of x_i to any cluster always violates a constraint, then exit with failure.

    (b) Recalculate centroids $\mu_1, \ldots, \mu_k$ taking into account the weight of the instances in X using Equation 7.5

5. Return final partitions.

FIGURE 7.6: Clustering under constraints using COP-KMeans.

link constraint between instances. Similarly, if constraints are generated by domain experts, some constraints may be ill-specified or even contradictory. The two algorithms in this subsection attempt to ignore noisy or inappropriate constraints by allowing constraints to be left unsatisfied but with a penalty. This involves a trade-off between finding the best clustering and satisfying as many constraints as possible. To achieve this, the penalty of ignoring a constraint must be in the same units as the measure for how good the clustering of the data is. The CVQE algorithm uses distance as the fundamental unit and the PKM uses probability. We now discuss these two algorithms.

7.4.2.1 CVQE

The core idea behind the CVQE algorithm is to penalize constraint violations using distance. If a must-link constraint is violated then the penalty is the distance between the two centroids of the clusters containing the two instances that should be together. If a cannot-link constraint is violated then the penalty is the distance between the cluster centroid the two instances are assigned to and its (the centroid's) distance to the nearest cluster centroid. These two penalty types give rise to a new objective function which is termed the Constrained Vector Quantization Error (CVQE) shown in Equation 7.6 where $g(x)$ returns the cluster index that instance x belongs to.

$$CVQE_j = \frac{1}{2} \sum_{x_i \in \mu_j} D(\mu_j, x_i)^2 \; + \tag{7.6}$$

$$\frac{1}{2} \sum_{x_i \in \mu_j, (x_i, x_a) \in C_=, g(x_i) \neq g(x_a)} D(\mu_j, \mu_{g(x_a)})^2$$

$$\frac{1}{2} \sum_{x_i \in \mu_j, (x_i, x_a) \in C_{\neq}, g(x_i) = g(x_a)} D(\mu_j, \mu_{h(g(x_a))})^2$$

These penalties were found by experimentation to be useful and others (39) (see next section) have improved upon these.

The first step of the constrained KMeans algorithm must minimize the new constrained vector quantization error. This is achieved by assigning instances so as to minimize the new error term. For instances that are not part of constraints, this involves performing a nearest cluster centroid calculation as before in regular KMeans. For pairs of instances in a constraint, for each possible combination of cluster assignments, the $CVQE$ is calculated and the instances are assigned to the clusters that minimally increases the $CVQE$. This is shown in Equation 7.7 and requires at most $O(k^2)$ calculations per assignment where δ is the Kronecker Delta function.

$$\forall x_i \notin C_= \cup C_{\neq} : \quad argmin_j D(x_i, \mu_j)^2 \tag{7.7}$$
$$\forall (x_a, x_b) \in C_= : argmin_{i,j} D(x_a, \mu_i)^2 + D(x_b, \mu_j)^2 + \neg\delta(a, b) * D(\mu_j, \mu_i)^2$$
$$\forall (x_a, x_b) \in C_{\neq} : argmin_{i,j} D(x_a, \mu_i)^2 + D(x_b, \mu_j)^2 + \delta(a, b) * D(\mu_j, \mu_{h(\mu_j)})^2$$

The second step is to update the cluster centroids so as to minimize the constrained vector quantization error. To achieve this we take the first order derivative of the error, set to zero, and solve. By setting the appropriate values of m_l we can derive the update rules for the must-link and cannot-link constraint violations. Solving for μ_j, we get the update rule shown in Equation 7.8.

$$\mu_j =$$
$$\frac{\sum_{x_i \in \pi_j} x_i + \sum_{(x_i, x_a) \in C_=, g(x_i) \neq g(x_a)} \mu_{g(x_a)} + \sum_{(x_i, x_a) \in C_{\neq}, g(x_i) = g(x_a)} \mu_{h(g(x_a))}}{|\mu_j| + \sum_{x_i \in \mu_j, (x_i, x_a) \in C_=, g(x_i) \neq g(x_a)} 1 + \sum_{s_i \in \pi_j, (x_i, x_a) \in C_{\neq}, g(x_i) \neq g(x_a)} 1} \tag{7.8}$$

The intuitive interpretation of the centroid update rule is that if a must-link constraint is violated, the cluster centroid is moved towards the other cluster containing the other instance. Similarly, the interpretation of the update rule for a cannot-link constraint violation is that cluster centroid containing both constrained instances should be moved to the nearest cluster centroid so that one of the instances eventually gets assigned to it, thereby satisfying the constraint.

7.4.3 LCVQE: An Extension to CVQE

Pelleg and Baras (39) create a variation of the assignment and update rules for CVQE that they term LCVQE. Though their algorithm was not derived to minimize a particular objective function, it was shown to improve performance on several standard datasets both in terms of accuracy and run-time. The two main extensions made by this algorithm over CVQE are: a) not computing all possible k^2 assignments but only a subset of reasonable assignments and b) Changing the penalty for a cannot-link constraint to be the distance from the most outlying (with respect to the cluster centroid) instance in the CL constraint to the cluster centroid nearest it.

The assignment step shown in Equation 7.9 and the centroid update rule are shown in Equation 7.10.

$$\forall x_i \quad \notin C_= \cup C_{\neq} : \quad argmin_j D(x_i, \mu_j)^2 \tag{7.9}$$

$$\forall (x_a, x_b) \in C_= : argmin_{[i=g(x_a), j=g(x_b)], [i=g(x_a), j=i], [i=j, j=g(x_b)]}$$
$$D(x_a, \mu_i)^2 + D(x_b, \mu_j)^2 + \neg\delta(a, b) * D(\mu_j, \mu_i)^2$$

$$\forall (x_a, x_b) \in C_{\neq} : argmin_{[i=g(x_a), j=g(x_b)], [i=g(x_a), j=i.D(x_a, g(x_a)) < D(x_b, g(x_b))]}$$
$$D(x_a, \mu_i)^2 + D(x_b, \mu_j)^2 + \delta(a, b) * D(\mu_j, \mu_{g(x_b)})^2$$

$$\mu_j = \tag{7.10}$$
$$\frac{\sum_{x_i \in \pi_j} [x_i + \sum_{\substack{(x_i, x_a) \in C_=, \\ g(x_i) \neq g(x_a)}} \mu_{g(x_a)} + \sum_{\substack{(x_i, x_a) \in C_{\neq}, \\ g(x_i) = g(x_a), D(x_i) < D(x_a)}} \mu_{g(x_a)}]}{|\mu_j| + \sum_{s_i \in \mu_j, (s_i, s_x) \in C_=, g(s_i) \neq g(s_x)} 1 + \sum_{s_i \in \mu_j, (s_i, s_x) \in C_{\neq}, g(s_i) \neq g(s_x)} 1}$$

7.4.4 Probabilistic Penalty – PKM

The PKM algorithm allows constraints to be violated during clustering, but enforces a probabilistic penalty of constraint violation. It is a special case of the HMRF-KMeans algorithm, which is described in detail in Section 7.6 — PKM is an ablation of HMRF-KMeans, doing constraint enforcement but not performing distance learning.

7.5   Learning Distance Function with Constraints

In this section, we will discuss two different approaches of using constraints for distance metric learning in constrained clustering, both of which can cluster text data using Euclidean distance on L_2-normalized text data.

7.5.1   Generalized Mahalanobis Distance Learning

Xing et al. (48) proposed a formulation for learning a parameterized Mahalanobis metric of the form $d(x_1, x_2) = \sqrt{(x_1 - x_2)^T A(x_1 - x_2)}$ from must-link and cannot-link constraints. They proposed the following semi-definite program (SDP) for the problem:

$$\min_A \sum_{(x_i, x_j) \in ML} ||x_i - x_j||_A^2 = \min_A \sum_{(x_i, x_j) \in ML} (x_i - x_j)^T A(x_i - x_j) \quad (7.11)$$

$$s.t., \sum_{(x_i, x_j) \in CL} ||x_i - x_j||_A \geq 1, A \succeq 0$$

Equation 7.11 learns A such that the must-link instances are brought closer together, while ensuring that the cannot-link instances are kept apart (SDP constraint on CL set) and the underlying metric still satisfies the triangle inequality (SDP constraint on A). Xing et al. (48) proposed an equivalent formulation of Equation 7.11:

$$\max_A g(A) = \sum_{(x_i, x_j) \in CL} ||x_i, x_j||_A \quad (7.12)$$

$$s.t., f(A) = \sum_{(x_i, x_j) \in ML} ||x_i, x_j||_A^2 A \leq 1 \rightarrow C_1 \quad (7.13)$$

$$A \succeq 0 \rightarrow C_2$$

Xing et al. (48) optimized Equation 7.12 using an alternate maximization algorithm, that had 2 steps: (1) gradient ascent – to optimize the objective; (2) iterated projection algorithm – to satisfy the inequality constraints. De Bie et al. (7) used a variant of Linear Discriminant Analysis (LDA) to find the Mahalanobis metric from constraints more efficiently than using an SDP. Experiments in both these papers showed that doing clustering with a distance metric learned from constraints gave improved performance over clustering without distance metric learning.

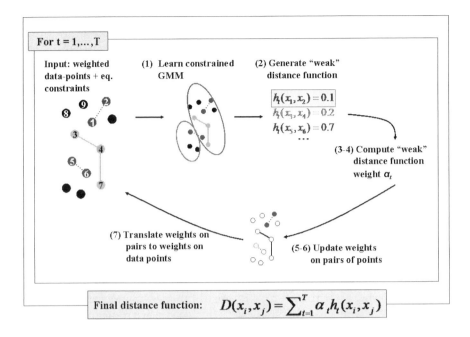

FIGURE 7.7: DistBoost algorithm.

7.5.2 Kernel Distance Functions Using AdaBoost

Hertz et al. (27) proposed a method for distance metric learning by using boosting in the product space of the input data space X. They posed the constrained metric learning problem as learning a function that took as input the instances in the product space $X \times X$, and output binary labels corresponding to must-link (1) and cannot-link constraints (0). They used boosting on the product space to learn this function, where boosting is a standard machine learning tool that combines the strength of an ensemble of "weak" learners (with low prediction accuracy) to create a "strong" learner (with high prediction accuracy) (24). The overall flow of the *DistBoost* algorithm of Hertz et al. (27) is outlined in Figure 7.7. In the first step, a constrained weighted EM algorithm is run on the dataset and constraints, to fit a Gaussian Mixture Model (GMM) over weighted unlabeled data and the given constraints. The key difference of constrained EM from ordinary EM is the E-step, which sums the assignment probabilities only over assignments that comply with the constraints. The output of the GMM is treated as a "weak" learner and is used to learn a "weak" distance function, where the distance $h(x_1, x_2)$ between two instances x_1 and x_2 is computed from their MAP assignment in the GMM as follows:

$$h(x_1, x_2) = \max_i p(y(x_1) = i|\Theta) \cdot \max_j p(y(x_2) = j|\Theta), \qquad (7.14)$$

where y_i is the label assignment for point x_i.

The *DistBoost* algorithm computes the weights of the "weak" distance functions using Boosting, and updates the weights on pairs of instances, which are translated to weights on individual data instances. This is again passed back to the input of the GMM-EM algorithm, and the process is repeated for multiple steps.

7.6   Satisfying Constraints and Learning Distance Functions

As mentioned in Section 7.2, there have been some algorithms that try to both enforce constraints and learn distance functions from constraints for partitional clustering algorithms, e.g., KMeans. In this section we will outline one such algorithm, which uses the framework of a generative probabilistic model, the Hidden Markov Random Field (HMRF) (6). It can cluster text documents using either cosine distance or Euclidean distance on L_2-normalized input data, doing both constraint satisfaction and distance learning in the process.

7.6.1   Hidden Markov Random Field (HMRF) Model

The Hidden Markov Random Field (HMRF) is a probabilistic generative model for semi-supervised constrained clustering, consisting of the following components: (1) an *observable* set $X = (x_1, \ldots, x_n)$ of random variables, corresponding to the given data instances X; (2) an *unobservable* (hidden) set $Y = (y_1, \ldots, y_n)$ of random variables, corresponding to cluster assignments of instances in X, $y_i \in (1, \ldots, K)$; (3) an *unobservable* (hidden) set of generative model parameters Θ, which consists of distance measure parameters A (typically a matrix or vector of weights) and cluster representatives $M = (\mu_1, \ldots, \mu_K)$: $\Theta = \{A, M\}$; (4) an *observable* set of constraint variables $C = (c_{12}, c_{13}, \ldots, c_{n-1,n})$. Each c_{ij} is a tertiary variable taking on a value from the set $(-1, 0, 1)$, where $c_{ij} = 1$ indicates that $(x_i, x_j) \in C_{ML}$, $c_{ij} = -1$ indicates that $(x_i, x_j) \in C_{CL}$, and $c_{ij} = 0$ corresponds to pairs (x_i, x_j) that are not constrained. The constraints are accompanied by associated violation costs W, where w_{ij} represents the cost of violating the constraint between instances x_i and x_j if such a constraint exists. Fig. 7.8 shows a simple example of an HMRF having five data instances partitioned into three clusters, while maximally respecting three pairwise constraints.

The joint probability of X, Y, and Θ, given C, in the described HMRF

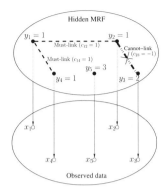

FIGURE 7.8: A hidden Markov random field.

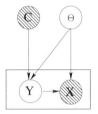

FIGURE 7.9: Graphical plate model of variable dependence.

model can be factorized as follows:

$$P(X, Y, \Theta | C) = P(\Theta | C) \, P(Y | \Theta, C) \, P(X | Y, \Theta, C) \qquad (7.15)$$

The graphical plate model (10) of the dependence between the random variables in the HMRF is shown in Figure 7.9. The prior probability of Θ is assumed to be independent of C, so that $P(\Theta | C) = P(\Theta)$. The probability of observing the label configuration Y depends on the constraints C and current generative model parameters Θ. Observed data instances corresponding to variables X are generated using the model parameters Θ based on cluster labels Y, independent of the constraints C. The variables X are assumed to be mutually independent: each x_i is generated individually from a conditional probability distribution $P(x_i | y_i, \Theta)$.

Basu et al. (6) show that the joint probability on the HMRF is equivalent to maximizing:

$$P(X, Y, \Theta | C) = P(\Theta) \left(\frac{1}{Z} \exp\left(- \sum_{c_{ij} \in C} v(i, j) \right) \right) \left(\prod_{i=1}^{n} p(x_i | y_i, \Theta) \right) \qquad (7.16)$$

They chose the following Gibbs potential for $P(Y | \Theta, C)$:

$$P(Y|\Theta, C) = \frac{1}{Z} \exp\left(-\sum_{i,j} v(i,j)\right) \qquad (7.17)$$

where each constraint potential function $v(i,j)$ has the following form inspired by the generalized Potts model (32) where f_{ML} and f_{CL} are the distances between the constrained points:

$$v(i,j) = \begin{cases} w_{ij} f_{ML}(i,j) & \text{if } c_{ij} = 1 \text{ and } y_i \neq y_j \\ w_{ij} f_{CL}(i,j) & \text{if } c_{ij} = -1 \text{ and } y_i = y_j \\ 0 & \text{otherwise} \end{cases} \qquad (7.18)$$

The joint probability formulation in Equation 7.16 provides a general framework for incorporating various distance measures in clustering by choosing a particular form of $p(x_i|y_i, \Theta)$, the probability density that generates the i-th instance x_i from cluster y_i. Basu et al. (6) restrict their attention to probability densities from the exponential family, where the conditional density for observed data can be represented as follows:

$$p(x_i|y_i, \Theta) = \frac{1}{Z_\Theta} \exp\left(-D(x_i, \mu_{y_i})\right) \qquad (7.19)$$

where $D(x_i, \mu_{y_i})$ is the Bregman divergence between x_i and μ_{y_i}, corresponding to the exponential density p, and Z_Θ is the normalizer (3). Different clustering models fall into this exponential form:

- If x_i and μ_{y_i} are vectors in Euclidean space, and D is the square of the L_2 distance parameterized by a positive semidefinite weight matrix A, $D(x_i, \mu_{y_i}) = \|x_i - \mu_{y_i}\|_A^2$, then the cluster conditional probability is a d-dimensional multivariate normal density with covariance matrix A^{-1}: $p(x_i|y_i, \Theta) = \frac{1}{(2\pi)^{d/2}|A|^{-1/2}} \exp(-\frac{1}{2}(\|x_i - \mu_{y_i}\|_A^2)$ (30);

- If x_i and μ_{y_i} are probability distributions, and D is KL-divergence $(D(x_i, \mu_{y_i}) = \sum_{m=1}^{d} x_{im} \log \frac{x_{im}}{\mu_{y_i m}})$, then the cluster conditional probability is a multinomial distribution (20).

The relation in Equation 7.19 holds even if D is not a Bregman divergence but a directional distance measure such as cosine distance, which is useful in text clustering. Then, if x_i and μ_{y_i} are vectors of unit length and D is one minus the dot-product of the vectors $\left(D(x_i, \mu_{y_i}) = 1 - \frac{\sum_{m=1}^{d} x_{im}\mu_{y_i m}}{\|x_i\|\|\mu_{y_i}\|}\right)$, then the cluster conditional probability is a von-Mises Fisher (vMF) distribution with unit concentration parameter (2), which is the spherical analog of a Gaussian.

Putting Equation 7.19 into Equation 7.16 and taking logarithms gives the following cluster objective function, minimizing which is equivalent to maximizing the joint probability over the HMRF in Equation 7.16:

$$\mathcal{J}_{\text{obj}} = \sum_{x_i \in X} D(x_i, \mu_{y_i}) + \sum_{c_{ij} \in C} v(i,j) - \log \mathrm{P}(\Theta) + \log Z + n \log Z_\Theta \quad (7.20)$$

Basu et al. (6) used Rayleigh priors for $\mathrm{P}(\Theta)$, and they ignored the normalizer terms. An optimal clustering is obtained by minimizing $\mathcal{J}_{\text{obj}}$ over the hidden variables Y and parameters Θ, which are comprised of cluster centroids M and distance measure parameters A (note that given the cluster assignments Y, the means $M = \{\mu_i\}_{i=1}^K$ are uniquely determined).

7.6.2   EM Algorithm

As discussed in Section 7.6.1, Basu et al. (6) minimize $\mathcal{J}_{\text{obj}}$ using a K-Means-type iterative algorithm HMRF-KMEANS. The outline of the algorithm is presented in Figure 7.10. The basic idea of HMRF-KMEANS is as follows: the constraints are used to obtain a good initialization of the clustering. Then in the E-step, given the current cluster representatives, every data instance is re-assigned to the cluster that minimizes its contribution to $\mathcal{J}_{\text{obj}}$. The E-step of HMRF-KMEANS uses an Iterated Conditional Modes (ICM) approach, which is a greedy strategy to sequentially update the cluster assignment of each instance, keeping the assignments for the other instances fixed. In the M-step, the cluster representatives $M = (\mu_1, \ldots, \mu_K)$ are re-estimated from the cluster assignments to minimize $\mathcal{J}_{\text{obj}}$ for the current assignment. The clustering distance measure is subsequently updated in the M-step to reduce the objective function by modifying the parameters of the distance measure.

Note that this corresponds to the generalized EM algorithm (38; 18), where the objective function is reduced but not necessarily minimized in the M-step. Effectively, the E-step minimizes $\mathcal{J}_{\text{obj}}$ over cluster assignments Y, the M-step (A) minimizes $\mathcal{J}_{\text{obj}}$ over cluster representatives M, and the M-step (B) reduces $\mathcal{J}_{\text{obj}}$ over the parameters of the distance measure. The E-step and the M-step are repeated till a specified convergence criterion is reached. Basu et al. (6) show that HMRF-KMEANS converges to a local optimum of $\mathcal{J}_{\text{obj}}$.

7.6.3   Improvements to HMRF-KMEANS

There have been multiple improvements to the initial HMRF-based probabilistic generative constrained clustering framework. Lange et al. (34) incorporated prior knowledge from both labels on the input data instances as well as constraints into their clustering model. They inferred the constraint potentials in the HMRF model from a Maximum Entropy solution of $P(Y)$ under constraints encoded in the label and constraint set, and replaced the ICM-based greedy assignment scheme in the E-step of HMRF-KMEANS by mean-field approximation. Lu et al. (35) proposed probabilistic EM-style assignments instead of winner-take-all KMeans-type assignments, and used Gibbs sampling in the E-step of their constrained EM algorithm.

Algorithm: HMRF-KMEANS
Input: Set of data points $X = \{x_i\}_{i=1}^n$, number of clusters K,
    set of *must-link* constraints $C_{ML} = \{(x_i, x_j)\}$,
    set of *cannot-link* constraints $C_{CL} = \{(x_i, x_j)\}$,
    distortion measures $\{D_h\}_{h=1}^K$, constraint violation costs W.
Output: Disjoint K-partitioning $\{X_h\}_{h=1}^K$ of X such that
    objective function $\mathcal{J}_{\mathrm{obj}}$ is (locally) minimized.
Method:
1. Initialize the K clusters centroids $\{\mu_h^{(0)}\}_{h=1}^K$, set $t \leftarrow 0$
2. Repeat until *convergence*
2a. **E-step:** Given $\{\mu_h^{(t)}\}_{h=1}^K$, re-assign cluster labels
    $\{y_i^{(t+1)}\}_{i=1}^n$ on the points $\{x_i\}_{i=1}^n$ to minimize $\mathcal{J}_{\mathrm{obj}}$.
2b. **M-step(A):** Given cluster labels $\{y_i^{(t+1)}\}_{i=1}^n$, re-calculate
    cluster centroids $\{\mu_h^{(t+1)}\}_{h=1}^K$ to minimize $\mathcal{J}_{\mathrm{obj}}$.
2c. **M-step(B):** Re-estimate distortion measures $\{D_h\}_{h=1}^K$ to reduce $\mathcal{J}_{\mathrm{obj}}$.
2d. $t \leftarrow t+1$

FIGURE 7.10: HMRF-KMEANS algorithm.

7.7   Experiments

This section describes the experiments that were performed to demonstrate the effectiveness of various types of constrained clustering algorithms on text data. We have taken one type of algorithm described earlier: constrained based, distance based, and both. We use the work of Basu and collaborators (6) that includes one algorithm of each type but retains the same underlying implementations. This means the insights we shall find when comparing the different algorithms are due to how the constraints are used rather than different initialization schemes for example. Experiments were run using both Euclidean distance and cosine distance, since different algorithms outlined in this chapter used different distance measures.

7.7.1   Datasets

We considered 3 text datasets that have the characteristics of being sparse, high-dimensional, and having a small number of instances compared to the dimensionality of the space. This is done for two reasons: (1) When clustering sparse high-dimensional data, e.g., text documents represented using the vector space model, it is particularly difficult to cluster small datasets, as observed by (20). The purpose of performing experiments on these subsets is to scale down the sizes of the datasets for computational reasons but at the same time not scale down the difficulty of the tasks. (2) Clustering small number of sparse high-dimensional data instances is a likely scenario in realistic applications. For example, when clustering the search results in a web-search engine like Vivísimo, typically the number of webpages that are being clustered is in the order of hundreds. However the dimensionality of the feature space, corresponding to the number of unique words in all the webpages, is in the order of thousands. Moreover, each webpage is sparse, since it contains only a small number of all the possible words. On such datasets, clustering algorithms can easily get stuck in local optima: in such cases it has been observed that there is little reassignments of documents between clusters for most initializations, which leads to poor clustering quality after convergence of the algorithm (20). Supervision in the form of pairwise constraints is most beneficial in such cases and may significantly improve clustering quality.

Three datasets were derived from the *20-Newsgroups* collection.[3] This collection has messages harvested from 20 different Usenet newsgroups, 1000 messages from each newsgroup. From the original dataset, a reduced dataset was created by taking a random subsample of 100 documents from each of the 20 newsgroups. Three datasets were created by selecting 3 categories from the reduced collection. *News-Similar-3* consists of 3 newsgroups on similar topics (comp.graphics, comp.os.ms-windows, comp.windows.x) with significant overlap between clusters due to cross-posting. *News-Related-3* consists of 3 newsgroups on related topics (talk.politics.misc, talk.politics.guns, and talk.politics.mideast). *News-Different-3* consists of articles posted in 3 newsgroups that cover different topics (alt.atheism, rec.sport.baseball, sci.space) with well-separated clusters. All the text datasets were preprocessed using the techniques outlined in Section 7.3.1.

Table 7.1 summarizes the properties of these datasets.

TABLE 7.1:   Text datasets used in experimental evaluation

	News-Different-3	*News-Related-3*	*News-Similar-3*
Instances	300	300	300
Dimensions	3251	3225	1864
Classes	3	3	3

7.7.2   Clustering Evaluation

Normalized mutual information (NMI) was used as the clustering evaluation measure. NMI is an external clustering validation metric that estimates the quality of the clustering with respect to a given underlying class labeling of

---

[3]http://www.ai.mit.edu/people/jrennie/20Newsgroups

the data: it measures how closely the clustering algorithm could reconstruct the underlying label distribution in the data (45). Therefore, the higher the NMI the better. If $\widehat{Y}$ is the random variable denoting the cluster assignments of the instances and Y is the random variable denoting the underlying class labels on the instances, then the NMI measure is defined as:

$$NMI = \frac{I(Y;\widehat{Y})}{(H(Y) + H(\widehat{Y}))/2} \qquad (7.21)$$

where $I(X;Y) = H(X) - H(X|Y)$ is the mutual information between the random variables X and Y, $H(X)$ is the Shannon entropy of X, and $H(X|Y)$ is the conditional entropy of X given Y (13). NMI effectively measures the amount of statistical information shared by the random variables representing the cluster assignments and the user-labeled class assignments of the data instances. Though various clustering evaluation measures have been used in the literature, NMI and its variants have become popular lately among clustering practitioners (22; 23; 37).

7.7.3   Methodology

Learning curves were generated using two-fold cross-validation performed over 20 runs on each dataset. In every trial, 50% of the dataset was set aside as the training fold. Every point on the learning curve corresponds to the number of constraints on pairs of data instances from the training fold. These constraints are obtained by randomly selecting pairs of instances from the training fold and creating must-link or cannot-link constraints depending on whether the underlying classes of the two instances are same or different. Unit constraint costs W were used for all constraints (original and inferred), since the datasets did not provide individual weights for the constraints. The clustering algorithm was run on the whole dataset, but NMI was calculated using instances in the test fold.

7.7.4   Comparison of Distance Functions

Figure 7.11 shows the results of running constrained PKM clustering on *News-Same-3* and *News-Different-3*, using both Euclidean and cosine distances. As shown in the figure, there is an improvement in the performance of the algorithm with cosine distance over Euclidean distance, which is consistent with previous research (40). Euclidean distance can be used if necessary for constrained text clustering (e.g., for the algorithms outlined in Section 7.4), with pre-normalization of the text documents. However, using cosine distance is recommended by practitioners for constrained clustering of text datasets in most domains, in which case algorithms like HMRF-KMEANS are more useful.

7.7.5 Experimental Results

We performed experiments on text datasets with HMRF-KMEANS, a combined constraint-based and distance-based algorithm, to study the effectiveness of each component of the algorithm. HMRF-KMEANS was compared with three ablations, as well as with unsupervised KMeans clustering. The following variants were compared:

- KMEANS-C-D-R is the complete HMRF-KMEANS algorithm that incorporates constraints in cluster assignments (C), includes distance learning (D), and also performs weight regularization (R) using a Rayleigh prior;

- KMEANS-C-D is the first ablation of HMRF-KMEANS that includes all components except for regularization of distance measure parameters;

- KMEANS-C is an ablation of HMRF-KMEANS that uses pairwise supervision for initialization and cluster assignments, but does not perform distance measure learning. This is equivalent to the PKM algorithm mentioned in Section 7.4.

- KMEANS is the unsupervised K-Means algorithm.

The goal of these experiments was to evaluate the utility of each component of the HMRF framework and identify settings in which particular components are beneficial. Figures 7.12, 7.13, and 7.14 present the results for the ablation experiments where weighted cosine distance was used as the distance measure.

As the results demonstrate, the full HMRF-KMEANS algorithm with regularization (KMEANS-C-D-R) outperforms the unsupervised K-Means baseline as well as the ablated versions of the algorithm. As can be seen from results for zero pairwise constraints in the figures, distance measure learning is beneficial even in the absence of any pairwise constraints, since it allows capturing the relative importance of the different attributes in the unsupervised data. In the absence of supervised data or when no constraints are violated, distance learning attempts to minimize the objective function by adjusting the weights given the distortion between the unsupervised data instances and their corresponding cluster representatives.

For these datasets, regularization is clearly beneficial to performance, as can be seen from the improved performance of KMEANS-C-D-R over KMEANS-C-D on all datasets. This can be explained by the fact that the number of distance measure parameters is large for high-dimensional datasets, and therefore algorithm-based estimates of parameters tend to be unreliable unless they incorporate a prior.

Overall, these results show that the HMRF-KMEANS algorithm effectively incorporates constraints for doing both distance learning and constraint satisfaction, each of which improves the quality of clustering for the text datasets considered in the experiments.

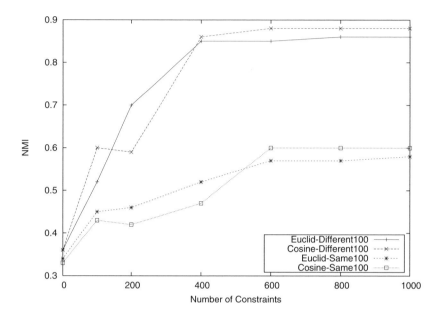

FIGURE 7.11: Comparison of cosine and Euclidean distance.

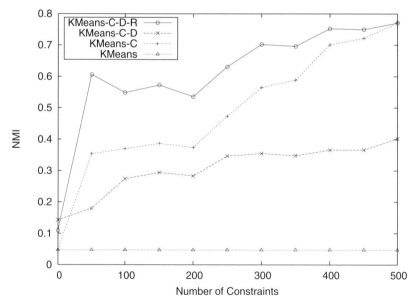

FIGURE 7.12: Results on *News-Different-3*.

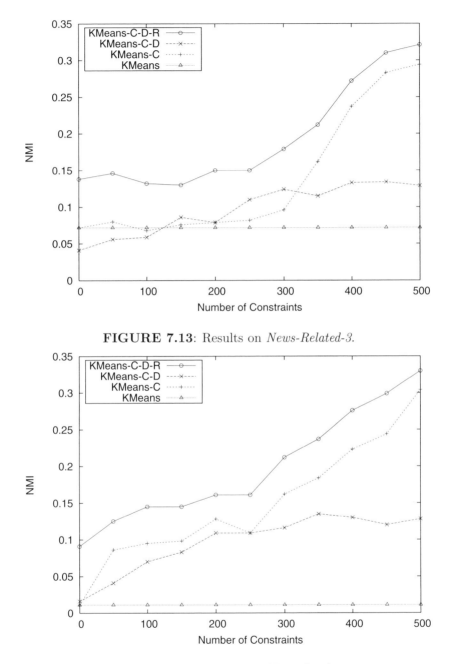

FIGURE 7.13: Results on *News-Related-3*.

FIGURE 7.14: Results on *News-Similar-3*.

7.8   Conclusions

In this book chapter, we gave an overview of different types of constrained partitional clustering algorithms and how they can be used for improved text clustering. We mainly focused on pairwise constraints and partitional clustering algorithms that use these constraints in different ways (e.g., constraint enforcement during inference, distance metric learning) for different distance measures (e.g., cosine distance, Euclidean distance). There are other types of constraints (e.g., size constraints on clusters (9)) and other categories of constrained clustering algorithms (e.g., hierarchical clustering (15), graph clustering (29; 33)), which we could not cover in this chapter. Experiment results on text datasets demonstrate that using constraints during clustering can significantly improve the quality of the results, and also indicate that using the cosine distance function is recommended for constrained clustering in the text domain.

References

[1] R. Baeza-Yates and B. Ribeiro-Neto. *Modern Information Retrieval*. ACM Press, New York, 1999.

[2] A. Banerjee, I. Dhillon, J. Ghosh, and S. Sra. Clustering on the unit hypersphere using von Mises-Fisher distributions. *Journal of Machine Learning Research*, 6:1345–1382, 2005.

[3] A. Banerjee, S. Merugu, I. Dhillon, and J. Ghosh. Clustering with Bregman divergences. *Journal of Machine Learning Research*, 6:1705–1749, 2005.

[4] A. Bar-Hillel, T. Hertz, N. Shental, and D. Weinshall. Learning distance functions using equivalence relations. In *Proceedings of ICML*, pages 11–18, Washington, DC, 2003.

[5] S. Basu, A. Banerjee, and R. J. Mooney. Semi-supervised clustering by seeding. In *Proceedings of ICML*, pages 19–26, 2002.

[6] S. Basu, M. Bilenko, and R. J. Mooney. A probabilistic framework for semi-supervised clustering. In *Proceedings of ACM SIGKDD*, pages 59–68, Seattle, WA, 2004.

[7] T. De Bie, M. Momma, and N. Cristianini. Efficiently learning the metric using side-information. In *Proc. of the 14th International Conference on*

Algorithmic Learning Theory (ALT2003), volume 2842 of *Lecture Notes in Artificial Intelligence*, pages 175–189. Springer, 2003.

[8] M. Bilenko and R. J. Mooney. Adaptive duplicate detection using learnable string similarity measures. In *Proceedings of ACM SIGKDD*, pages 39–48, Washington, DC, 2003.

[9] P. S. Bradley, K. P. Bennett, and A. Demiriz. Constrained K-means clustering. Technical Report MSR-TR-2000-65, Microsoft Research, May 2000.

[10] W. L. Buntine. Operations for learning with graphical models. *Journal of Artificial Intelligence Research*, 2:159–225, 1994.

[11] H. Chang and D.-Y. Yeung. Locally linear metric adaptation for semi-supervised clustering. In *Proceedings of 21st International Conference on Machine Learning (ICML-2004)*, 2004.

[12] D. Cohn, R. Caruana, and A. McCallum. Semi-supervised clustering with user feedback. Technical Report TR2003-1892, Cornell University, 2003.

[13] T. M. Cover and J. A. Thomas. *Elements of Information Theory*. Wiley-Interscience, 1991.

[14] I. Davidson, M. Ester, and S. S. Ravi. Efficient incremental clustering with constraints. In *Proceedings of the Thirteen ACM Conference on Data Mining and Knowledge Discovery*, 2007.

[15] I. Davidson and S. S. Ravi. Hierarchical clustering with constraints: Theory and practice. In *Proceedings of the Nineth European Principles and Practice of KDD (PKDD)*, pages 59–70, 2005.

[16] I. Davidson and S. S. Ravi. Clustering with constraints: Feasibility issues and the k-means algorithm. In *Proceedings of the 2005 SIAM International Conference on Data Mining (SDM-05)*, 2005.

[17] A. Demiriz, K. P. Bennett, and M. J. Embrechts. Semi-supervised clustering using genetic algorithms. In *Proceedings of ANNIE*, pages 809–814, 1999.

[18] A. P. Dempster, N. M. Laird, and D. B. Rubin. Maximum likelihood from incomplete data via the EM algorithm. *JRSSB*, 39:1–38, 1977.

[19] I. S. Dhillon, J. Fan, and Y. Guan. Efficient clustering of very large document collections. In *Data Mining for Scientific and Engineering Applications*. Kluwer Academic Publishers, 2001.

[20] I. S. Dhillon and Y. Guan. Information theoretic clustering of sparse co-occurrence data. In *Proceedings of ICDM*, pages 517–521, 2003.

[21] I. S. Dhillon and D. S. Modha. Concept decompositions for large sparse text data using clustering. *Machine Learning*, 42:143–175, 2001.

[22] B. E. Dom. An information-theoretic external cluster-validity measure. Research Report RJ 10219, IBM, 2001.

[23] X. Fern and C. Brodley. Random projection for high dimensional data clustering: A cluster ensemble approach. In *Proceedings of 20th International Conference on Machine Learning (ICML-2003)*, 2003.

[24] Y. Freund and R. E. Schapire. Experiments with a new boosting algorithm. In Lorenza Saitta, editor, *Proceedings of the Thirteenth International Conference on Machine Learning (ICML-96)*, pages 148–156. Morgan Kaufmann, July 1996.

[25] J. Ghosh and A. Strehl. *Grouping Multidimensional Data: Recent Advances in Clustering*, chapter Similarity-based Text Clustering: A Comparitive Study. Springer Berlin Heidelberg, 2006.

[26] M. Goldszmidt and M. Sahami. A probabilistic approach to full-text document clustering. Technical Report ITAD-433-MS-98-044, SRI International, 1998.

[27] T. Hertz, A. Bar-Hillel, and D. Weinshall. Boosting margin based distance functions for clustering. In *Proceedings of 21st International Conference on Machine Learning (ICML-2004)*, 2004.

[28] M. Hiu, C. Law, A. Topchy, and A. K. Jain. Model-based clustering with probabilistic constraints. In *Proceedings of the 2005 SIAM International Conference on Data Mining (SDM-05)*, 2005.

[29] S. D. Kamvar, D. Klein, and C. D. Manning. Spectral learning. In *Proceedings of the Eighteenth International Joint Conference on Artificial Intelligence (IJCAI-2003)*, pages 561–566, Acapulco, Mexico, 2003.

[30] M. Kearns, Y. Mansour, and A. Y. Ng. An information-theoretic analysis of hard and soft assignment methods for clustering. In *Proceedings of UAI*, pages 282–293, 1997.

[31] D. Klein, S. D. Kamvar, and C. Manning. From instance-level constraints to space-level constraints: Making the most of prior knowledge in data clustering. In *Proceedings of ICML*, pages 307–314, Sydney, Australia, 2002.

[32] J. Kleinberg and E. Tardos. Approximation algorithms for classification problems with pairwise relationships: Metric labeling and Markov random fields. In *Proceedings of FOCS*, pages 14–23, 1999.

[33] B. Kulis, S. Basu, I. Dhillon, and R. J. Mooney. Semi-supervised graph clustering: A kernel approach. Proceedings of 22nd International Conference on Machine Learning (ICML-2005), 2005.

[34] T. Lange, M. H. C. Law, A. K. Jain, and J. M. Buhmann. Learning with constrained and unlabeled data. In *CVPR*, pages 731–738. San Diego, CA, 2005.

[35] Z. Lu and T. Leen. Semi-supervised learning with penalized probabilistic clustering. In *Advances in Neural Information Processing Systems*, 2005.

[36] Z. Lu and T. K. Leen. Semi-supervised learning with penalized probabilistic clustering. In *Advances in Neural Information Processing Systems 17*, 2005.

[37] M. Meila. Comparing clusterings by the variation of information. In *Proceedings of the 16th Annual Conference on Computational Learning Theory*, pages 173–187, 2003.

[38] R. M. Neal and G. E. Hinton. A view of the EM algorithm that justifies incremental, sparse, and other variants. In Michael I. Jordan, editor, *Learning in Graphical Models*, pages 355–368. MIT Press, 1998.

[39] D. Pelleg and D. Baras. K-means with large and noisy constraint sets. In *ECML*, 2007.

[40] M. Sahami. Personal communication, September 2007.

[41] G. Salton and M. J. McGill. *Introduction to Modern Information Retrieval*. McGraw-Hill, New York, 1983.

[42] M. Seeger. Learning with labeled and unlabeled data, 2000.

[43] E. Segal, H. Wang, and D. Koller. Discovering molecular pathways from protein interaction and gene expression data. *Bioinformatics*, 19:i264–i272, July 2003.

[44] J. Sinkkonen and S. Kaski. Semisupervised clustering based on conditional distributions in an auxiliary space. Technical Report A60, Helsinki University of Technology, 2000.

[45] A. Strehl, J. Ghosh, and R. Mooney. Impact of similarity measures on web-page clustering. In *Workshop on Artificial Intelligence for Web Search (AAAI 2000)*, pages 58–64, July 2000.

[46] K. Wagstaff and C. Cardie. Clustering with instance-level constraints. In *Proceedings of the Seventeenth International Conference on Machine Learning*, pages 1103–1110, Palo Alto, CA, 2000. Morgan Kaufmann.

[47] K. Wagstaff, C. Cardie, S. Rogers, and S. Schroedl. Constrained K-Means clustering with background knowledge. In *Proceedings of ICML*, pages 577–584, 2001.

[48] E. P. Xing, A. Y. Ng, M. I. Jordan, and S. Russell. Distance metric learning, with application to clustering with side-information. In *NIPS 15*, 2003.

[49] X. Zhu. Semi-supervised learning literature survey. Technical Report 1530, Computer Sciences, University of Wisconsin-Madison, 2005. http://www.cs.wisc.edu/~jerryzhu/pub/ssl_survey.pdf.

Chapter 8

Adaptive Information Filtering

Yi Zhang

8.1   Introduction

A financial analyst wants to be alerted of any information that may affect the price of the stock he is tracking; an agent working in the Homeland Security Department wants to be alerted of any information related to potential terror attacks; a customer call center representative wants to answer customer calls about problems that he can handle; and a student wants to be alerted of fellowship or financial aid opportunities appropriate for her/his circumstances.

In these examples, the user preferences are comparatively stable and represent a long term information need, the information source is dynamic, information arrives sequentially over time, and the information needs to be delivered to the user as soon as possible. Traditional *ad hoc* search engines, which are designed to help the users to pull out information from a comparatively static information source, are inadequate to fulfill the requirements of these tasks. Instead, a filtering system can better serve the user. A filtering system is an autonomous agent that delivers good information to the user in a dynamic environment. As opposed to forming a ranked list, it estimates whether a piece of information matches the user needs as soon as the information arrives and pushes the information to the user if the answer is "yes," so a user can be alerted of any important information on time.

A typical information filtering system is shown in Figure 8.1. In this figure, a piece of information is a document. A user's information needs are

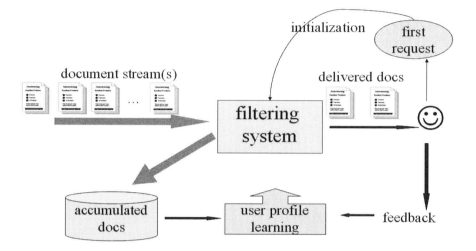

FIGURE 8.1: A typical filtering system. A filtering system can serve many users, although only one user is shown in the figure. Information can be documents, images, or videos. Without loss of generality, we focus on text documents in this chapter.

represented in a user profile. The profile contains one or more classes, such as "stock" or "music," and each class corresponds to one information need. When a user has a new information need, he/she sends to the system an initial request, such as a query or an example of what he/she wants. The system then initializes and creates a new online classifier in the user's profile to serve this information need. As future documents arrive, the system delivers documents the classifier considered relevant to the user. The user may then read the delivered documents and provide explicit feedback, such as identifying a document as "good" or "bad." The user also provides some implicit feedback, such as deleting a document without reading it or saving a document. The filtering system uses the user feedback accumulated over time to update the user profile.

Adaptive filtering vs. retrieval: Standard *ad hoc* retrieval systems, such as search engines, let users use short queries to pull information out of a repository. These systems treat all users the same given the same query. Most IR systems return back documents that match a user query. They assume that a user knows what he/she wants, and what words to use to describe it whenever he/she has an information need. However, a user often does not know these or thinks he/she needs to know one thing but actually needs something else. For example, a financial analyst may search for news in order to check whether the earnings of a company matches the projected earnings. However, also relevant to this task is the large number of customer complaints about the company's product in the blog space. Another example is a research scientist often wants to keep up-to-date with what is happening within a research field, but not looking for a specific answer.

If the information need of a user is more or less stable over a long period of time, a filtering system is a good environment to learn user profiles (also called user models) from a fair amount of user feedback that can be accumulated over time. In other words, the adaptive filtering system can serve the user better by learning user profiles while interacting with the user, thus information delivered to the user can be personalized to an individual user's information needs automatically. Even if the user's interest drifts or changes, the adaptive filtering system can still adapt to the user's new interest by constantly updating the user profile from training data, creating new classes automatically, or letting the user create/delete classes.

Adaptive filtering vs. collaborative filtering: Collaborative filtering is an alternative approach used by *push* system to provide personalized recommendations to users. Adaptive filtering, which is also called content based filtering, assumes what a user will like is similar to what the user liked before, and thus make recommendations for one user based on the user's feedback about past documents. Collaborative filtering assumes users have similar tastes on some items may also have similar preferences on other items, and thus make recommendations for one user based on the feedback from other users that are similar to this user. Memory-based heuristics and model based approaches have been used in collaborative filtering task (29) (22) (10). This chapter does not intend to compare adaptive filtering with collaborative filtering or claim which one is better. We think each complements the other. Adaptive filtering is extremely useful for handling new documents/items with little or no user feedback, while collaborative filtering leverages information from other users with similar tastes and preferences in the past. Researchers have found that a recommendation system will be more effective when both techniques are combined. However, this is beyond the scope of this chapter and thus not discussed here.

Adaptive filtering vs. Topic Detection and Tracking: The supervised tracking task at the Topic Detection and Tracking (TDT) Workshops is a forum closely related to information filtering (1). TDT research focuses on discovering topically related material in streams of data. TDT is different from adaptive filtering in several aspects. In TDT, a topic is user independent and defined as an event or activity, along with all directly related events and activities. In adaptive filtering, an information need is user specific and has a broader definition. A user information needs may be a topic about a specific subject, such as "2004 presidential election," or not, such as "weird stories." However, TDT-style topic tracking and TREC-style adaptive filtering have

TABLE 8.1:   The values assigned to
relevant and non-relevant documents that the
filtering system did and did not deliver. R^-,
R^+, N^+, and N^- correspond to the number
of documents that fall into the corresponding
category. A_R, A_N, B_R, and B_N correspond to
the credit/penalty for each element in the
category.

	Relevant	*Non-Relevant*
Delivered	R^+, A_R	N^+, A_N
Not Delivered	R^-, B_R	N^-, B_N

much in common, especially if we treat a topic as a form of user information
need. Since a separate chapter in this book is devoted to TDT, we refer the
readers to that chapter for research on TDT.

This chapter is organized as follows. Section 8.2 introduces the standard
evaluation measures used in the TREC adaptive filtering task. Section 8.3
introduces commonly used retrieval models and adaptive filtering approaches.
Section 8.4 describes how to solve the "cold start" problem for new users using
Bayesian prior learned from other users. Section 8.5 introduces techniques to
avoid redundant information while filtering. This chapter ends with discussion
and references to other important topics not covered in details in this book.

8.2   Standard Evaluation Measures

In the information retrieval community, the performance of an *ad hoc* retrieval system is typically evaluated using relevance-based recall and precision
at a certain cut-off of the ranked result. Taking a 20-document cut-off as an
example:

$$precision = \frac{the\ number\ of\ relevant\ documents\ among\ the\ top\ 20}{20} \quad (8.1)$$

$$recall = \frac{the\ number\ of\ relevant\ documents\ in\ the\ top\ 20}{all\ relevant\ documents\ in\ the\ corpus} \quad (8.2)$$

What is a good cut off number is unknown. In order to compare different
algorithms without a specific cut off, the mean of the precision scores after
each relevant document is retrieved, which is called Mean Average Precision
(MAP), is often used.

However, the above evaluation measures are not appropriate for filtering.
Instead of a ranking list, a filtering system makes an explicit binary decision

of whether to accept or reject a document for each profile. A *utility function* is usually used to model user satisfaction and evaluate a system. A general form of the linear utility function used in the recent Text REtrieval Conference (TREC) Filtering Track (46) is shown below.

$$U = A_R \cdot R^+ + A_N \cdot N^+ + B_R \cdot R^- + B_N \cdot N^- \qquad (8.3)$$

This model corresponds to assigning a positive or negative value to each element in the categories of Table 8.1, where R^-, R^+, N^+, and N^- correspond to the number of documents that fall into the corresponding category, A_R, A_N, B_R, and B_N correspond to the credit/penalty for each element in the category. Usually, A_R is positive, and A_N is negative. In the TREC-9, TREC-10, and TREC-11 Filtering Tracks, the following utility function was used:

$$T11U = T10U = T9U = 2R^+ - N^+ \qquad (8.4)$$

If we use the T11U utility measure directly and get the final result by averaging across user profiles, profiles with many delivered documents will dominate the final result. So a normalized version T11SU was also used in TREC-11:

$$T11SU = \frac{max(\frac{T11U}{MaxU}, MinNU) - MinNU}{1 - MinNU} \qquad (8.5)$$

where $MaxU = 2 * (R^+ + R^-)$ is the maximum possible utility,[1] and $MinNU$ was set to -0.5 in TREC-11. If the score is below $MinNU$, the $MinNU$ is used, which simulates the scenario that the users stop using the system when the performance is too poor.[2]

Notice that in a real scenario, we could define user-specific utility functions to model user satisfaction and evaluate filtering systems. A better choice of A_R, A_N, B_R, and B_N would depend on the user, the task, and the context. For example, when a user is reading news with a wireless phone, he may have less tolerance for non-relevant documents delivered and prefer higher precision, and thus use a utility function with larger penalty for non-relevant documents delivered, such as $U_{wireless} = R^+ - 3N^+$. When a user is doing research about a certain topic, he may have a high tolerance for non-relevant documents delivered and prefer high recall, and thus use a utility function with less penalty for non-relevant documents delivered, such as $U_{research} = R^+ - 0.5N^+$. When monitoring potential terrorist activities, missing information might be crucial and B_R may be a big non-zero negative value.

In addition to the linear utility measure, other measures such as F-beta (46) defined by van Rijsbergen and DET curves (37) are also used in the research

---

[1] Notice the normalized version does take into consideration undelivered relevant documents. Therefore, it also provides some information about the recall of the system implicitly.

[2] This is not exactly the same, since in TREC the system is evaluated at the very end of the filtering process.

community. Measures that consider novelty or properties of a document have also been proposed by researchers (65).

8.3   Standard Retrieval Models and Filtering Approaches

In this section, we first review some existing information retrieval models since most of them have been adapted, or can be adapted, for the information filtering task. Then we review three common filtering approaches for learning user profiles from explicit user feedback.

We introduce these existing approaches and their drawbacks here, so that the readers can get a better understanding of the common practices in adaptive filtering. This section also provides the context and motivation of the research work described in the following sections. As there is a large amount of literature about standard retrieval models and filtering approaches, we will only review them concisely. For more detail about these models, the readers are referred to other papers or books.

8.3.1   Existing Retrieval Models

Information filtering has a long history dating back to the 1970s. It was created as a subfield of the more general information retrieval field, which was originally established to solve the ad hoc retrieval task.[3] For this reason, early work tended to view filtering and retrieval as "two sides of the same coin" (9). The duality argument is based on the assumptions that documents and queries are interchangeable. This dual view has been questioned (49) (12) by challenging the interchangeability of documents and queries due to their asymmetries of representation, ranking, evaluation, iteration, history, and statistics. However, the influence of retrieval models on filtering is still large, because the retrieval models were comparatively well studied and the two tasks share many common issues, such as how to handle words and tokens, how to represent a document, how to represent a user query, how to understand relevance, and how to use relevance feedback. So it is worthwhile to look at various models used in IR and how relevance feedback is used in these models.

In the last several decades, many different retrieval models have been developed to solve the *ad hoc* retrieval task. In general, there are three major classes of IR models:

---

[3]Historically, information retrieval was first used to refer to the *ad hoc* retrieval task, and then was expanded to refer to the broader information seeking scenario that includes filtering, text classification, question answering, and more.

8.3.1.1 Boolean models

The *Boolean model* is the simplest retrieval model based on Boolean algebra and set theory. The concept is very simple and intuitive. The drawbacks of the Boolean model are in two aspects: 1) The users may have difficulty to express their information needs using Boolean expressions; and 2) The retrieval system can hardly rank documents since a document is predicted to be either relevant or non-relevant without any notion of degree of relevance. Nevertheless, the Boolean model is widely used in commercial search engines because of its simplicity and efficiency. How to use relevance feedback from the user to refine a Boolean query is not straightforward, so the Boolean model was extended for this purposes (34).

8.3.1.2 Vector space models

The *vector model* is a widely implemented IR model, most famously built in the SMART system (52). It represents documents and user queries in a high dimensional space indexed by "indexing terms," and assumes that the relevance of a document can be measured by the similarity between it and the query in the high dimensional space (51). In the vector space framework, relevance feedback is used to reformulate a query vector so that it is closer to the relevant documents, or for query expansion so that additional terms from the relevant documents are added to the original query. The most famous algorithm is the Rocchio algorithm (50), which represents a user query using a linear combination of the original query vector, the relevant documents centroid, and the non-relevant documents centroid.

A major criticism for the vector space model is that its performance depends highly on the representation, while the choice of representation is heuristic because the vector space model itself does not provide a theoretical framework on how to select key terms and how to set weights of terms.

8.3.1.3 Probabilistic models

Probabilistic models, such as the *Binary Independence Model (BIM)* ((44)), provide direct guidance on term weighting and term selection based on probability theory. In these probabilistic models, the probability of a document d is relevant to a user query q is modelled explicitly (43) (44) (23). Using relevance feedback to improve parameter estimation in probabilistic models is straightforward according to the definition of the models, because they presuppose relevance information.

In recent decades many researchers proposed IR models that are more general, while also explaining already existing IR models. For example, *Inference networks* have been successfully implemented in the well known INQUERY retrieval system (57). Bayesian networks extend the view of inference networks. Both models represent documents and queries using acyclic graphs. Unfortunately, both models do not provide a sound theoretical framework to

learn the structure of the graph or to estimate the conditional probabilities defined on the graphs, and thus the model structure and parameter estimations
are rather *ad hoc* (24). Another example is the *language modeling approach*,
which is a statistical approach that models the document generation process.
This approach is a very active research area in the IR community since the
late 90's (20).

8.3.2   Existing Adaptive Filtering Approaches

The key component of an adaptive filtering system is the user profile used by
the system to make the decision of whether to deliver a document to the user
or not. In the early research work as well as some recent commercial filtering
systems, a user profile is represented as Boolean logic (25). With the growing
computation power and the advance of research in the information retrieval
community in the last 20 years, filtering systems have gone beyond simple
Boolean queries and represent a user profile as either a vector, a statistical
distribution of words, or something else. Much of the research on adaptive
filtering is focused on learning a user profile from explicit user feedback on
whether the user likes a document or not while interacting with the user. In
general, there are two major approaches.

8.3.2.1   Filtering as retrieval + thresholding

A typical retrieval system has a static information source, and the task is
to return a ranking of documents in response to a short-term user request.
Because of the influence of the retrieval models, some existing filtering systems
use "retrieval scoring+thresholding" approach for filtering and build adaptive
filtering based on algorithms originally designed for the retrieval task. A
filtering system uses a retrieval algorithm to score each incoming document
and delivers the document to the user if and only if the score is above a
dissemination threshold. Some examples of retrieval models that have been
applied to the adaptive filtering task are: Rocchio, language models, Okapi,
and pseudo relevance feedback (3) (12) (35) (5) (19) (54).

A threshold is not needed in a retrieval task, because the system only needs
to return a ranked list of documents. A major research topic in the adaptive
filtering community is on how to set dissemination thresholds (48) (7) (63)
(6) (72) (68). The criteria of thresholds are often expressed in an easy to
understand way, such as the utility function described in Section 8.2. At
each time point, the system learns a threshold from the relevance judgements
collected so far. For example, one direct utility optimization technique is
to compute the utility on the training data for each candidate threshold, and
choose the threshold that gives the maximum utility. Score distribution based
approach assumes generative models of scores for relevant documents and
non-relevant documents. For example, one can assume the scores of relevant
documents follow a Gaussian distribution, and the scores for non-relevant

documents follow an exponential distribution. Training data can be used to estimate the model parameters, and the threshold can be found by optimizing the expected utility under the estimated model (7). However, an adaptive filtering system only receives feedback for documents delivered/rated by the user; thus model estimation techniques based on random sampling assumption usually lead to biased estimation and should be avoided (72).

8.3.2.2 Filtering as text classification

Text classification is another well studied area. A typical classification system learns a classifier from a labeled training dataset, and then classifies unlabeled testing documents into different classes. A popular approach is to treat filtering as a text classification task by defining two classes: relevant vs. non-relevant. The filtering system learns a user profile as a classifier and delivers a document to the user if the classifier thinks it is relevant or the probability of relevance is high. The state of the art text classification algorithms, such as support vector machines (SVM), K nearest neighbors (K-NN), neural networks, logistic regression, and Winnow, have been used to solve this binary classification task (32) (13) (46) (64) (71)(54) (38) (61) (30) (55).

Instead of minimizing classification error, an adaptive filtering system needs to optimize the standard evaluation measure, such as a user utility. For example, in order to optimize the utility measure $T11U = 2R^+ - N^+$ (Equation 8.4), a filtering system usually delivers a document to the user if the probability of relevance is above 67% (45). Some machine learning approaches, such as logistic regression or neural networks, estimate the probability of relevance directly, which makes it easier to make the binary decision of whether to deliver a document.

Many standard text classification algorithms do not work well for a new user, which usually means no or few training data points. Some new approaches have been developed for initialization. For example, researchers have found that retrieval techniques, such as Rocchio, work well at the early stage of filtering when the system has very few training data. Statistical text classification techniques, such as logistic regression, work well at the later stage of filtering when the system has accumulated enough training data. Techniques have been developed to combine different algorithms, and their results are promising (71). Yet another example discussed in the following section is to initialize the profile of a new user based on training data from existing users.

It is worth mentioning that when adapting a text classification technique to the adaptive filtering task, one needs to pay attention that the classes are extremely unbalanced, because most documents are not relevant. The fact that the training data are not sampled randomly is also a problem that has not been well studied.

8.4   Collaborative Adaptive Filtering

One major challenge of building a recommendation or personalization system is that the profile learned for a particular user is usually of low quality when the amount of data from that particular user is small. This is known as the "cold start" problem. This means that any new user must endure poor initial performance until sufficient feedback from that user is provided to learn a reliable user profile.

There has been much research on improving classification accuracy when the amount of labeled training data is small. The semi-supervised learning approach combines unlabeled and labeled data together to achieve this goal. Another approach is using domain knowledge. Researchers have modified different learning algorithms, such as Naïve-Bayes (33), logistic regression (21), and SVMs (62), to integrate domain knowledge into a text classifier. The third approach is borrowing training data from other resources (16) (21). The effectiveness of these different approaches is mixed, due to how well the underlying model assumption fits the data.

This section introduces one well-received approach to improve recommendation system performance for a particular user: borrowing information from other users through a Bayesian hierarchical modeling approach. Several researchers have demonstrated that this approach effectively trades off between shared and user-specific information, thus alleviating poor initial performance for each user (76) (67) (74).

Assume there are M users in the adaptive filtering system. The task of the system is to deliver documents that are relevant to each user. For each user, the system learns a user model from the user's history. In the rest of this section, the following notations are used to represent the variables in the system.

$m = 1, 2, ..., M$**:** The index for each individual user. M is the total number of users.

w_m**:** The user model parameter associated with user m. w_m is a K dimensional vector.

$j = 1, 2, ..., J_m$**:** The index for a set of data for user m. J_m is the number of training data for user m.

$D_m = \{(x_{m,j}, y_{m,j})\}$**:** A set of data associated with user m. $x_{m,j}$ is a K dimensional vector that represents the mth user's jth training document.[4] $y_{m,j}$ is a scalar that represents the label of document $x_{m,j}$.

$k = 1, 2, ..., K$**:** The dimensional index of input variable x.

---

[4]The first dimension of x is a dummy variable that always equals to 1.

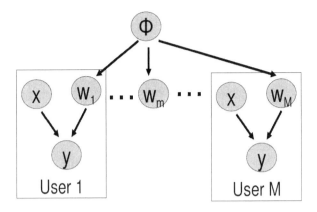

FIGURE 8.2: Illustration of dependencies of variables in the hierarchical model. The rating, y, for a document, x, is conditioned on the document and the user model, w_m, associated with the user m. Users share information about their models through the prior, $\Phi = (\mu, \Sigma)$.

The Bayesian hierarchical modeling approach has been widely used in real-world information retrieval applications. Generalized Bayesian hierarchical linear models, a simple set of Bayesian hierarchical models, are commonly used and have achieved good performance on collaborative filtering (67) and content-based adaptive filtering (76) (74) tasks. Figure 8.2 shows the graphical representation of a Bayesian hierarchical model. In this graph, each user model is represented by a random vector w_m. Assume a user model is sampled randomly from a prior distribution $P(w|\Phi)$. The system can predict the user label y of a document x given an estimation of w_m (or w_m's distribution) using a function $y = f(x, w)$. The model is called generalized Bayesian hierarchical linear model when $y = f(w^T x)$ is any generalized linear model such as logistic regression, SVM, and linear regression. To reliably estimate the user model w_m, the system can borrow information from other users through the prior $\Phi = (\mu, \Sigma)$.

Now we look at one commonly used model where $y = w^T x + \epsilon$, where $\epsilon \sim N(0, \sigma_\epsilon^2)$ is a random noise (67) (76). Assume that each user model w_m is an independent draw from a population distribution $P(w|\Phi)$, which is governed by some unknown hyperparameter Φ. Let the prior distribution of user model w be a Gaussian distribution with parameter $\Phi = (\mu, \Sigma)$, which is the commonly used prior for linear models. $\mu = (\mu_1, \mu_2, ..., \mu_K)$ is a K dimensional vector that represents the mean of the Gaussian distribution, and Σ is the covariance matrix of the Gaussian. Usually, a Normal distribution $N(0, aI)$ and an Inverse Wishart distribution $P(\Sigma) \propto |\Sigma|^{-\frac{1}{2}b} \exp(-\frac{1}{2}\mathrm{ctr}(\Sigma^{-1}))$ are used as hyperprior to model the prior distribution of μ and Σ respectively.

I is the K dimensional identity matrix, and a, b, and c are real numbers. With these settings, we have the following model for the system:

1. μ and Σ are sampled from $N(0, aI)$ and $IW_\nu(aI)$, respectively.

2. For each user m, w_m is sampled randomly from a Normal distribution: $w_m \sim N(\mu, \Sigma^2)$

3. For each item $x_{m,j}$, $y_{m,j}$ is sampled randomly from a Normal distribution: $y_{m,j} \sim N(w_m^T x_{m,j}, \sigma_\epsilon^2)$.

Let $\theta = (\Phi, w_1, w_2, ..., w_M)$ represent the parameters of this system that needs to be estimated. The joint likelihood for all the variables in the probabilistic model, which includes the data and the parameters, is:

$$P(D, \theta) = P(\Phi) \prod_m P(w_m | \Phi) \prod_j P(y_{m,j} | x_{m,j}, w_m) \qquad (8.6)$$

For simplicity, we assume a, b, c, and σ_ϵ are provided to the system.

Researchers have shown that the Bayesian hierarchical modeling approach has a statistical significant improvement over the regularized linear regression model on several real world datasets. They observed a negative correlation between the number of training data for a user and the improvement the system gets. This suggests that the borrowing information from other users has more significant improvements for users with less training data, which is as expected. However, the strength of the correlation differs over data sets, and the amount of training data is not the only characteristic that will influence the final performance.

One major concern about the hierarchical Bayesian modeling approach is the computation complexity. This problem has been addressed by exploiting the sparsity of the data space. A fast learning algorithm has been developed and tested on a real world dataset (480,189 users, 159,836 features, and 100 million ratings). All the user models can be learned in about 4 hours using a single CPU PC(2GB memory, P4 3GHz), and the learned models perform much better than regularized linear regression models. This demonstrates that the hierarchical Bayesian modeling technique can efficiently handle a large number of users and is used in a large-scale commercial system. More details of the fast learning algorithm is beyond the scope of this chapter, and we refer the reader to Zhang and Koren 2007 (74) for more information.

8.5   Novelty and Redundancy Detection

Although there is an extensive body of research on adaptive information filtering, most of it is focused on identifying relevant documents. A common complaint about information filtering systems is that they do not distinguish between documents that contain new relevant information and documents that contain information that is relevant but already known. This is a serious problem, since a practical filtering system usually handles multiple document sources with significant amounts of redundant information. For example, a financial analyst only wants news stories that may affect the stock market, a market research analyst only wants new complaints about the product, and a newspaper subscriber does not have time to read hundreds of similar news stories from different agencies about the same topic. In all these scenarios, topical relevancy is not enough because the users want *new* information. An information filtering system would provide better service to its users if it can filter out relevant documents that do not contain any new information.

The decision about whether a document contains new information depends on whether the relevant information in a document is covered by information in documents delivered previously. This complicates the filtering problem. The relevance of a document is traditionally a stateless Boolean value. A document either is or is not relevant, without regard as to where the document appears in the stream of documents. Decisions about redundancy and novelty depend very much on where in the stream a document appears.

Relevance and redundancy are significantly different concepts that require different solutions. A system that delivers documents that are novel and relevant must identify documents that are similar to previously delivered relevant documents in the sense of having a same topic, but also dissimilar to the previously delivered documents in the sense of containing new information. If the task is to deliver relevant documents, the learning algorithm will try to recognize documents similar to the delivered relevant documents (training data). Indeed, traditional evaluation of filtering systems (e.g., the TREC Adaptive Filtering track (47) (46)) actually rewards systems for delivering redundant documents. If the task is to deliver only documents containing novel information, the learning algorithm must avoid documents that are similar to those already delivered. These two goals are in some sense contradictory, and it may be unrealistic to expect a single component to satisfy them both.

This suggests the redundancy problem needs a solution that's very different from the traditional adaptive information filtering models. We discuss some possible solutions in this section. We use the following notation throughout this section. All notation is defined with respect to a particular user profile.

- A, B: sets of documents
- d_t: a document that arrives at time t and that is being evaluated for redundancy.
- D_t: the set of all documents delivered for the profile by the time d_t arrives, not including d_t.
- d_j: usually refers to a relevant document that was delivered before d_t arrived.

When acquiring redundancy judgements and developing algorithms, we assume the redundancy of a new document d_t depends on the documents the user saw before d_t arrived. We also assume the documents the user saw before d_t arrived are the set of all documents delivered to the user profile by the time d_t arrives. We use $R(d_t) = R(d_t|D_t)$ to measure the redundancy of d_t.

One approach to novelty/redundancy detection is to cluster all previously delivered documents D_t, and then to measure the redundancy of the current document d_t by its distance to each cluster. This approach would be similar to solutions for the TDT First Story Detection problem (2). This approach is sensitive to clustering accuracy, and is based on strong assumptions about the nature of redundancy.

Another approach is to measure redundancy based on the distance between the new document and each previously delivered document (document-document distance). This approach was developed by some researchers who argue that it may be more robust than clustering, and may be a better match to how users view redundancy. Because they found that it is easiest for a user to identify a new document as being redundant with a single previously seen document, and harder to identify it as being redundant with *a set* of previously seen documents. The calculation of $R(d_t|D_t)$ is simplified by setting it equal to the value of the maximally similar value in all $R(d_t|d_j)$.

$$R(d_t|D_t) = max_{d_j \in D_t} R(d_t|d_j)$$

In the extreme case when d_t and d_j are exact duplicates ($d_t = d_j$), it is obvious that $R(d_t|d_j)$ should have a high value since a duplicate document is maximally redundant. One natural way to measure $R(d_t|d_j)$ is using measures of similarity/distance/difference between d_t and d_j.

One practical concern of redundancy estimation is the size of D_t could be very large. To reduce the computation cost during redundancy decisions, D_t can be truncated to the most recent documents delivered for a profile.

One possibly subtle problem characteristic is that redundancy is not a symmetric metric. d_j may cause d_k to be viewed as redundant, but if the presentation order is reversed, d_k and d_j may both be viewed as containing novel information. A simple example is a document d_k that is a subset (e.g., a paragraph) of a longer document d_j. This problem characteristic motivates exploration of asymmetric forms of traditional similarity/distance/difference measures.

Several different approaches to redundancy detection have been proposed and evaluated (73)(4). The simple set distance measure is designed for Boolean, set based document models. The geometric distance (cosine similarity) measure is a simple metric designed for vector space document models. Several variations of KL divergence and related smoothing algorithms are more complex metrics designed to measure differences in probabilistic document models.

8.5.1 Set Difference

If each document is represented as a set of words, the set difference measure can be used to measure the redundancy of a new document. The novelty of a new document d_t is measured by the number of new words in the smoothed set representation of d_t. If a word w_k occurred frequently in document d_t but less frequently in an old document d_j, it is likely that new information not covered by d_j is covered by d_t.

Thus we can have the following measure for the novelty of the current document d_t with respect to an old document d_j.

$$R(d_t|d_j) = \|d_t \bigcap \overline{d_j}\| \qquad (8.7)$$

We are not using the true difference between two sets

$$\|d_t \bigcap \overline{d_j}\| + \|\overline{d_t} \bigcap d_j\|$$

here because the words in

$$\|\overline{d_t} \bigcap d_j\|$$

shouldn't contribute to the novelty of d_t.

Different variations of the set representation of a document have been proposed. The simplest approach is to include a word in a set d_j if and only if the document contains the word. An alternative approach is to include a word in a set representation if and only if the number of times the word occurs in a document is larger than a threshold. However, some words are expected to be frequent in a new document because they tend to be frequent in the corpus, or because they tend to be frequent in all relevant documents. Stop words such as "the," "a," and "and" are examples of words that tend to be frequent in a corpus. There may also be topic-related stopwords, which are words that behave like stopwords in relevant documents, even if they are not stopwords in the corpus as a whole. To compensate for stop words, a third approach is to smooth a new document's word frequencies with word counts from *all* previously seen documents and word counts from *all delivered* (presumed relevant) documents (73).

8.5.2 Geometric Distance

If each document is represented as a vector, several different geometric distance measures, such as Manhattan distance and Cosine distance (31), can be used to measure the redundancy of a new document.

For example, prior research show that cosine distance, a symmetric measure related to the angle between two vectors (26), works reasonably well for redundancy detection. Represent d as a vector $d = (w_1(d), w_2(d), .., w_K(d))^T$, then:

$$R(d_t|d_j) = cosine(d_t, d_j) \tag{8.8}$$

$$= \frac{d_t \bullet d_j}{\| d_t \| \| d_j \|} \tag{8.9}$$

$$= \frac{\sum_{k=1}^{K} w_{k,t} w_{k,j}}{\sqrt{\sum_{k=1}^{K} w_{k,t}^2} \sqrt{\sum_{k=1}^{K} w_{k,j}^2}} \tag{8.10}$$

If we use $tf * idf$ score as the weight of each dimension of the document vector, we have $w_{k,j} = tf_{w_k, d_j} * idf_{w_k}$,

Where:

- $idf_{w_k} = \dfrac{log(\frac{C+0.5}{df_{w_k}})}{log(C+1.0)}$

- tf_{w_k, d_j} :   the number of times word w_k occurs in document d_j

- df_{w_k} :   the number of times word w_k occurs in documents the system processed

- C :   the total number of documents the system processed

8.5.3   Distributional Similarity

If each document is represented as a probabilistic document model, distribution similarity can be used to measure the redundancy of a new document. Probabilistic language models, which are widely used in speech recognition, have been very popular in the information retrieval community over the last 10 years (e.g., (20)). The strong theoretical foundation of language models enables a variety of new capabilities, including redundancy detection. In the language model approach, a document is represented by a word distribution. Kullback-Leibler divergence, a distributional similarity measure, is a natural way to measure the redundancy of one document given another.

Representing document d as a unigram language model θ_d

$$R(d_t|d_j) = -KL(\theta_{d_t}, \theta_{d_j}) \tag{8.11}$$

$$= -\sum_{w_k} P(w_k|\theta_{d_t}) log(\frac{P(w_k|\theta_{d_j})}{P(w_k|\theta_{d_t})}) \tag{8.12}$$

where θ_d is the language model for document d, and is a multinomial distribution.

θ_d can be found based on maximum likelihood estimation (MLE):

$$P(w_k|d) = \frac{tf_{w_k, d}}{\sum_{w_k} tf_{w_k, d}}$$

The problem with using MLE is that if a word never occurs in document d, it will get a zero probability ($P(w_k|d) = 0$). Thus a word in d_t but not in d_j will make $KL(\theta_{d_t}, \theta_{d_j}) = \infty$.

Smoothing techniques are necessary to adjust the maximum likelihood estimation so that the KL-based measure is more appropriate. Research shows that retrieval and filtering performance is highly sensitive to smoothing parameters when using language models. Several smoothing methods have been applied to *ad hoc* information retrieval, text classification problems, and novelty detection (69)(73).

8.5.4   Summary of Novelty Detection

The work described above is focused on the redundancy measure, and it is somewhat user independent in the sense that our redundancy measures only calculate a score indicating the degree of redundancy in a document given a history of delivered documents. They do not actually make a decision as to whether a document is considered redundant or novel.

A **redundancy threshold** is needed in order to classify a document as redundant or novel. When human assessors are asked to make redundancy decisions given the same topics and document streams, they sometimes disagreed. In some cases the disagreement was based on differences in the assessors' internal definition of redundancy. However, more often one assessor might feel that a document d_t should be considered redundant if a previously seen document d_j covered 80% of d_t; the other assessor might not consider it redundant unless the coverage was more than 95%. A person's tolerance for redundancy can be modeled with a user-dependent threshold that converts a redundancy score into a redundancy decision. User feedback about which documents are redundant can serve as training data. Over time the system can learn to estimate the probability that a new document with a given redundancy score would be considered redundant. This probability can be expressed as $P(\text{user j thinks } d_t \text{ is redundant}|R(d_t|D_t))$.

8.6   Other Adaptive Filtering Topics

While learning user profiles is an advantage of a filtering system, it is also a major research challenge in the adaptive filtering research community. Common learning algorithms require a significant amount of training data. However, a real-world filtering system must work as soon as the user uses the system, when the amount of training is extremely small or zero.[5] How should a good filtering system learn user profiles efficiently and effectively with limited user supervision while filtering? In order to solve this problem, researchers working on adaptive filtering have tried to develop a robust learning algorithm that can work reasonably well when the amount of training data is small and more effective with more training data (66) (71). Some filtering systems explore what the user likes while satisfying a user immediate information need and trade off exploration and exploitation (75) (15). Some filtering systems consider many aspects of a document besides relevance, such as novelty, readability, and authority (70) (65). Some filtering systems use multiple forms of evidence, such as user context and implicit feedback from the user, while interacting with a user (70) (41).

This chapter does not cover all adaptive filtering topics in detail due to the space limit and also because they are less "text" oriented. To finish this section, some missed important topics are listed as follows, and the readers are referred to the papers cited for more details

8.6.1   Beyond Bag of Words

Most of the existing adaptive filtering approaches are focused on identifying relevant documents using distance measures defined in a document space indexed by text features such as keywords. This is a very simple and limited view of user modeling, without considering user context or other property of a document, such as whether a document is authoritative or whether it is novel to the user. However, even this simplest filtering task is still very hard, and existing filtering systems do not work effectively. Bayesian graphical modeling, a complex data driven user modeling approach, has been used to learn from implicit and explicit user feedback and to satisfy complex user criteria (70).

8.6.2   Using Implicit Feedback

For most of adaptive filtering work described in this section, we assume the system learns from explicit user feedback on whether a document delivered is relevant or not. There is much related work on using implicit feedback in the information retrieval community and the user modeling community. The work in these areas can be categorized according to the behavior category and minimum scope and have been reviewed recently (27). There are many possible behaviors (view, listen, scroll, find, query, print, copy, paste, quote, mark up, type, and edit) on different scope (segment, object, and class) for system designers to choose from. Implicit feedback has also been explored

---

[5]It is possible the system needs to begin working given a short user query and no positive instance.

for the task of filtering (40) (11) (39) (42) (70). (40) suggested a list of potential implicit feedbacks. (11) built a personal news agent that used time-coded feedback from the user to learn a user profile. (39) investigated implicit feedback for filtering newsgroup articles.

8.6.3 Exploration and Exploitation Trade Off

Most of the filtering systems deliver a document if and only if the expected immediate utility of delivering it is greater than the expected utility of not delivering it. However, delivering a document to the user has two effects: 1) it satisfies the user's information need immediately, and 2) it helps the system better satisfy the user in the future by learning from the relevance feedback about this document provided by the user. An adaptive information filtering approach is not optimal if it fails to recognize and model this second effect. Some researchers have followed this direction. (15) considers exploration benefit while filtering and carries out exploration and exploitation trade-off. (75) studies the second aspect and models the long term benefit of delivering a document as expected utility improvement as a result of improved model. However, exploration and exploitation trade off is a problem far from being solved.

8.6.4 Evaluation beyond Topical Relevance

Utility is an approximation of the user's criteria of a good document. Given a utility measure, a system can achieve the objective of maximizing the user's satisfaction through utility maximization using mathematical or statistical techniques. A good utility measure is critical, because no system can do well with an inappropriate objective. In the IR community, utility is usually defined over relevance. Relevance was meant to represent a document's ability to satisfy the needs of a user. However, this concept is very abstract and hard to model, thus usually reduced to a narrow definition of "topical relevance" or "related to the matter at hand (aboutness)" (45) (59). On the other hand, "presenting the documents in order of estimated relevance" without considering the incremental value of a piece of information is not appropriate (58). Researchers have studied criteria such as information-novelty for retrieval (17), summarization (14), filtering (73), and topic detection and tracking (4). Prior research on what is a user's perception/criteria has found that a wide range of factors (such as personal knowledge, topicality, quality, novelty, recency, authority, and author qualitatively) affect human judgments of relevance (8) (36) (56) (60) (53). We also discussed how to estimate novelty in this chapter, which is just an example of many of the important criteria for the user besides relevance, such as readability (18) and authority (28). How to build and evaluate a filtering system to optimize a more complex user criteria that goes beyond "topical relevance" or "aboutness" is still a challenging research problem for the adaptive filtering community.

8.7 Acknowledgments

The author would like to thank Jamie Callan, Thomas Minka, Yiming Yang, Wei Xu, Stephen Robertson, Chengxiang Zhai, James Allan, Sarah Tyler, Philip Zigoris, and Jonathan Koren for their contributions to the work reported in this chapter. This research was supported in part by National Science Foundation IIS-0713111, AFOSR/AFRL, an IBM Fellowship, and the industry sponsors of the Information Retrieval and Knowledge Management Lab at University of California Santa Cruz. Any opinions, findings, conclusions, or recommendations expressed in this paper are the author's, and do not necessarily reflect those of the sponsors.

References

[1] J. Allan, J. Carbonell, G. Doddington, J. Yamron, and Y. Yang. Topic detection and tracking pilot study. In *Topic Detection and Tracking Workshop Report*. 2001.

[2] J. Allan, V. Lavrenko, and H. Jin. First story detection in tdt is hard. In *Proceedings of the 9th International Conference on Information and Knowledge Management*, pages 374–381, 2000.

[3] J. Allan, R. Papka, and V. Lavrenko. On-line new event detection and tracking. In *Proceedings of 21st Annual International ACM SIGIR Conference on Research and Development in Information Retrieval*, 1998.

[4] J. Allan, C. Wade, and A. Bolivar. Retrieval and novelty detection at the sentence level. In *Proceedings of the 26th Annual International ACM SIGIR Conference on Research and Development in Information Retrieval*, July 2003.

[5] A. Anghelescu, E. Boros, D. Lewis, V. Menkov, D. Neu, and P. Kantor. Rutgers filtering work at trec 2002: Adaptive and batch. In *Proceedings of the Eleventh Text REtrieval Conference (TREC-11)*, 2002.

[6] A. Arampatzis. *Adaptive and Temporally-Dependent Document Filtering*. PhD thesis, Katholieke Universiteit Nijmegen, Nijmegen, Netherland, 2001.

[7] A. Arampatzis and A. Hameren. The score-distribution threshold optimization for adaptive binary classification task. In *Proceedings of the 24th Annual International ACM SIGIR Conference on Research and Development in Information Retrieval*, pages 285–293, 2001.

[8] C. L. Barry. User-defined relevance criteria: An exploratory study. In *Journal of the American Society for Information Science*, 45(3), 1994.

[9] N. Belkin and B. Croft. Information filtering and information retrieval: two sides of the same coin? In *Communications of the ACM*, 1992.

[10] R. Bell, Y. Koren, and C. Volinsky. Modeling relationships at multiple scales to improve accuracy of large recommender systems. In *KDD '07: Proceedings of the 13th ACM SIGKDD International Conference on Knowledge Discovery and Data Mining*, pages 95–104, New York, NY, USA, 2007. ACM Press.

[11] D. Billsus and M. J. Pazzani. A personal news agent that talks, learns and explains. In *AGENTS '99: Proceedings of the Third Annual Conference on Autonomous Agents*, pages 268–275. ACM Press, 1999.

[12] J. Callan. Document filtering with inference networks. In *Proceedings of the Nineteenth Annual International ACM SIGIR Conference on Research and Development in Information Retrieval*, pages 262–269, 1996.

[13] N. Cancedda, N. Cesa-Bianchi, A. Conconi, C. Gentile, C. Goutte, T. Graepel, Y. Li, J. M. Renders, J. S. Taylor, and A. Vinokourov. Kernel method for document filtering. In *The Eleventh Text REtrieval Conference (TREC11)*. National Institute of Standards and Technology, special publication 500-249, 2003.

[14] J. Carbonell and J. Goldstein. Automatic text summarization of multiple documents. In *Proceedings of the 21th Annual International ACM SIGIR Conference on Research and Development in Information Retrieval*, 1998.

[15] K. M. A. Chai, H. L. Chieu, and H. T. Ng. Bayesian online classifiers for text classification and filtering. In *Proceedings of 25th Annual International ACM SIGIR Conference on Research and Development in Information Retrieval*. ACM, 2002.

[16] C. Chelba and A. Acero. Adaptation of maximum entropy capitalizer: Little data can help a lot. In D. Lin and D. Wu, editors, *Proceedings of EMNLP 2004*, pages 285–292, Barcelona, Spain, July 2004. Association for Computational Linguistics.

[17] H. Chen and D. R. Karger. Less is more: probabilistic models for retrieving fewer relevant documents. In *SIGIR '06: Proceedings of the 29th Annual International ACM SIGIR Conference on Research and Development in Information Retrieval*, pages 429–436, New York, NY, USA, 2006. ACM Press.

[18] K. Collins-Thompson and J. Callan. Predicting reading difficulty with statistical language models. *Journal of the American Society for Information Science and Technology*, 56(13), 2005.

[19] K. Collins-Thompson, P. Ogilvie, Y. Zhang, and J. Callan. Information filtering, novelty detection, and named-page finding. In *Proceedings of the Eleventh Text REtrieval Conference (TREC-11)*, 2002.

[20] B. Croft and J. Lafferty, editors. *Language Modeling for Information Retrieval.* Kluwer, 2002.

[21] A. Dayanik, D. D. Lewis, D. Madigan, V. Menkov, and A. Genkin. Constructing informative prior distributions from domain knowledge in text classification. In *SIGIR '06: Proceedings of the 29th Annual International ACM SIGIR Conference on Research and Development in Information Retrieval*, pages 493–500, New York, NY, USA, 2006. ACM Press.

[22] J. Delgado and N. Ishii. Memory-based weighted majority prediction for recommender systems. In *ACM SIGIR'99 Workshop on Recommender Systems*, 1999.

[23] N. Fuhr. Probabilistic models in information retrieval. In *The Computer Journal*, volume 35(3), pages 243–255, 1992.

[24] R. Fung and B. D. Favero. Applying bayesian networks to information retrieval. *Communications of the ACM*, 38(3):42–ff., 1995.

[25] E. M Housman. Selective dissemination of information. In Carlos, A. Cuandra, editor, *Annual Review of Information Science and Technology. Vol. 8. American Society for Information Science*, 1973.

[26] W. P. Jones and G. W. Furnas. Pictures of relevance. *Journal of the American Society for Information Science*, 1987.

[27] D. Kelly and J. Teevan. Implicit feedback for inferring user preference: a bibliography. *SIGIR Forum*, 37(2):18–28, 2003.

[28] J. Kleinberg. Authoritative sources in a hyperlinked environment. In *Proc. 9th ACM-SIAM Symposium on Discrete Algorithms*, 1998.

[29] J. A. Konstan, B. N. Miller, D. Maltz, J. L. Herlocker, L. R. Gordon, and J. Riedl. GroupLens: Applying collaborative filtering to Usenet news. *Communications of the ACM*, 40(3):77–87, 1997.

[30] K.-S. Lee, K. Kageura, and A. Aizawa. TREC 11 experiments at NII: The effects of virtual relevant documents in batch filtering. In *Proceeding of the Eleventh Text REtrieval Conference (TREC-11)*, 2002.

[31] L. Lee. Measures of distributional similarity. In *Proceedings of the 37th ACL*, 1999.

[32] D. Lewis. Applying support vector machines to the TREC-2001 batch filtering and routing tasks. In *Proceedings of the Eleventh Text REtrieval Conference (TREC-11)*, 2002.

[33] B. Liu, X. Li, W. S. Lee, and P. Yu. Text classification by labeling words. In *Proceedings of The Nineteenth National Conference on Artificial Intelligence (AAAI-2004)*, July 25-29, 2004.

[34] R. M. Losee and A. Bookstein. Integrating boolean queries in conjunctive normal form with probabilistic retrieval models. In *Information Processing and Management*, 1988.

[35] L. Ma, Q. Chen, S. Ma, M. Zhang, and L. Cai. Incremental learning for profile training in adaptive document filtering. In *Proceedings of the Eleventh Text REtrieval Conference (TREC-11)*, 2002.

[36] K. L. Maglaughlin and D. H. Sonnenwald. User perspectives on relevance criteria: A comparison among relevant, partially relevant, and not-relevant judgments. In *Journal of the American Society for Information Science and Technology*, 2003.

[37] A. Martin, G. Doddington, T. Kamm, and M. Ordowski. The DET curve in assessment of detection task performance. In *Proceedings of EuroSpeech*, 1997.

[38] P. McNamee, C. Piatko, and J. Mayfield. JHU/APL at TREC 2002: Experiments in filtering and arabic retrieval. In *Proceedings of the Eleventh Text REtrieval Conference (TREC-11)*, 2002.

[39] M. Morita and Y. Shinoda. Information filtering based on user behavior analysis and best match text retrieval. In *Proceedings of the 17th Annual International ACM SIGIR Conference on Research and Development in Information Retrieval*, pages 272–281. Springer-Verlag New York, Inc., 1994.

[40] D. M. Nichols. Implicit rating and filtering. In *Proceedings of the Fifth DELOS Workshop on Filtering and Collaborative Filtering*, 1997.

[41] D. Oard and J. K. Contact. User modeling for information access based on implicit feedback, *Tech Reports in Computer Science and Engineering*, HCIL-TR-2000-11, University of Maryland, College Park, 2000.

[42] D. W. Oard and J. Kim. Modeling information content using observable behavior. In *ASIST 2001 Annual Meeting*.

[43] V. Rijbergen and J. C. A theoretical basis for the use of co-occurrence data in information retrieval. In *Journal of Documentation*, pages 106–119, 1976.

[44] S. Robertson and K. S. Jones. Relevance weighting of search terms. In *Journal of the American Society for Information Science*, volume 27, pages 129–146, 1976.

[45] S. Robertson and I. Soboroff. The TREC-10 Filtering track final report. In *Proceedings of the Tenth Text REtrieval Conference (TREC-10)*,

pages 26–37. National Institute of Standards and Technology, special publication 500-250, 2002.

[46] S. Robertson and I. Soboroff. The TREC 2002 filtering track report. In *Proceedings of the Eleventh Text REtrieval Conference (TREC-11)*, 2002.

[47] S. Robertson and S. Walker. Microsoft Cambridge at TREC-9: Filtering track. In *Proceedings of the Ninth Text REtrieval Conference (TREC-9)*, pages 361–368. National Institute of Standards and Technology, special publication 500-249, 2001.

[48] S. Robertson and S. Walker. Threshold setting in adaptive filtering. *Journal of Documentation*, pages 312–331, 2000.

[49] S. Robertson. On theoretical argument in information retrieval. Salton Award Lecture given at SIGIR 2000, July 2000.

[50] J. J. Rocchio. Relevance feedback in information retrieval. In *The SMART Retrieval System– Experiments in Automatic Document Processing*, pages 313–323. Prentice Hall, 1971.

[51] G. Salton and C. Buckley. Term-weighting approaches in automatic text retrieval, *Information Processing and Management: an International Journal*, 24(5), 1988.

[52] G. Salton and M. McGill. *Introduction to Modern Information Retrieval*. McGraw-Hill, 1983.

[53] L. Schamber and J. Bateman. User criteria in relevance evaluation: Toward development of a measurement scale. In *ASIS 1996 Annual Conference Proceedings*, October 1996.

[54] M. Srikanth, X. Wu, and R. Srihari. UB at TREC 11: Batch and adaptive filtering. In *Proceedings of the Eleventh Text REtrieval Conference (TREC-11)*, 2002.

[55] M. Stricker, F. Vichot, G. Dreyfus, and F. Wolinski. Training context-sensitive neural networks with few relevant examples for the TREC-9 routing. In *The Ninth Text REtrieval Conference (TREC9)*. National Institute of Standards and Technology, special publication 500-249, 2000.

[56] A. Tombros, I. Ruthven, and J. M. Jose. How users assess web pages for information seeking. *J. Am. Soc. Inf. Sci. Technol.*, 56(4):327–344, 2005.

[57] H. R. Turtle. *Inference Networks for Document Retrieval*. PhD thesis, University of Massachusetts, October 1990.

[58] H. R. Varian. Economics and search (invited talk at SIGIR 1999), 1999.

[59] E. M. Voorhees and L. P. Buckland, editors. *NIST Special Publication 500-251: The Eleventh Text REtrieval Conference (TREC 2002)*. Department of Commerce, National Institute of Standards and Technology, 2002.

[60] P. Wang. *A cognitive model of document selection of real users of IR Systems*. PhD thesis, University of Maryland, 1994.

[61] L. Wu, X. Huang, J. Niu, Y. Xia, Z. Feng, and Y. Zhou. FDU at TREC 2002: Filtering, Q&A, web and video tasks. In *Proceedings of the Eleventh Text REtrieval Conference (TREC-11)*, 2002.

[62] X. Wu and R. K. Srihari. Incorporating prior knowledge with weighted margin support vector machines. In *Proc. ACM Knowledge Discovery Data Mining Conf.(ACM SIGKDD 2004)*, Aug. 2004.

[63] Y. Yang and B. Kisiel. Margin-based local regression of adaptive filtering. In *Proceedings of the Twelveth International Conference on Information Knowledge Management (CIKM 2003)*. ACM Press, 2003.

[64] Y. Yang, S. Yoo, J. Zhang, and B. Kisiel. Robustness of adaptive filtering methods in a cross-benchmark evaluation. In *Proceedings of the 28th Annual International ACM SIGIR Conference on Research and Development in Information Retrieval*, 2005.

[65] Y. Yang, A. Lad, Ni Lao, A. Harpale, B. Kisiel, and M. Rogati. Utility-based information distillation over temporally sequenced documents. In *SIGIR '07: Proceedings of the 30th Annual International ACM SIGIR Conference on Research and Development in Information Retrieval*, pages 31–38, New York, NY, USA, 2007. ACM Press.

[66] Kai Yu, Volker Tresp, and Anton Schwaighofer. Learning gaussian processes from multiple tasks. In *ICML '05: Proceedings of the 22nd International Conference on Machine Learning*, pages 1012–1019, New York, NY, USA, 2005. ACM Press.

[67] K. Yu, V. Tresp, and S. Yu. A nonparametric hierarchical bayesian framework for information filtering. In *SIGIR '04: Proceedings of the 27th Annual International ACM SIGIR Conference on Research and Development in Information Retrieval*, pages 353–360. ACM Press, 2004.

[68] C. Zhai, P. Jansen, and E. Stoica. Threshold calibration in CLARIT adaptive filtering. In *Proceedings of Seventh Text REtrieval Conference (TREC-7)*, pages 149–157. National Institute of Standards and Technology, special publication 500-242, 1999.

[69] C. Zhai and J. Lafferty. A study of smoothing methods for language models applied to ad hoc information retrieval. In *Proceedings of the 24th Annual International ACM SIGIR Conference on Research and Development in Information Retrieval*, pages 334–342, September 2001.

[70] Y. Zhang and J. Callan. Combine multiple forms of evidence while filtering. In *Proceedings of Human Language Technology Conference and Conference on Empirical Methods in Natural Language Processing*, 2005.

[71] Y. Zhang. Using Bayesian priors to combine classifiers for adaptive filtering. In *Proceedings of the 27th Annual International ACM SIGIR Conference on Research and Development in Information Retrieval*, 2004.

[72] Y. Zhang and J. Callan. Maximum likelihood estimation for filtering thresholds. In *Proceedings of the 24th Annual International ACM SIGIR Conference on Research and Development in Information Retrieval*, pages 294–302, 2001.

[73] Y. Zhang, J. Callan, and T. Minka. Novelty and redundancy detection in adaptive filtering. In *Proceedings of the 25th ACM SIGIR Conference*, 2002.

[74] Y. Zhang and J. Koren. Efficient bayesian hierarchical user modeling for recommendation systems. In *Proceedings of the 30st Annual International ACM SIGIR Conference on Research and Development in Information Retrieval*, 2007.

[75] Y. Zhang, W. Xu, and J. Callan. Exploration and exploitation in adaptive filtering based on bayesian active learning. In *Proceedings of the International Conference on Machine Learing (ICML 2003)*, 2003.

[76] P. Zigoris and Y. Zhang. Bayesian adaptive user profiling with explicit & implicit feedback. In *Conference on Information and Knowledge Management 2006*, 2006.

Symbol Description

$\vec{x}$	a TF-IDF vector, representing a passage
y	the class label of a passage, indicating its relevance (yes or no) to a query
$\vec{w}*$	a vector of regression coefficients, serving as a query profile or "class model"
f_{RL}	the solution of regularized logistic regression, the mapping function from any passage to the estimated conditional probability for the passage to be relevant to a query
$\vec{h}_i$	a TF-IDF vector, representing a historical passage
$H(t)$	the user history at time t, defined over a sequence of historical passages
$f_{ND}(\vec{x})$	the novelty scoring function applied to an input passage
$f_{AR}(\vec{x})$	the anti-redundancy scoring function
$DCG(n)$	the Discounted Cumulated Gain of a ranked list of n passages
$DCU(n)$	the Discounted Cumulated Utility of a ranked list of n passages
$NDCU$	the Normalized DCU
$PNDCU$	the Penalized NDCU
$G(d_i, q)$	the gain for reading document d_i with respect to query q
$U(p_i, q)$	the utility for reading passage p_i with respect to query q
$C(p_i)$	the set of nuggets contained in passage p_i
β	the dampening factor that penalizes re-occurrences of a nugget in ranked passages
λ	the weight balancing the NDCU term with the penalty on ranked-list length in utility assessment

Chapter 9

Utility-Based Information Distillation

Yiming Yang and Abhimanyu Lad

9.1   Introduction

Utility-based information distillation is a new challenge in information retrieval, focusing on effective ways to combine technologies from adaptive filtering (AF), novelty detection, anti-redundant passage ranking and flexible user feedback. The ultimate goal is to improve the true utility of the system, as well as to support effective and efficient user feedback. To see why utility-based distillation is a practically important problem and an open challenge for research, let us briefly outline the related work in Adaptive filtering and Topic Detection and Tracking, and visit some limitations of the current solutions.

9.1.1   Related Work in Adaptive Filtering (AF)

Adaptive filtering is the task of online prediction of the relevance of each new document in a temporally ordered sequence, with respect to a pre-specified topic or query. Here we use the terms "topic" and "query" interchangeably as synonyms. Based on the initial query words or topic description, and a few positive examples of on-topic documents, the system maintains a *profile* for each topic. The profile is incrementally updated whenever relevance feedback is received from the user. The learning nature of AF systems makes them more powerful than standard search engines without adaptation. A variety of supervised learning algorithms (e.g., Rocchio-style classifiers, Exponential-Gaussian models, local regression and logistic regression approaches) have been studied in adaptive settings with explicit and implicit relevance feedback, and on benchmark datasets from TREC (Text Retrieval Conferences) and the TDT (Topic Detection and Tracking) evaluation forum (1; 5; 8; 18; 25; 31; 29). Regularized logistic regression (26), for example, is one of the strong-performing methods in terms of both effectiveness and efficiency, and is easy to scale for frequent adaptations over large datasets such as the TREC-10 corpus with over 800,000 documents and 84 topics.

9.1.2   Related Work in Topic Detection and Tracking (TDT)

Topic Detection and Tracking (TDT) research focuses on automated detection and tracking of news events from multiple sources of temporally ordered stories (2). TDT has two primary tasks: topic tracking and novelty detection. The topic tracking task, although defined independently, is almost identical to the adaptive filtering task except that user feedback is assumed to be not available, although pseudo-relevance feedback (PRF) by the system is allowed. PRF means that the system takes the top-ranking documents in a retrieved list for a topic as truly relevant in its profile adaptation for that topic. PRF may be useful when training examples are sparse and when true relevance feedback is not sufficient (26).

Novelty detection (ND), the other primary task in TDT, aims to detect the first report of each new event from temporally ordered news stories. The task is also called First-Story Detection (FSD) or New Event Detection (NED). There has been a significant body of work for addressing ND problems. Yang et al. (23) examined incremental clustering for grouping documents into events, and used the cosine similarity in combination with some time-decaying function to measure the novelty of new documents with respect to historical events. Zhang et al. (30) developed a Bayesian statistic framework for modeling the growing number of events over time in a non-parametric Dirichlet process. Yang et al. (24) studied effective use of Named Entities in the modeling of novelty of documents conditioned on events and higher-level topics. Zhang et al. (32) compared alternative measures for sentence-level novelty detection conditioned on perfect knowledge of document-level relevance; cosine similarity worked the best in their experiments. Allan et al. (3) argued for the importance of comparing novelty measures under a more realistic assumption, i.e., under the condition that sentence-level relevance is not available but predicted by a system. Kuo et al. (12) developed a indexing-tree strategy for speedy computation and investigated the use of Named Entities.

9.1.3 Limitations of Current Solutions

Despite the substantial accomplishments in both AF and TDT, significant problems remain unsolved regarding how to optimize utility of the system in terms of the relevance and novelty of returned documents for users attention, and how to make user feedback most effective and least costly. The following issues, specifically, might seriously limit the true utility of an AF or ND system in real-world applications:

- Users have a 'passive' role. That is, he or she reacts to the system only if the system makes a 'yes' decision on a document, by confirming or rejecting the system decision. A more active alternative would be to allow the user to review a ranked list of system-selected candidates each time, making human judgments more effective in discriminating hard cases between true positives and false alarms for profile adaptation. To support this, modeling the uncertainty of a ranked document being read by the user becomes an issue (for which little research has been done in AF and ND) because we can no longer assume a deterministic process for user relevance feedback.

- The unit for receiving user relevance judgments has been restricted to a document in conventional AF and ND. However, a real user may be willing to provide more informative, fine-grained feedback via highlighting some smaller pieces of text as relevant and/or novel. To support such interaction, the system may provide passage ranking based on relevance where passage length may vary (as documents, paragraphs, sentences or n-consecutive word windows), depending on applications, datasets and user preferences. Further, the system needs to learn from labeled pieces of text of arbitrary span instead of just allowing labeled documents. How to train, optimize and evaluate such a system is an open challenge.

- System-selected documents are often highly redundant. A major news event, for example, would be reported by multiple sources repeatedly for a while, making most of the information content in those articles redundant with each other. A relevance-driven AF system would select all these redundant documents for user feedback, wasting the user's time while offering little gain. Clearly, novelty detection (ND) and anti-redundancy ranking of documents or passages would help in principle. However, how to leverage both relevance and novelty assessments for unified utility optimization and for effective user interactions with the system is a main challenge in information distillation.

In the rest of the chapter, we present our recent work in utility-based information distillation, addressing the above limitations and challenges (27). Specifically, with a new distillation system called CAFÉ, CMU Adaptive Filtering Engine, we define a task-oriented distillation process, analyze issues and propose new solutions for utility optimization and utility-based evaluation. Section 9.2 outlines the information distillation process with a concrete example. Section 9.3 describes CAFÉ with the core components of adaptive filtering, novelty detection, anti-redundant passage ranking and the support to fine-grained user feedback. Section 9.4 discusses issues with respect to evaluation methodology and proposes our new solutions. Section 9.5 describes our extension of the TDT4 benchmark corpus with manually annotated "answer keys" (Section 9.4) which are necessary for evaluating systems that procedure flexible-length passages. Section 9.6 presents our experiments and results. Section 9.7 concludes the study and gives future perspectives.

9.2   A Sample Task

Consider a news event – the escape of seven convicts from a Texas prison in December 2000 and their capture a month later. Assuming a user were interested in this event since its early stage, the information need could be: 'Find information about the escape of convicts from Texas prison, and information related to their recapture.' The associated lower-level questions could be:

- How many prisoners escaped?

- Where and when were they sighted?

- Who are their known contacts inside and outside the prison?

- How are they armed?

- Do they have any vehicles?

- What steps have been taken so far?

We call such an information need a *task* and the associated questions as the *queries* in this task. A distillation system is supposed to monitor the incoming documents, process them chunk by chunk in a temporal order, select potentially relevant and novel passages from each chunk with respect to each query and present a ranked list of passages to the user. Passage ranking here is based on how relevant a passage is with respect to the current query, how novel it is with respect to the current user history (of his or her interactions with the system) and how redundant it is compared to other passages with a higher rank in the list.

The user may provide feedback via a highlighting interface – he or she may highlight arbitrary spans of text and label them as 'Relevant,' 'Not Relevant,' or 'Already Seen.' Only the highlighted pieces are used by the system to update its model ("profile") of the current query. Depending on the type of user feedback, the system takes one of the following actions:

- If the feedback type is 'Relevant,' use the highlighted piece of text as a positive example in the adaptation of the query profile, and also add it to the user's history.

- If the feedback type is 'Not-relevant,' use the highlighted piece of text as a negative example in the adaptation of the query profile, and also add it to the user's history.

- If the feedback type is 'Already Seen,' do not use the text for positive or negative feedback; just add it to the user history.

As soon as the query profile is updated, the system re-issues a search and returns another ranked list of passages where the previously seen passages are either removed or ranked low, based on user preference. For example, if the user highlights '...officials have posted a $100,000 reward for their capture...' as relevant answer to the query "What steps have been taken so far?", then the highlighted piece is used as an additional positive training example in the adaptation of the query profile. This piece of feedback is also added to the user history as a seen example, so that the system will be unlikely to place another passage mentioning '$100,000 reward' in the future at the top of the ranked list. However, an article mentioning '...officials have doubled the reward money to $200,000...' might be ranked high since it is both relevant to the (updated) query profile and novel with respect to the (updated) user history. The user may modify the original queries or add a new query during the process; the query profiles will be changed accordingly. Clearly, novelty detection is very important for the utility of such a system because of the iterative search. Without novelty detection, the old relevant passages would be shown to the user repeatedly in each ranked list.

Through the above example, we can see the main properties of our new framework for utility-based information distillation over temporally ordered documents. Our framework combines and extends the power of adaptive filtering (AF), *ad hoc* retrieval (IR) and novelty detection (ND). Compared to standard IR, our approach has the power of incrementally learning long-term information needs and modeling a sequence of queries within a task. Compared to conventional AF, it enables a more active role of the user in refining his or her information needs and requesting new results by allowing relevance and novelty feedback via highlighting of arbitrary spans of text in passages returned by the system.

Compared to past work, this is the first evaluation of ND in a utility-based framework, integrated with adaptive filtering for sequenced queries that allows flexible user feedback over ranked passages. The combination of AF, IR and ND with the new extensions raises an important research question regarding evaluation methodology: how can we measure the utility of such an information distillation system? Existing metrics in standard IR, AF and ND are insufficient, and new solutions must be explored, as we will discuss in Section 9.4. First, we describe the technical cores of our system.

9.3   Technical Cores

Our system consists of the AF component for incremental learning of query profiles, the passage retrieval component for estimating the relevance of each passage with respect to a query profile, the novelty detection component for assessing the novelty of each passage with respect to the user history, and the anti-redundancy component for minimizing redundancy among the ranked passages.

9.3.1   Adaptive Filtering Component

We use a state-of-the-art algorithm in the field – the regularized logistic regression method which had the best results on several benchmark evaluation corpora for AF (26). Logistic regression (LR) is a supervised learning algorithm for statistical classification. Based on a training set of labeled instances, it learns a class model which can then by used to predict the labels of unseen instances. Its performance as well as efficiency in terms of training time makes it a good candidate when frequent updates are required to the class model, as is the case in adaptive filtering, where the system must learn from each new feedback provided by the user. Regularized logistic regression has the optimization criteria as follows:

$$\vec{w}_{map} = \underset{\vec{w}}{\operatorname{argmin}} \left\{ \sum_{i=1}^{n} s(i) \log(1 + e^{-y_i \vec{w} x_i}) + \lambda ||\vec{w}||^2 \right\}$$

The first term in the objective function is for reducing training-set errors, where $s(i)$ takes three different values (pre-specified constants) for query, positive and negative documents respectively. This is similar Rocchio where different weights are given to the three kinds of training examples: topic descriptions (queries), on-topic documents and off-topic documents. The second term in the objective function is for *regularization*, equivalent to adding a Gaussian prior to the regression coefficients with a zero mean and covariance variance matrix $\frac{1}{2}\lambda I$ where I is the identity matrix. Tuning $\lambda(\leq 0)$ is theoretically justified for reducing model complexity (the effective degree of freedom) and avoiding over-fitting on training data. The solution of the modified objective function is called the Maximum A Posteriori (MAP) estimate, which reduces to the maximum likelihood solution for standard LR if $\lambda = 0$. (See (26) and (29) for computational complexity, parameter tuning and implementation issues.)

In adaptive filtering, each query is considered as a class, and the class model – a set of regression coefficients corresponding to individual terms – is the query profile as viewed by the system. As for the training set, we use the query itself as the initial positive training example of the class, and the user-highlighted pieces of text (marked as Relevant or Not-relevant) during feedback as additional training examples. To address the *cold start* issue in the early stage before any user feedback is obtained, the system uses a small sample from a retrospective corpus as the initial negative examples in the training set. The details of using logistic regression for adaptive filtering (assigning different weights to positive and negative training instances, and regularizing the objective function to prevent overfitting on training data) are presented in (26).

The class model $\vec{w}^*$ learned by Logistic Regression, or the query profile, is a vector whose dimensions are individual terms and whose elements are the regression coefficients, indicating how influential each term is in the query profile. The query profile is updated whenever a new piece of user feedback is received. A temporally decaying weight can be applied to each training example, as an option, to emphasize the most recent user feedback.

9.3.2 Passage Retrieval Component

We use standard IR techniques in this part of our system. Incoming documents are processed in chunks, where each chunk can be defined as a fixed span of time or as a fixed number of documents, as preferred by the user. For each incoming document, corpus statistics like the IDF (Inverted Document Frequency) of each term are updated. We use a state-of-the-art named entity identifier and tracker (9; 15) to identify person and location names, and merge them with co-referent named entities seen in the past. Then the documents are segmented into passages, which can be a whole document, a paragraph, a sentence, or any other continuous span of text, as preferred. Each passage is represented using a vector of TF-IDF (Term Frequency–Inverse Document Frequency) weights, where term can be a word or a named entity.

Given a query (represented using its profile as described in Section 9.3.1), the system computes a relevance score (the posterior probability of belonging to class '+1') for each passage $\vec{x}$ using the logistic regression solution $\vec{w}^*$:

$$f_{RL}(\vec{x}) \equiv P(y = 1|\vec{x}, \vec{w}^*) = \frac{1}{(1 + e^{-\vec{w}^* \cdot \vec{x}})} \qquad (9.1)$$

Passages are ordered by these relevance scores and the ones with scores above a relevance threshold (tuned on a training set) comprise the *relevance list* that is passed on to the next step – novelty detection.

9.3.3   Novelty Detection Component

To avoid showing information that the user has already seen, the system maintains a *user history* $H(t)$, which contains all the spans of text h_i that the user highlighted (as feedback) during their past interactions with the system, up to the current time t. Each passage in the *relevance list* (Section 9.3.2) is compared to the user history for novelty assessment.

Denoting the history as

$$H(t) = \left\{ \vec{h}_1, \vec{h}_2, ..., \vec{h}_t \right\},\qquad(9.2)$$

the novelty score of a new candidate passage $\vec{x}$ is computed as:

$$f_{ND}(\vec{x}) = 1 - \max_{i \in 1..t} \left\{ \cos(\vec{x}, \vec{h}_i) \right\}\qquad(9.3)$$

where both candidate passage x and highlighted spans of text h_i are represented as TF-IDF vectors.

The novelty score of each passage is compared to a pre-specified threshold (also tuned on a training set), and any passage with a score below this threshold is removed from the *relevance list*.

9.3.4   Anti-Redundant Ranking Component

Although the novelty detection component ensures that only *novel* (previously unseen) information remains in the *relevance list*, this list might still contain the same novel information at multiple positions of the ranked list. Suppose, for example, that the user has already read about a $100,000 reward for information about the escaped convicts. A new piece of news that the award has been increased to $200,000 is novel since the user hasn't read about it yet. However, multiple news sources would report this information and we might end up showing (redundant) articles from all these sources in a ranked list. Hence, a ranked list should also be made non-redundant with respect to its own contents. We use a simplified version of the Maximal Marginal Relevance method, originally developed for combining relevance and novelty in text retrieval and summarization (6). Our procedure starts with the current list of passages sorted by relevance (Section 9.3.2) and filtered by Novelty Detection component (Section 9.3.3), and generates a new non-redundant list as follows:

1. Take the top passage in the current list as the top one in the new list.

2. Add the next passage $\vec{x}$ in the current list to the new list only if

$$f_{AR}(\vec{x}) > t$$

   where

$$f_{AR}(\vec{x}) = 1 - \max_{p_i \in L_{new}} \left\{ \cos(\vec{x}, p_i) \right\}$$

   and L_{new} is the set of passages already selected in the new list.

3. Repeat step 2 until all the passages in the current list have been examined.

After applying the abovementioned algorithm, each passage in the new list is sufficiently dissimilar to others, thus favoring diversity rather than redundancy in the new ranked list. The anti-redundancy threshold t is tuned on a training set.

9.4 Evaluation Methodology

The approach we proposed above for information distillation raises important issues regarding evaluation methodology. Firstly, since our system allow the output to be passages at different leves of granularity (e.g., k-sentence windows where k may vary) instead of a fixed level, it is not possible to have pre-annotated relevance judgments at all such granularity levels. Secondly, since we wish to measure the *utility* of the system output as a combination of both relevance and novelty, traditional relevance-only based measures must be replaced by measures that penalize the repetition of the same information in the system output across time. Thirdly, since the output of the system is ranked lists, we must reward those systems that present useful information (both relevant and previously unseen) using shorter ranked lists, and penalize those that present the same information using longer ranked lists. None of the existing measures in *ad hoc* retrieval, adaptive filtering, novelty detection or other related areas (text summarization and question answering) have desirable properties in all the three aspects. Therefore, we must develop a new one.

9.4.1 Answer Keys

To enable the evaluation of a system whose output consists of passages of arbitrary length, we borrow the concept of *answer keys* from the Question Answering (QA) community, where systems are allowed to produce arbitrary spans of text as answers. Answer keys define *what* should be present in a system response to receive credit, and are comprised of a collection of *information nuggets*, i.e., factoid units about which human assessors can make binary decisions of whether or not a system response contains them.

Defining answer keys and the associated binary decisions is a conceptual task that requires semantic mapping (22), since a system can present the same piece of information in many different ways. Hence, QA evaluations have relied on human assessors, making them costly, time consuming and not scalable to large query sets, document collections and extensive system evaluations with various parameter settings.

9.4.1.1   Automating evaluations based on answer keys

Automatic evaluation methods would allow for faster system building and tuning, as well as provide an objective and affordable way of comparing various systems. Recently, such methods have been proposed, more or less, based on the idea of n-gram co-occurrences. Pourpre (13) assigns a fractional recall score to a system response based on its unigram overlap with a given nugget's description. For example, a system response 'A B C' has recall 3/4 with respect to a nugget with description 'A B C D.' However, such an approach is unfair to systems that present the same information but using words other than A, B, C and D. Another open issue is how to weight individual words in measuring the closeness of a match. For example, consider the question "How many prisoners escaped?" In the nugget 'Seven prisoners escaped from a Texas prison,' there is no indication that 'seven' is the keyword, and that it must be matched to get any relevance credit. Using IDF values does not help, since 'seven' will generally not have a higher IDF than words like 'texas' and 'prison' – an observation of ours supported by the results reported by the authors of Pourpre. Also, redefining the nugget as just 'seven' does not solve the problem since now it might spuriously match any mention of 'seven' out of context. Nuggeteer (16) works on similar principles but makes binary decisions about whether a nugget is present in a given system response by tuning a threshold. However, it is also plagued by 'spurious relevance' since not all words of the nugget description (or known correct responses) are *central* to the nugget.

9.4.1.2   Nugget-matching rules

We propose a reliable automatic method for determining whether a snippet of text contains a given nugget, based on *nugget-matching rules*, which are generated using a semi-automatic procedure explained below. These rules are essentially boolean queries that will only match against snippets that contain the nugget. For instance, a candidate rule for matching answers to "How many prisoners escaped?" is (Texas AND seven AND escape AND (convicts OR prisoners)), possibly with other synonyms and variants in the rule. For a corpus of news articles, which usually follow a typical formal prose, it is surprisingly easy to write such simple rules to match expected answers, if assisted by an appropriate tool.

We propose a two-stage approach, inspired by Autoslog (17), that combines the strength of humans in identifying semantically equivalent expressions and the strength of the system in gathering statistical evidence from a human-annotated corpus of documents. In the first stage, human subjects annotated (using a highlighting tool) portions of on-topic documents that contained answers to each nugget.[1] In the second stage, subjects used our rule generation

---

[1]LDC (21) already provides relevance judgments for 100 topics on the TDT4 corpus. We

tool to create rules that would match the annotations for each nugget. The tool allows users to enter a boolean rule as a disjunction of conjunctions (e.g., `((a AND b) OR (a AND c AND d) OR (e))`). Given a candidate rule, our tool uses it as a boolean query over the entire set of on-topic documents and calculates its recall and precision with respect to the annotations that it is expected to match. Hence, the subjects can start with a simple rule and iteratively refine it until they are satisfied with its recall and precision. We observed that it was very easy for humans to improve the precision of a rule by tweaking its existing conjunctions (adding more `AND`s), and improving the recall by adding more conjunctions to the disjunction (adding more `OR`s).

Note that the annotations generated in the first stage cannot themselves be used reliably for automatic evaluations. System generated passages might partially overlap with such annotations, making it non-trivial to automatically determine whether the system response actually contains the corresponding nugget. This problem is alleviated by the rule creation stage which succinctly captures various ways of answering a question, while avoiding matching incorrect (and out of context) responses. Human involvement in the rule creation ensures high quality generic rules which can then be used to evaluate arbitrary system responses reliably.

As an example, let's try to create a rule for the nugget which says that seven prisoners escaped from the Texas prison. We start with a simple rule – (`seven`). When we input this into the rule generation tool, we realize that this rule matches many spurious occurrences of `seven` (e.g. '...seven states...') and thus gets a low precision score. We can further qualify our rule – `Texas AND seven AND convicts`. Next, by looking at the 'missed annotations,' we realize that some news articles mentioned "...seven prisoners escaped...." We then replace `convicts` with the disjunction (`convicts OR prisoners`). We continue tweaking the rule in this manner until we achieve a sufficiently high recall and precision – i.e., the (small number of) misses and false alarms can be safely ignored.

9.4.2 Evaluating the Utility of a Sequence of Ranked Lists

Once we have a reliable way to determine the presence of nuggets in a given span of text, we can assign a relevance score to each system-produced passage. However, each such passage will now get a *graded* score since it can contain multiple nuggets. Moreover, a user perceives lesser utility when presented with the same nugget repeatedly. We first describe a recently proposed measure for evaluating a ranked list of documents in terms of their *relevance* to the query, and extend it to evaluate the *utility* of a sequence of ranked lists of passages produced by our system.

Discounted Cumulated Gain (DCG) (11) is an intuitive measure of the total

---

further ensured that these judgments are exhaustive on the entire corpus using pooling.

gain obtained by a user by going through a ranked list, from the top, up to a given position. It allows for graded relevance, and discounts the gain received at lower ranks to favor systems that place highly relevant documents near the top of the ranked list. The DCG score at rank n is calculated as follows:

$$DCG(n) = \sum_{i=1}^{n} G(d_i, q)/\log_b(i + b - 1) \qquad (9.4)$$

where d_i is the i-th document in the ranked list, $G(d_i, q)$ is the graded relevance of document d_i with respect to the query q and parameter b is a pre-specified constant to control the discount rates with respect to the position of each document in the ranked list. The DCG score is normalized with respect to the ideal (best possible) DCG to get the Normalized Discounted Cumulated Gain (NDCG). To obtain a single score for the system's performance on a query, the NDCG scores at all ranks are averaged. Given a test set of queries, the per-query NDCG scores are further averaged to produce a global score.

In our evaluation scheme, we make two changes to the standard NDCG metric, which we will describe in detail:

1. Replace graded document relevance $G(d_i, q)$ with graded passage utility $U(p_i, q)$ that takes both nugget-based relevance and novelty into account.

2. Penalize longer ranked lists to account for the effort spent by the user in going through the system output.

9.4.2.1   Graded passage utility

To account for the presence of nuggets as well as whether the nuggets have been seen by the user in the past, we calculate the gain received from each passage in terms of *utility* $U(p_i, q)$, instead of *relevance* $G(d_i, q)$. Thus, we define Discounted Cumulated Utility (DCU) as:

$$DCU(n) = \sum_{i=1}^{n} U(p_i, q)/\log_b(i + b - 1) \qquad (9.5)$$

which is normalized with respect to the ideal DCU to get the Normalized Discounted Cumulated Utility (NDCU). $U(p_i, q)$ is calculated as:

$$U(p_i, q) = \sum_{j \in C(p_i)} w_j \qquad (9.6)$$

where $C(p_i)$ is the set of nuggets contained in passage p_i, determined using the rules as described in 9.4.1.2. Each nugget N_j has an associated weight w_j, which determines the utility derived by seeing that nugget in a system-produced passage. These weights are initially set to be equal, but could also be initialized based on the pyramid approach (14) to assign different levels of importance to nuggets.

Since the repeated occurrences of the same piece of information are less useful (or not useful at all) to the user, we *dampen* the weight w_j of each nugget N_j whenever it occurs in a system-produced passage, so that subsequent occurrences receive lower utility. That is, for each nugget N_j, its weight is updated as $w_j = w_j * \beta$, where p is a preset dampening factor. When $\beta = 1$, no utility dampening occurs and each occurrence of the same nugget is given equal score, as with traditional relevance based methods. At the other extreme, $\beta = 0$ causes only the first occurrence of a nugget to be scored, ignoring all its subsequent occurrences. As a middle ground, a small non-zero dampening factor can be used if the user prefers to see some redundancy, perhaps as an indicator of importance or reliability of the presented information.

These nugget weights are preserved between evaluation of successive ranked lists produced by the system, since the users are expected to remember what the system showed them in the past. Hence, systems that show novel items (i.e., items not seen in the past) and also produce non-redundant ranked lists (i.e., do not display very similar passages at multiple positions in the same ranked list) are favored by such an evaluation scheme.

9.4.2.2 Ranked list length penalty

Each passage selected by the system for the user's attention has an associated cost in terms of user time and effort to review it. Therefore, an adaptive filtering system must learn to limit the length of its ranked list to balance this cost against the gain, as measured by NDCU. However, NDCU as such is a recall oriented measure giving no incentive to a system to limit the ranked list length, since each additional passage in the list can only increase the utility score. Hence, we assign a penalty to longer ranked lists, and calculate Penalized Normalized Discounted Utility (PNDCU) as follows:

$$PNDCU = \lambda \cdot NDCU + (1 - \lambda) \cdot (1 - log_m(l + 1)) \qquad (9.7)$$

where l is the length of the system-produced ranked list, and m is the maximum ranked list length allowed. λ controls the trade-off between the gain and cost of going through the system's output.

9.5 Data

TDT4 was the evaluation benchmark corpus in TDT2002 and TDT2003. The corpus consists of over $90,000$ news articles from multiple sources (AP, NYT, CNN, ABC, NBC, MSNBC, Xinhua, Zaobao, Voice of America, PRI the World, etc.) published between October 2000 and January 2001, in three languages – Arabic, English and Mandarin. Speech-recognized and machine-translated versions of the non-English articles were provided as well.

LDC (21) has annotated the corpus with 100 topics, that correspond to various news events in this time period. Out of these, we selected a subset of 12 actionable events, and defined corresponding tasks for them.[2] For the Texas prison break event, for example, we defined a hypothetical task – 'Find information about the escape of convicts from Texas prison, and information related to their recapture'. For each task, we manually defined a profile consisting of an initial set of (5 to 10) queries (e.g. 'number of escaped convicts,' 'their last known locations,' 'actions taken by police so far,' etc.), a free-text description of the user history, i.e., what the user already knows about this event that should not be repeated by the system, and a list of known on-topic and off-topic documents (if available) as training examples.

For each query, we generated answer keys and corresponding nugget matching rules using the procedure described in Section 9.4.1.2. Thus we had a total of 120 queries, with an average of 7 nuggets per query.

9.6 Experiments and Results

9.6.1 Baselines

We used Indri (20), a popular language-model based retrieval engine, as a baseline for comparison with our system. Indri supports standard search engine functionality, including pseudo-relevance feedback (PRF) (4; 7), and is representative of a typical query-based retrieval system. Indri does not support any kind of novelty detection.

We compare Indri (System A) with PRF turned on and off, against our system (system B) with user feedback, novelty detection and anti-redundant ranking turned on and off.

9.6.2 Experimental Setup

We divided the TDT4 corpus spanning 4 months into 10 *chunks*, each defined as a period of 12 consecutive days. At any given point of time in the distillation process, each system accesses the past data up to the current point, and produces a ranked list of up 50 passages per query.

The 12 tasks defined on the corpus were divided into a training and test

---

[2]URL: http://nyc.lti.cs.cmu.edu/downloads

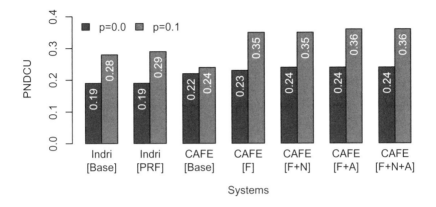

FIGURE 9.1: PNDCU Scores of Indri and CAFÉ for two dampening factors (p), and various settings (PRF: Pseudo Relevance Feedback, F: Feedback, N: Novelty Detection, A: Anti-Redundant Ranking).

set containing 6 tasks each. Each system was allowed to use the training set to tune its parameters for optimizing PNDCU (equation 9.7), including the ranked list length for both Indri and our own system, and the novelty and anti-redundancy thresholds for our system.

The PNDCU for each system run is calculated automatically. User feedback was also simulated: relevance judgments for each system-produced passage (as determined by the nugget matching rules described in section 9.4.1.2) were used as user feedback in the adaptation of query profiles and user histories.

9.6.3 Results

In Figure 9.1, we show the PNDCU scores of the two systems under various settings. These scores are averaged over all chunks of the six tasks in the test set, and are calculated with two dampening factors (see Section 9.4.2.1): $\beta = 0$ and 0.1, to simulate no tolerance and small tolerance for redundancy, respectively.

Allowing user feedback in our system improves the utility substantially when the user is willing to allow some redundancy $(\beta = 0.1)$, whereas the improvement is smaller when no redundancy is allowed $(\beta = 0)$. This is not surprising – when the user gives positive feedback on an item, the system favors that item in its query model and tends to show it repeatedly in the future. It is informative to evaluate such systems using our utility measure (with $p = 0$) which accounts for novelty and thus gives a more realistic picture

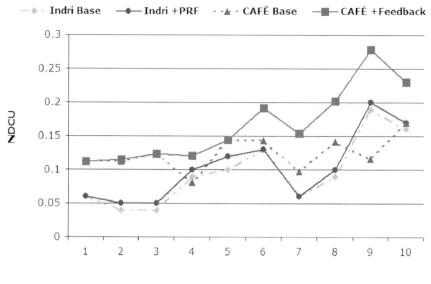

Chunk Number

FIGURE 9.2: Performance of CAFÉ and Indri across chunks.

of how well a system can generalize from user feedback, rather than using traditional IR measures like recall and precision which give an incomplete picture of improvement when using feedback.

Since documents were processed chunk by chunk, it would be interesting to see how the performance of systems improves over time. Figures 9.2 shows the performance trends for both the systems across chunks. While the performance with and without feedback on the first few chunks is expected to be close, for subsequent chunks, the performance curve with feedback enabled rises above the one with the no-feedback setting. The performance trends are not consistent across all chunks because on-topic documents are not uniformly distributed over all the chunks, making some queries 'easier' than others in certain chunks. Moreover, since Indri uses pseudo-relevance feedback while our system uses feedback based on actual relevance judgments, the improvement in case of Indri is less dramatic than that of our system.

When PNDCU is measured with $\beta = 0$ (no redundancy allowed), enabling novelty detection and anti-redundant ranking with feedback shows an improvement of 4.3% compared to when only feedback is enabled. Of course, a smaller improvement (2.8%) is natural when using $\beta = 0.1$ since the user now prefers to see repetition in the ranked passages.

In a realistic setting, users may sometimes want to see the same information from multiple sources, as an indicator of its importance or reliability. In such a case, they might choose to turn off novelty detection and anti-redundant ranking, or ask the system to reveal the documents that were suppressed by the system due to their redundancy to the current document they are viewing.

9.7 Concluding Remarks

In this chapter we presented the first investigation on utility-based information distillation with a system that learns long-lasting information needs from fine-grained user feedback over a sequence of ranked lists. We focused on how to combine adaptive filtering, novelty detection, anti-redundancy ranking and fine-grained feedback in a unified framework for utility optimization. We developed a new scheme for automated evaluation of such a system with simulated user feedback, which consists of 1) a semi-automatic procedure for acquiring rules that allow automatically matching nuggets against system responses, and 2) a modified NDCG metric for assessing the utility of ranked passages as a weighted combination of relevance and novelty. The importance of utility-based information dislillation is that it combines relevance with novelty in a *user-centric* adaptive system.

Open challenges we have not included here but plan to address in future work include: 1) modeling user's behavior (with uncertainty) in browsing ranked lists as an extension of our current utility optimzation framework, and 2) dynamic thresholding on system-produced ranked lists for utility optimization over iterative user-system interactions.

Evaluation of utility-based information distillation with true users is another important subject we did not include due to the space limitation. Some work on distillation evaluation with real users is reported in a separate paper (10).

9.8 Acknowledgments

Contributers to the presented work include Ni Lao, Abhay Harpale, Bryan Kisiel, Monica Rogati, Jian Zhang and Jaime Carbonell at the Carnegie Mellon University who participated in the method design, system implementation and/or automated evaluations of the CAFÉ system, and Peter Brusilowsky, Daqing He, Rosta Farzan, Jonathan Grady, Jaewook Ahn, and Yefei Peng at the University of Pittsburgh who colloborated in generating the extended TDT4 annotations and conducted user studies with CAFÉ. This work is supported in parts by Defense Advanced Research Project Agency (DARPA) under contracts NBCHD030010 and W0550432, and the National

Science Foundation (NSF) under grants IIS-0434035, IIS-0704689 and IIS-0704628. Any opinions, findings, conclusions or recommendations expressed in this material are those of the authors and do not necessarily reflect the views of the sponsors.

References

[1] J. Allan. Incremental relevance feedback for information filtering. *Proceedings of the 19th Annual International ACM SIGIR Conference on Research and Development in Information Retrieval*, pages 270–278, 1996.

[2] J. Allan, J. Carbibekkm G. Doddington, J. Yamron, and Y. Yang. Topic detection and tracking pilot studyL Final Report. In *DARPA Broadcast News Transcription and Understanding Workshop*, pages 194–218, 1998.

[3] J. Allan, C. Wade, and A. Bolivar. Retrieval and novelty detection at the sentence level. *Proceedings of the ACM SIGIR conference on Research and Development in Information Retrieval*, 2003.

[4] C. Buckley, G. Salton, and J. Allan. Automatic retrieval with locality information using SMART. *NIST special publication*, (500207):59–72, 1993.

[5] J. Callan. Learning while filtering documents. *Proceedings of the 21st Annual International ACM SIGIR Conference on Research and Development in Information Retrieval*, pages 224–231, 1998.

[6] J. Carbonell and J. Goldstein. The use of MMR, diversity-based reranking for reordering documents and producing summaries. *Proceedings of the 21st Annual International ACM SIGIR Conference on Research and Development in Information Retrieval*, pages 335–336, 1998.

[7] E. Efthimiadis. Query Expansion. *Annual Review of Information Science and Technology (ARIST)*, 31:p121–87, 1996.

[8] J. Fiscus and G. Duddington. Topic detection and tracking overview. *Topic Detection and Tracking: Event-based Information Organization*, pages 17–31.

[9] R. Florian, H. Hassan, A. Ittycheriah, H. Jing, N. Kambhatla, X. Luo, N. Nicolov, and S. Roukos. A statistical model for multilingual entity detection and tracking. *NAACL/HLT*, 2004.

[10] D. He, P. Brusilovsky, J. Ahn, J. Grady, R. Farzan, Y. Peng, Y. Yang, and M. Rogati. An evaluation of adaptive filtering in the context of

realistic task-based information exploration. In *Information Processing and Management,* 2007.

[11] K. Järvelin and J. Kekäläinen. Cumulated gain-based evaluation of IR techniques. *ACM Transactions on Information Systems (TOIS),* 20(4):422–446, 2002.

[12] J. Kuo, L. Zi, and W. Gang. New event detection based on indexing-tree and named entities. In *Proceedings of the ACM SIGIR Conference on Research and Development in Information Retrieval,* pages 215–222, 2007.

[13] J. Lin and D. Demner-Fushman. Automatically evaluating answers to definition questions. *Proceedings of the 2005 Human Language Technology Conference and Conference on Empirical Methods in Natural Language Processing (HLT/EMNLP 2005),* 2005.

[14] J. Lin and D. Demner-Fushman. Will pyramids built of nuggets topple over. *Proceedings of HLT-NAACL,* 2006.

[15] X. Luo, A. Ittycheriah, H. Jing, N. Kambhatla, and S. Roukos. A mention-synchronous coreference resolution algorithm based on the bell tree. *Proc. of ACL,* 4:136–143, 2004.

[16] G. Marton. Nuggeteer: Automatic nugget-based evaluation using descriptions and judgements. *HLT/NAACL,* 2006.

[17] E. Riloff. Automatically constructing a dictionary for information extraction tasks. *Proceedings of the Eleventh National Conference on Artificial Intelligence,* pages 811–816, 1993.

[18] S. Robertson and S. Walker. Microsoft Cambridge at TREC-9: Filtering track. *The Ninth Text REtrieval Conference (TREC–9),* pages 361–368.

[19] R. Schapire, Y. Singer, and A. Singhal. Boosting and Rocchio applied to text filtering. *Proceedings of the 21st Annual International ACM SIGIR Conference on Research and Development in Information Retrieval,* pages 215–223, 1998.

[20] T. Strohman, D. Metzler, H. Turtle, and W. Croft. Indri: A language model-based serach engine for complex queries. *Proceedings of the International Conference on Intelligence Analysis,* 2004.

[21] The Linguistic Data Consortium. http://www.ldc.upenn.edu/.

[22] E. Voorhees. Overview of the TREC 2003 Question Answering Track. *Proceedings of the Twelfth Text REtrieval Conference (TREC 2003),* 2003.

[23] Y. Yang, T. Pierce, and J. Carbonell. A study on retrospective and online event detection. In *Proceedings of the 21st Annual International*

ACM SIGIR Conference on Research and Development in Information Retrieval, pages 28–36, 1998.

[24] Y. Yang, J. Zhang, J. Carbonell, and C. Jin. Topic-conditioned novelty detection. In *Proceedings of the 8th ACM SIGKDD International Conference*, pages 688–693, 2002.

[25] Y. Yang and B. Kisiel. Margin-based local regression for adaptive filtering. *Proceedings of the Twelfth International Conference on Information and Knowledge Management*, pages 191–198, 2003.

[26] Y. Yang, S. Yoo, J. Zhang, and B. Kisiel. Robustness of adaptive filtering methods in a cross-benchmark evaluation. *Proceedings of the 28th Annual International ACM SIGIR Conference on Research and Development in Information Retrieval*, pages 98–105, 2005.

[27] Y. Yang, A. Lad, N. Lao, A. Harpale, B. Kisiel, M. Rogati, J. Zhang, J. Carbonell, P. Brusilovsky, and D. He. Utility-based information distillation over temporally sequenced documents. In *Proceedings of the ACM SIGIR Conference on Research and Development in Information Retrieval*, pages 31–38, 2007.

[28] C. Zhai, W. Cohen, and J. Lafferty. Beyond independent relevance: methods and evaluation metrics for subtopic retrieval. *Proceedings of the 26th Annual International ACM SIGIR Conference on Research and Development in Information Retrieval*, pages 10–17, 2003.

[29] J. Zhang and Y. Yang. Robustness of regularized linear classification methods in text categorization. *Proceedings of the 26th Annual International ACM SIGIR Conference on Research and Development in Information Retrieval*, pages 190–197, 2003.

[30] J. Zhang, Z. Ghahramani and Y. Yang. A probabilistic model for online document clustering with application to novelty detection *Advances in Neural Information Processing Systems (NIPS)*, 2004.

[31] Y. Zhang. Using bayesian priors to combine classifiers for adaptive filtering. *Proceedings of the 27th Annual International Conference on Research and Development in Information Retrieval*, pages 345–352, 2004.

[32] Y. Zhang, J. Callan, and T. Minka. Novelty and redundancy detection in adaptive filtering. *Proceedings of the 25th Annual International ACM SIGIR Conference on Research and Development in Information Retrieval*, 2002.

Chapter 10

Text Search-Enhanced with Types and Entities

Soumen Chakrabarti, Sujatha Das, Vijay Krishnan, and Kriti Puniyani

10.1 Entity-Aware Search Architecture

Until recently, large-scale text and Web search systems regarded a document as a sequence of string tokens. Queries were also comprised of string tokens, and the search engine's job was to assign a score to each document based on the extent of matches between query and document tokens, the rarity of the query tokens in the corpus, and, more recently, the "prestige" of the Web document in the social network of hyperlinks.

Several parallel and interrelated developments have changed this state of affairs in the last few years. Some smaller scale search applications were already more heavily invested in computational linguistics and natural language processing (NLP), and those technologies are being imported into and scaled up to benefit large-scale search. Machine learning techniques for tagging entities mentioned in unstructured text have become quite sophisticated, scalable and robust. XML is often used to represent typed entity-relationship graphs, and query engines for XML already support graph idioms that are common in entity extraction and NLP.

Gradually, Web search engines have turned to quite a bit of *interpretation* of string tokens against the backdrop of our physical world. A five-digit number is interpreted as a zipcode in some contexts. Many named entities are recognized and exploited:

- Recognizing that a query is a person name triggers a "diversity" objective that makes sure the first page lists different persons sharing the name.

- Recognizing that the query is a disease name triggers a canned response from structured records about causes, symptoms and cures.

- A navigational query that matches businesses in certain broad sectors triggers a purpose-differentiated first response, e.g., with links for downloading software, booking tickets, contacting service staff, etc.

Entities and relations form complex networks in our mind, and yet, search engines seem limited to the paradigms of entering the information need into a small text box, and getting the response in the form of a ranked list of URLs with snippets. Many research systems have tried to get past this simplistic interface, but its simplicity and convenience frequently trump a more thoughtful design. It appears that any enhancement to the query input interface must be evolutionary, and allow a fallback to the rudimentary text-box whenever desired.

However, even the smallest hint of type information in the query helps immensely. Informal study of Web search query logs reveals many sessions of 3–8 queries where some words remain fixed, such as *Nikon Coolpix*, while others come and go, such as *weight, light, heavy, gm, oz*, etc. Clearly, the user wishes to determine the weight of a given camera, and is trying hard to express this information need through a "telegraphic" Web query. We have built a prototype metasearch tool where there are *two* query boxes. In one, the user enters the type of the answer desired, such as *city*. In the other, the user enters ordinary words to be matched, such as *India, Australia, cricket*. This is an approximate representation of the question "In which cities are cricket matches being played between India and Australia?" Informally, we have found improvements to response quality if the user takes the trouble of separating the uninstantiated answer type from words to be matched. For one thing, responses are not page URLs, but instances of type *city*.

10.1.1 Guessing Answer Types

In the area of *question answering* (QA), queries are expected to be relatively coherent questions already, such as "What is the height of Mount Everest?" A large-scale search engine would largely, if not completely, ignore the valuable prepositions and articles that give away the type (here, *height*) of the desired answer. In the first part of this article (Section 10.2), we will present a technique to extract the answer type (also called **atype** for short) from a well-formed question. The atypes are provided to the system as a directed acyclic graph (DAG) of types, edges representing transitive "is-a" relations, e.g., Einstein is-a physicist is-a scientist.

10.1.2 Scoring Snippets

The second challenge is in making use of the atype to define a scoring strategy. In traditional Information Retrieval (IR), documents and queries are represented as vectors, and cosine similarity (or tweaks to it) define ranking. Most later IR systems reward a document with a better score if the query words appear close to each other. We continue to model the corpus as a linear sequence of tokens, but some tokens are now attached to nodes in our atype DAG (see Figure 10.1). Apart from general concepts, there may be *surface patterns* (such as a token having exactly four digits, or beginning with an uppercase letter) that are strong indicators of the type of the entity mentioned in a token.

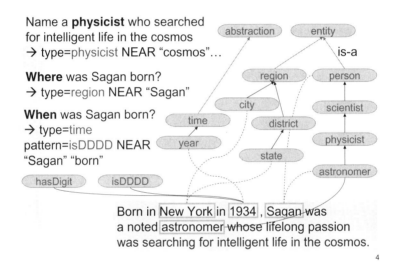

FIGURE 10.1 (SEE COLOR INSERT FOLLOWING PAGE 130.): Document as a linear sequence of tokens, some connected to a type hierarchy. Some sample queries and their approximate translation to a semi-structured form are shown.

In Figure 10.1, one or more nodes a in the atype DAG has/have been designated as desired atypes for the given query. Some *candidate tokens* in the corpus are descendants of a. We have to score and rank these candidates. The merit of a candidate is decided by its proximity (defined as the number of intervening tokens) to other tokens that match the non-atype part of the query. In Section 10.3 we present a machine learning approach to design a proximity scoring function of this form. We show that this has higher accuracy than using a standard IR system to score fixed text windows against the query.

10.1.3   Efficient Indexing and Query Processing

Having decided on a ranking function, the third problem is to build indexes and design a query-processing algorithm. The scoring paradigm indicated above leads to an interesting performance trade-off. We can expand the query atype to all ground instantiations, but this will be very expensive, especially for very broad atypes. Or we can index all atype ancestors of each token, but that will lead to unacceptable bloating of the index. Can we hit a practical middle ground? That is the topic of Section 10.4.

Figure 10.2 shows our overall system. The modules with heavy dotted outlines are described at length here.

10.1.4   Comparison with Prior Work

Related work exists in several areas: question answering (QA), information retrieval (IR) and databases (DB). The key difference from standard QA systems is that we are not after a black-box solution; instead, we wish to approximately "translate" well-formed questions into a semi-structured form, and then give precise semantics for executing this form of semi-structured queries. The notion of an atype appears often in the QA literature. Meanwhile, many projects in the IR and DB communities deal with fast top-k queries over feature vectors or tuples, but they do not consider lexical proximity. XML search systems need to support path reachability queries, but we know of no system that integrates reachability with lexical proximity and supports a graceful trade-off between index space and query time.

10.2   Understanding the Question

Well-formed questions that seek a single entity or attribute of a given type can be a great help to the search engine, as compared to 2–3 word "telegraphic" queries.

Most successful QA systems first map the question to one or few likely atype. This step is called "question classification" or "answer type identification." The answer type is usually picked from a hand-built taxonomy having dozens to hundreds of answer types (17; 18; 25; 41; 13).

There are two major approaches to question classification. Earlier, rule-based classification was used. A manually-constructed set of rules mapped the question to a type. The rules exploited clues such as the wh-word (who, where, when, how many) and the head of noun phrases associated with the main verb (what is the tallest *mountain* in . . .). Rule-based systems are difficult to maintain and can be brittle.

More recently, question classification, following other prominent tasks in

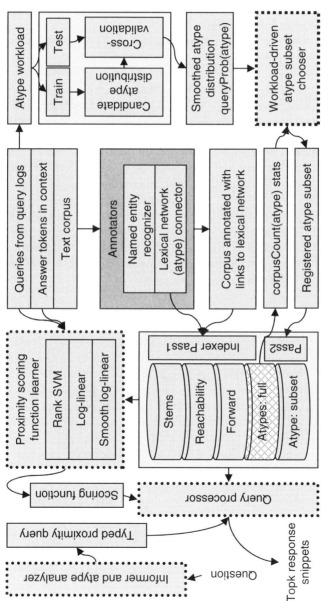

FIGURE 10.2 (SEE COLOR INSERT FOLLOWING PAGE 130.): The IR4QA system that we describe in this paper.

NLP (such as part-of-speech tagging and sentence parsing), is increasingly being achieved through machine learning. Li and Roth (27), Hacioglu and Ward (16) and Zhang and Lee (40) have used supervised learning for question classification.

The use of machine learning has enabled the above systems to handle larger datasets and more complex type systems. A benchmark available from UIUC[1] is now standard. It has 6 coarse and 50 fine answer types in a two-level taxonomy, together with 5500 training and 500 test questions. Webclopedia (18) has also published its taxonomy with over 140 types.

Compared to other areas of text mining, question classification has benefited from machine learning somewhat less than one might expect.

Li and Roth (27) used question features like tokens, parts of speech (POS), chunks (non-overlapping phrases) and named entity (NE) tags. Some of these features, such as part-of-speech, may themselves be generated from sophisticated inference methods. Li and Roth achieved 78.8% accuracy for 50 classes. On using a hand-built dictionary of "semantically related words" (unpublished, to our knowledge) the accuracy improved to 84.2%. It seems desirable to use only off-the-shelf knowledge bases and labeled training data consisting of questions and their atypes. Designing and maintaining the dictionary may be comparable in effort to maintaining a rule base.

Support Vector Machines (SVMs) (38) have been widely successful in many other learning tasks. SVMs were applied to question classification shortly after the work of Li and Roth. Hacioglu and Ward (16) used linear support vector machines with a very simple set of features: question word 2-grams. E.g., the question "What is the tallest mountain in Africa?" leads to features *what is, is the, the tallest,* ..., etc., which can be collected in a bag of 2-grams. (It may help to mark the beginning 2-gram in some special way.) They did not use any named-entity tags or related word dictionary. Early SVM formulations and implementations usually handled two classes. Hacioglu and Ward used a technique by Dietterich and Bakiri (12) to adapt two-class SVMs to the multiclass setting in question classification. The high-level idea is to represent class labels with carefully chosen numbers, represent the numbers in the binary system and have one SVM predict each bit position. This is called the "error-correcting output code" (ECOC) approach. The overall accuracy was 80.2–82%, slightly higher than Li and Roth's baseline.

Zhang and Lee (40) used linear SVMs with all possible question word q-grams, i.e., the above question now leads to features *what, what is, what is the,* ..., *is, is the, is the tallest,* ..., etc. They obtained an accuracy of 79.2% without using ECOC, slightly higher than the Li and Roth baseline but somewhat lower than Hacioglu and Ward. Zhang and Lee went on to design an ingenious kernel on question parse trees, which yielded visible gains for the 6 coarse labels in the UIUC classification system. The accuracy gain

---

[1] http://l2r.cs.uiuc.edu/~cogcomp/Data/QA/QC/

for the 50 fine-grained classes was surprisingly small. The authors explain this in the following terms: "the syntactic tree does not normally contain the information required to distinguish between the various fine categories within a coarse category."

10.2.1 Answer Type Clues in Questions

We contend that the above methods for generating features from the question overload the learner with too many features too far from the critical question tokens that reveal the richest clues to the atype.

In fact, our experiments show that a very short (typically 1–3 word) subsequence of question tokens are adequate clues for question classification, at least by humans. We call these segments **informer spans**. This is certainly true of the most trivial atypes (*Who* wrote Hamlet? or *How many* dogs pull a sled at Iditarod?) but is also true of more subtle clues (How much does a rhino *weigh*?). Informal experiments revealed the surprising property that *only one* segment is enough. In the above question, a human does not even need the *how much* clue (which hints at only a generic quantity) once the word *weigh* is available. In fact, "How much does a rhino *cost*?" has an identical syntax but an atype that is a completely different subtype of "quantity," not revealed by *how much* alone. The only exceptions to the single-span hypothesis are multi-function questions like "What is the *name* and *age* of . . .," which should be assigned to multiple answer types. In this paper we consider questions where one type suffices.

Consider another question with multiple clues: *Who* is the *CEO* of IBM? In isolation, the clue *who* merely tells us that the answer might be a person or country or perhaps an organization, while *CEO* is perfectly precise, rendering *who* unnecessary. All of the above applies *a forteriori* to *what* and *which* clues, which are essentially uninformative on their own, as in "What is the *distance* between Pisa and Rome?"

The informer span is very sensitive to the structure of clauses, phrases and possessives in the question, as is clear from these examples (informers italicized): "What is Bill Clinton's wife's *profession*," and "What *country*'s president was shot at Ford's Theater." Depending on sentence structure, the informer can be near to or far from question triggers like *what*, *which* and *how*.

The choice of informer spans also depends on the target classification system. Initially we wished to handle definition questions separately, and marked no informer tokens in "What is digitalis." However, *what is* is an excellent informer for the UIUC question class marked "definition" `DESC:def`.

Before we get into the job of annotating the question with the informer segment, we summarize the accuracy obtained by some of the approaches reviewed earlier, as well as by a linear SVM that was provided with suitable features generated from the informer segment (details in Section 10.2.3). If "perfect" informer spans are labeled by hand, and features generated only

Algorithm	6-class	50-class
Li and Roth	[1]	78.8[2]
Hacioglu et al., SVM+ECOC	–	80.2–82
Zhang & Lee, LinearSVMq	87.4	79.2
Zhang & Lee, TreeSVM	90	–
SVM, "perfect" informer	**94.2**	**88**
SVM, CRF-informer	**93.4**	**86.2**

FIGURE 10.3: Summary of % accuracy for UIUC data. [1] SNoW accuracy without the related word dictionary was not reported. With the related-word dictionary, it achieved 91%. [2] SNoW with a related-word dictionary achieved 84.2% but the other algorithms did not use it. Our results are summarized in the last two rows; see text for details.

from these spans, a simple linear SVM beats all earlier approaches. This confirms our suspicion that the earlier approaches suffered because they generated spurious features from low-signal portions of the question.

10.2.2   Sequential Labeling of Type Clue Spans

In a real system, the atype informer span needs to be marked automatically in the question. This turns out to be a more difficult problem. Syntactic pattern-matching and heuristics widely used in QA systems are not very good at capturing informer spans, as we shall see in Section 10.2.4.

We will model the generation of the question token sequence as a Markov chain. An automaton makes probabilistic transitions between hidden states y, one of which is an "informer generating state," and emits tokens x. We observe the tokens and have to guess which were produced from the "informer generating state." Recent work has shown that conditional random fields (CRFs) (26; 35) have a consistent advantage over traditional HMMs in the face of many redundant features. We refer the reader to the above references for a detailed treatment of CRFs.

Two common HMMs are used for text annotation and information extraction. The first is the "in/out" model with two states. One ("in") state generates tokens that should be annotated as the informer span. The other ("out") state generates the remaining tokens. All transitions between the two states must be allowed, which means that multiple "in" or informer spans are possible in the output, which goes against our intuition above. The second HMM is the 3-state "begin/in/out" (BIO) model, also widely used in information extraction. The initial state cannot be "2" in the 3-state model; all states can be final. These transitions allow at most one informer span. The two state machines are shown in Figure 10.4.

The BIO model is better than the in/out model for much the same reasons as in information extraction, but we give some specific examples for

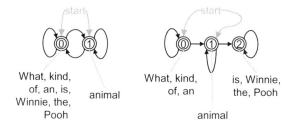

FIGURE 10.4: 2- and 3-state transition models.

completeness. Consider these question pairs:

1a What country is the largest producer of wheat?

1b Who is the largest producer of wheat?

2a Which president was the winner of the tenth election?

2b Name the winner of the tenth election

In 1b and 2b, for want of better informers, we would want *producer* and *winner* to be flagged as informers, but in 1a and 2a, *country* and *president* would be more useful informers.

The $i \pm 1$ context of *producer* is identical in 1a and 1b, as is the $i \pm 1$ context of *winner* in 2a and 2b. Any 2-state model that depends on positions $i \pm 1$ to define features will fail to distinguish between 1a and 1b, or 2a and 2b, and might mark both *country* and *producer* in 1a, and *president* and *winner*. From Figure 10.3, we see that generating features from parts of the question that are not informer tokens can reduce accuracy. Therefore, we would like to identify the single most likely informer span. By design, the BIO model will never annotate more than one contiguous segment.

The tree kernels used by Zhang *et al.* exploited the property that questions with similar parse trees are likely to have the informer span over similar token positions. We will therefore use the parse tree of the question to generate features that will be used in a conditional HMM. Unlike Zhang *et al.*, we will pay attention only to selected parts of the parse tree.

10.2.2.1 Parse tree and multiresolution feature table

Figure 10.5 shows a sample parse tree output by the Stanford Lexicalized Parser (23). The tree has been organized in levels. The non-terminal symbols of the tree follow the Penn Treebank tag convention (see `http://www.cis.upenn.edu/~treebank/` for details).

To employ max-margin methods for labeling (40), a suitable kernel has to be defined between two such trees. In case of a general CRF, we would be

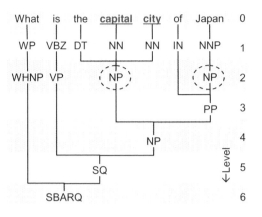

FIGURE 10.5: Stanford Parser output example.

i	1	2	3	4	5	6	7
y_i	0	0	0	1	1	2	2
x_i	What	is	the	capital	city	of	Japan
$\ell \downarrow$	\multicolumn{7} Features for x_is
1	WP,1	VBZ,1	DT,1	NN,1	NN,1	IN,1	NNP,1
2	WHNP,1	VP,1	NP,1	**NP**,1	NP,1	Null,1	**NP,2**
3	Null,1	Null,1	Null,1	Null,1	Null,1	PP,1	PP,1
4	Null,1	Null,1	NP,1	NP,1	NP,1	NP,1	NP,1
5	Null,1	SQ,1	SQ,1	SQ,1	SQ,1	SQ,1	SQ,1
6	SBARQ	SBARQ	SBARQ	SBARQ	SBARQ	SBARQ	SBARQ

FIGURE 10.6: A multi-resolution tabular view of the question parse showing `tag` and `num` attributes in each cell. *capital city* is the informer span with $y = 1$.

interested in associating a binary label (informer token or not) with the leaf nodes of the parse tree. It is tempting to cast this as a structured prediction problem where the graph is the parse tree itself, and the edges of the parse tree express Markov dependencies. A straightforward implementation of this approach may limit the exploitation of long-range features observable from the parse tree. For example, we may observe from training data that informer spans occur more often near the beginning of the question, but are rarely the first word. In other words, there is a distribution over token positions where the informer span occurs. Also consider the information latent in the parse tree at multiple levels of resolution. For example, in Figure 10.5, to label *city* as part of the informer span, it may help us more to know that the next chunk *of Japan* has POS "PP" at level 3, than to know that the next token *of* has POS "IN" at level 1.

   To exploit these valuable clues, we will first express the question parse tree as a table, then generate CRF features from the table. The table for the parse tree in Figure 10.5 is shown in Figure 10.6.

10.2.2.2 Cells and attributes

A labeled question comprises the token sequence $x_i; i = 1, \ldots$ and the label sequence $y_i, i = 1, \ldots$. Each x_i leads to a column vector of observations. Therefore we use matrix notation to write down x: A table cell is addressed as $x[i, \ell]$ where i is the token position (column index) and ℓ is the level or row index, 1–6 in this example. (Although the parse tree can be arbitrarily deep, we found that using features from up to level $\ell = 2$ was adequate.)

Intuitively, much of the information required for spotting an informer can be obtained from the part of speech of the tokens and phrase/clause attachment information. Conversely, specific word information is generally sparse and potentially misleading; the same word may or may not be an informer depending on its position, e.g., "What birds eat snakes?" and "What snakes eat birds?" have the same words but different informers. Accordingly, we observe two properties at each cell:

tag: The syntactic class assigned to the cell by the parser, e.g., $x[4, 2].\texttt{tag} = $ NP. It is well known that POS and chunk information are major clues to informer-tagging, specifically, informers are often nouns or noun phrases.

num: Many heuristics exploit the fact that the first NP is known to have a higher chance of containing informers than subsequent NPs. To capture this positional information, we define **num** of a cell at $[i, \ell]$ as one plus the number of distinct contiguous chunks to the left of $[i, \ell]$ with **tags** equal to $x[4, 2].\texttt{tag}$. E.g., at level 2 in the table above, *the capital city* forms the first NP, while *Japan* forms the second NP. Therefore $x[7, 2].\texttt{num} = 2$.

In conditional models, it is notationally convenient to express features as functions on (x_i, y_i). To one unfamiliar with CRFs, it may seem strange that y_i is passed as an argument to features. At training time, y_i is indeed known, and at testing time, the CRF algorithm efficiently finds the most probable sequence of y_is using a Viterbi search. True labels are not revealed to the CRF at testing time.

Cell features `IsTag` **and** `IsNum`**:** E.g., the observation "$y_4 = 1$ and $x[4, 2].\texttt{tag} = $ NP" is captured by the statement that "position 4 fires the feature $\texttt{IsTag}_{1,\text{NP},2}$" (which has a boolean value). There is an $\texttt{IsTag}_{y,t,\ell}$ feature for each (y, t, ℓ) triplet, where y is the state, t is the POS, and ℓ is the level. Similarly, for every possible state y, every possible **num** value n (up to some maximum horizon) and every level ℓ, we define boolean features $\texttt{IsNum}_{y,n,\ell}$. E.g., position 7 fires the feature $\texttt{IsNum}_{2,2,2}$ in the 3-state model, capturing the statement "$x[7, 2].\texttt{num} = 2$ and $y_7 = 2$".

Adjacent cell features `IsPrevTag` **and** `IsNextTag`: Context can be exploited by a CRF by coupling the state at position i with observations at positions adjacent to position i (extending to larger windows did not help). To capture this, we use more boolean features: position 4 fires the feature $\texttt{IsPrevTag}_{1,\text{DT},1}$ because $x[3,1].\texttt{tag} = \texttt{DT}$ and $y_4 = 1$. Position 4 also fires $\texttt{IsPrevTag}_{1,\text{NP},2}$ because $x[3,2].\texttt{tag} = \texttt{NP}$ and $y_4 = 1$. Similarly we define a $\texttt{IsNextTag}_{y,t,\ell}$ feature for each possible (y, t, ℓ) triple.

State transition features `IsEdge`: Position i fires feature $\texttt{IsEdge}_{u,v}$ if $y_{i-1} = u$ and $y_i = v$. There is one such feature for each state-pair (u, v) allowed by the transition graph. In addition we have sentinel features $\texttt{IsBegin}_u$ and $\texttt{IsEnd}_u$ marking the beginning and end of the token sequence.

Handling compound words: At first we collapsed compounds like `New_York_City` (if found in WordNet) into a single token. Initial experiments showed that compound detection is generally useful, but hurts accuracy when it is wrong. (This is almost universal of front-end token processors.) We then enhanced our code to detect a compound alert feature, but not collapse the tokens. Instead, for every position i and state pair y_1, y_2, we fired a special feature (i.e., set the value to 1) if the compound detector claimed that x_{i-1} and x_i were parts of the same compound. This gave the CRF a robust bias toward labeling a compound with a common state, without making this hard policy, and boosted our accuracy slightly.

10.2.2.3   Heuristic informer annotation

Even if one concedes that informers provide valuable features, one may question whether the elaborate mechanism using parse trees and CRFs is necessary. In the literature, much simpler heuristics are often used to directly extract the atype from a question. Singhal *et al.* (36) pick the head of the first noun phrase detected by a shallow parser. Ramakrishnan *et al.* (32) use the head of the noun phrase adjoining the main verb. The LASSO (31), FALCON (17) and Webclopedia (18) systems use dozens to hundreds of (unpublished to our knowledge) hand-built pattern-matching rules on the output of a full-scale parser.

We would like to play off our CRF-based informer annotator against such a heuristic annotator. We know of no readily available public code that implements the latter class, so we implemented the following rules:

How: For questions starting with *how*, we use the bigram starting with *how* unless the next word is a verb.

Wh: If the wh-word is not *how*, *what* or *which*, use the wh-word in the question as a separate feature.

WHNP: For questions having *what* and *which*, use the WHNP if it encloses a noun. WHNP is the Noun Phrase corresponding to the Wh-word, given by the Stanford parser.

NP1: Otherwise, for *what* and *which* questions, the first (leftmost) noun phrase is added to yet another feature.

We name apart the features in the cases above, so that there is no ambiguity regarding the rule that fired to create a feature.

10.2.3 From Type Clue Spans to Answer Types

We will generate features from the whole question as well as the segment designated as the informer span, but these features will be "named apart" so that the learner downstream can distinguish between these features. Figure 10.7 shows the arrangement, an instance of stacked or meta learning (8). The first-level learner is a CRF, and the second-level learner is a linear SVM.

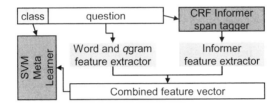

FIGURE 10.7: The meta-learning approach.

During training, there are two broad options:

1. For each training question, obtain both the true informer span and the question class as supervised data. Train the question classifier by generating features from the known informer span. Independently, train a CRF as in Section 10.2.2 to identify the informer span. Collecting training data for this option is tedious because the trainer has to identify not only the atype but also the informer span for every question.

2. For a relatively small number of questions, provide hand-annotated informer spans to train the CRF. For a much larger number of questions, provide only the question class but not the informer span. The trained CRF is used to choose an informer span which could be potentially incorrect.

Not only is the second approach less work for the trainer, but it can also give more robust accuracy when deployed. If the CRF makes systematic mistakes in tagging, the SVM is given a chance to correlate these mistakes to the true label. In contrast, in the first approach, the SVM may see test data that is distributionally different from the training data, and training data is of higher quality because the informer spans are human-generated. For these reasons, we implemented the second option. We have anecdotal evidence that the accuracy of the second approach is somewhat higher, because we subject the SVM to the limitations of the CRF output uniformly during both training and testing.

The SVM used is a linear multi-class one-vs-one SVM[2], as in the Zhang and Lee (40) baseline. We do not use ECOC (16) because the reported gain is less than 1%. Through tuning, we found that the SVM "*C*" parameter (used to trade between training data fit and model complexity) must be set to 300 to achieve published baseline numbers.

10.2.3.1   Informer q-gram features

Our main modification to earlier SVM-based approaches is in generating features from informers. In earlier work, word features were generated from word q-grams. We can apply the same method to the informer span, e.g., for the question "What is the *height* of Mount Everest?" where *height* is the informer span, we generate a feature corresponding to *height*. (We will also generate regular word features; therefore we have to tag the features so that 'height' occurring inside the informer span generates a distinct feature from 'height' occurring outside the informer span.)

As in regular text classification, the goal is to reveal to the learner important correlations between informer features and question classes, e.g., the UIUC label system has a class called NUMBER:distance. We would expect informers like *length* or *height* to be strongly correlated with the class label NUMBER:distance.

10.2.3.2   Informer hypernym features

Another set of features generated from informer tokens proves to be valuable. The class label NUMBER:distance is correlated with a number of potential informer q-grams, such as *height, how far, how long, how many miles*, etc. In an ideal setting, given very large amounts of labeled data, all such correlations can be learnt automatically. In real life, training data is limited. As a second example, the UIUC label system has a single coarse-grained class called HUMAN:individual, whereas questions may use diverse atype informer tokens like *author, cricketer* or *CEO*.

There are prebuilt databases such as WordNet (30) where explicit hypernym-hyponym (x is a kind of y) relations are cataloged as a directed acyclic graph of types. For example, *author, cricketer, CEO* would all connect

---

[2]http://www.csie.ntu.edu.tw/~cjlin/libsvm/

to a common ancestor node called *person* (strictly speaking, `person#n#1`, the first noun sense of the string *person*).

In the above example, if we walked up the WordNet hierarchy and included all hypernyms (generalizations) of informer tokens in our bag of features, we would get a much stronger correlation between the informer hypernym feature `person#n#1` and the question class label `HUMAN:individual`. In our implementation we look up an informer token and walk up to more general types, and include all of them in the bag of features. For example, if the informer token is *CEO*, we would include in the feature bag all these features: `corporate_executive#n#1`, `executive#n#1`, `administrator#n#1`, `head#n#4`, `leader#n#1`, `person#n#1`, `organism#n#1`, `living_thing#n#1`, `object#n#1`, `physical_entity#n#1`, `causal_agent#n#1`, `entity#n#1`. Some features, such as beyond `person#n#1` above, are too general, and they will be found to have poor correlation with the class label `HUMAN:individual`, enabling the SVM to ignore them. For informer spans having more than one token, we look up WordNet not only for individual informer tokens but also informer *q*-grams, because some tokens may be part of compounds, as in "Which breed of *hunting dog* ...," "Which European *prime minister* ...," "What is the *conversion rate* ..." and "Which *mountain range* ...."

10.2.3.3   Supplementary word features

If informer extraction were perfect, extracting other features from the rest of the question would appear unnecessary. As we have discussed before, because the informer span annotator is a learning program, it will make mistakes. Moreover, we use no word sense disambiguation (WSD) while processing informer tokens. *How long* ... may refer to both time and space, and *Which bank* ... may be about rivers or financial institutions. When we connect informer tokens to WordNet and expand to ancestors, we may amplify the ambiguities.

For the above reasons, it is a good idea to include additional features from regular question words. The word feature extractor selects unigrams and *q*-grams from the question. In our experiments, $q = 1$ or $q = 2$ worked best; but, if unspecified, all possible *q*grams were used. As with informers, we can also use hypernyms of regular words as SVM features.

10.2.4   Experiments

To keep our performance numbers directly comparable to earlier work, we used the dataset from UIUC[3] (27) that is now somewhat standard in question classification work. It has 6 coarse and 50 fine answer types in a two-level taxonomy, together with 5500 training and 500 test questions. We had two volunteers independently tag the 6000 UIUC questions with informer spans.

---

[3]`http://l2r.cs.uiuc.edu/~cogcomp/Data/QA/QC/`

Agreement between the volunteers was almost perfect. We will call these designated informer spans "perfect" informers.

10.2.4.1   Informer span tagging accuracy

Each question has a known set I_k of informer tokens, and gets a set of tokens I_c flagged as informers by the CRF. For each question, we can grant ourselves a reward of 1 if $I_c = I_k$, and 0 otherwise. This strict equality check can be harsh, because the second-level SVM classifier may well classify correctly despite small perturbations in the feature bag derived from informers. In Section 10.2.3.1, informer-based features were placed in a separate bag. Therefore, the *overlap* between I_c and I_k would be a reasonable predictor of question classification accuracy. We use the Jaccard similarity $|I_k \cap I_c|/|I_k \cup I_c|$.

Features used	Fraction $I_c = I_k$	Jaccard overlap
IsTag	0.368	0.396
+IsNum	0.474	0.542
+IsPrevTag+IsNextTag	0.692	0.751
+IsEdge+IsBegin+IsEnd	**0.848**	**0.867**

FIGURE 10.8: Effect of feature choices.

Feature ablation study: Figure 10.8 shows the effect of using diverse feature sets on the accuracy of the SVM, measured both ways. We make the following observations:

- By themselves, `IsTag` features are quite inadequate at producing acceptable accuracy.

- `IsNum` features improve accuracy 10–20%.

- `IsPrevTag` and `IsNextTag` ("+Prev +Next") add over 20% of accuracy.

- `IsEdge` transition features help exploit Markovian dependencies and add another 10–15% accuracy, showing that sequential models are indeed required.

Benefits from non-local chunk features: We have commented before on the potential benefits from our feature design procedure in Section 10.2.2.1. To test if such an elaborate procedure is actually beneficial, we limited the number of levels from Figure 10.5 that were converted into CRF features. Figure 10.9 shows the results. "1" corresponds to features generated from only the leaf level of the parse tree. Clearly adding non-local features from higher levels in the tree helps, at least up to level two (but the degradation thereafter from excess features is small). In fact, Figure 10.9 gives us the hope that a full parse of the question may not be needed; a parser that can recover chunk information up to level two, even from grammatically ill-formed questions, will do fine.

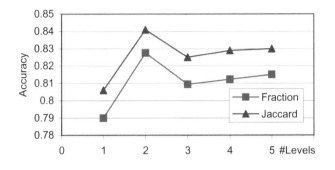

FIGURE 10.9: A significant boost in question classification accuracy is seen when two levels of non-local features are provided to the SVM, compared to just the POS features at the leaf of the parse tree.

Effect of number of CRF states: The last two columns of Figure 10.10 show that the 3-state CRF performs much better than the 2-state CRF. The gain comes mainly from difficult questions that start with *what* and *which*. In such questions, *what* and *which* are not useful in themselves, and the real clues are surrounded by other important word clues, e.g., "What is the name of Saturn's largest *moon*?" vs. "What *mammal* lays eggs?" etc. Deciphering these patterns benefits most from the three-state CRF.

Comparison with heuristic rules: Figure 10.10 also compares the Jaccard accuracy of informers found by the CRF vs. informers found by the heuristics described in Section 10.2.2.3. Again we see a clear superiority of the CRF approach.

Unlike the heuristic approach, the CRF approach is relatively robust to the parser emitting a somewhat incorrect parse tree, which is not uncommon. The heuristic approach picks the "easy" informer, *who*, over the better one, *CEO*, in "Who is the CEO of IBM." Its bias toward the NP-head can also be a problem, as in "What country's *president* ...."

Type	#Quest.	Heuristic Informers	2-state CRF	3-state CRF
what	349	57.3	68.2	83.4
which	11	77.3	83.3	77.2
when	28	75.0	98.8	100.0
where	27	84.3	100.0	96.3
who	47	55.0	47.2	96.8
how_*	32	90.6	88.5	93.8
rest	6	66.7	66.7	77.8
Total	500	62.4	71.2	86.7

FIGURE 10.10: Effect of number of CRF states, and comparison with the heuristic baseline (Jaccard accuracy expressed as %).

10.2.4.2 Question classification accuracy

Because our classification system is two-level (CRF followed by SVM), our evaluation will also be in two stages. First, we will evaluate the accuracy of the SVM assuming "perfect" (i.e., human-generated) informer spans are available during both training and testing. Second, we will evaluate the more realistic setting with the CRF providing the informer span.

Benefits from "perfect" informers: Figure 10.11 shows that the baseline word unigram SVM is already quite competitive with the best previous numbers, and exploiting perfect informer spans beats all known numbers. It is clear that both *informer q-grams* and *informer hypernyms* are very valuable features for question classification. The fact that no improvement was obtained with *question bigrams* over using *question hypernyms* highlights the importance of not using all question tokens uniformly, but recognizing that some of them have a special role to play in predicting the atype.

Figure 10.12 is the final summary of this section. Column (a) shows the performance of an SVM question classifier that does not use informers, but uses only word bigrams and their hypernyms. Columns (b), (c) and (d) show the accuracies obtained with *only* informer-based features. Column (b) uses manually tagged "perfect" informers. Column (c) uses heuristic informers, which often perform worse, especially for *what* and *which* questions. Informer spans tagged by the CRF perform somewhere between perfect informers and heuristic informers. However, columns (e), (f) and (g) show the best-performing settings where informer features are used in conjunction with the baseline features from all question bigrams and their hypernyms. Again, CRF-tagged informers are somewhere between perfect and heuristic informers, but closer to perfect informers on average.

Features	Coarse	Fine
Question trigrams	91.2	77.6
All question *q*grams	87.2	71.8
All question unigrams	88.4	78.2
Question bigrams	91.6	79.4
+informer q-grams	94.0	82.4
+informer hypernyms	**94.2**	**88.0**
Question unigrams + all informer	93.4	88.0
Only informer	92.2	85.0
Question bigrams + hypernyms	91.6	79.4

FIGURE 10.11: Percent accuracy with linear SVMs, "perfect" informer spans and various feature encodings. The 'Coarse' column is for the 6 top-level UIUC classes and the 'fine' column is for the 50 second-level classes.

10.3   Scoring Potential Answer Snippets

In Section 10.2 we established that atypes can be inferred from a natural language question with high accuracy. The atype extraction step is an important part of question preprocessing, because it lets us partition question tokens into

- Tokens that express the user's information need as a type to be instantiated, but which need not literally appear in a correct response document or snippet, and

- Tokens that the user expects to literally match correct response documents or snippets—we call these **selector** tokens.

For example, the question "What is the distance between Paris and Rome?" gets partitioned into

- Atype `NUMBER:distance` (UIUC system) or `distance#n#3` (WordNet system)

- Selectors *Paris* and *Rome* that can be used to shortlist documents and snippets that qualify to be scored

In this section we set up a machine learning framework to assign scores to snippets that potentially answer the question.

In traditional Information Retrieval, the extent of match between the query q and a candidate document d is often measured as the cosine of the angle between q and d represented as vectors in the Vector Space Model (33). Each word in the lexicon is represented by an axis in the vector space. Words

Type	#Quest.	B (Bigrams)	Only Informers			B+ Perf.Inf	B+ H.Inf	B+ CRF.Inf
			Perf.Inf	H.Inf	CRF.Inf			
6 coarse classes								
what	349	88.8	89.4	69.6	79.3	91.7	87.4	91.4
which	11	72.7	100.0	45.4	81.8	100.0	63.6	81.8
when	28	100.0	100.0	100.0	100.0	100.0	100.0	100.0
where	27	100.0	96.3	100.0	96.3	100.0	100.0	100.0
who	47	100.0	100.0	100.0	100.0	100.0	100.0	100.0
how_*	32	100.0	96.9	100.0	100.0	100.0	100.0	100.0
rest	6	100.0	100.0	100.0	66.7	100.0	66.7	66.7
Total	500	91.6	92.2	77.2	84.6	94.2	90.0	93.4
50 fine classes								
what	349	73.6	82.2	61.9	78.0	85.1	79.1	83.1
which	11	81.8	90.9	45.4	73.1	90.9	54.5	81.8
when	28	100.0	100.0	100.0	100.0	100.0	100.0	100.0
where	27	92.6	85.2	92.6	88.9	88.9	92.5	88.9
who	47	97.9	93.6	93.6	93.6	100.0	100.0	97.9
how_*	32	87.5	84.3	81.2	78.1	87.5	90.6	90.6
rest	6	66.7	66.7	66.7	66.7	100.0	66.7	66.7
Total	500	79.4	85.0	69.6	78.0	88.0	82.6	86.2
		a	b	c	d	e	f	g

FIGURE 10.12: Summary of % accuracy broken down by broad syntactic question types. a: question bigrams, b: perfect informers only, c: heuristic informers only, d: CRF informers only, e–g: bigrams plus perfect, heuristic and CRF informers.

are given different weights based on their rareness in the corpus (rare words get a larger weight), and some query words are eliminated because they are stopwords like *the* and *an*, but otherwise all query words are treated equally while computing the similarity between q and d. Such a scoring scheme does not work for us, because the atype or informer tokens are fundamentally different from the selector tokens in their purpose, and have to be treated very differently by the scoring function. Second, vector-space scoring evolved over more than a decade, and the scoring choices are backed by probabilistic arguments (37). But for scoring snippets, no such guiding principles are available.

In this section, we will first set up a parametric scoring model based on the lexical proximity between occurrences of instances of the question atype and occurrences of question selectors in short snippets in the corpus. We will then set up a learning problem to estimate the parameters of the scoring function from training data. Finally, we will describe our experiences with some TREC question answering benchmarks.

10.3.1 A Proximity Model

Consider the query "Who invented television?" which translates to atype `person#n#1` and (after stemming) selectors *television* and *invent** (meaning any suffix of *invent* is to be matched). Figure 10.13 shows a sample snippet that contains the answer at (relative) token offset 0.

The answer token is a descendant of the node `person#n#1` in WordNet. John Baird may not be explicitly coded into the WordNet database as a person, but a great deal of work on information extraction and named entity tagging (35) has produced reliable automated annotators that can connect the segment *John Baird* to the type node `person#n#1` in WordNet.

If the candidate (compound) token $w = $ *John Baird* is assigned relative offset 0, the selector stems are at token offsets -6, -4 and -1 in Figure 10.13. We will take an activation spreading approach to scoring token position 0. Each occurrence of a selector s gets an infusion of energy, $energy(s)$ and radiates it out along the linear token sequence, in both directions. The gap between candidate position w and a selector occurrence is denoted $gap(w, s)$. The selector occurrence s transfers

$$energy(s) \; decay(gap(w, s))$$

to the candidate token. The gap between a candidate token w and a matched selector s, called $gap(w, s)$, is one plus the number of intervening tokens. $decay(g)$ is a suitable function of the gap g.

10.3.1.1 *energy* and *decay*

Each matched selector s has an associated positive number called its **energy**, denoted $energy(s)$. A common notion of energy is the inverse

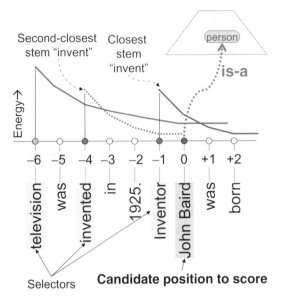

FIGURE 10.13 (SEE COLOR INSERT FOLLOWING PAGE 130.):
Setting up the proximity scoring problem.

document frequency or IDF standard in IR: the number N of documents in the corpus divided by the number N_s of documents containing the selector token s. This is a linear form of IDF. We implemented the more commonly used logarithmic form $\log(1 + N/N_s)$.

In many graph-based scoring systems such as OBJECTRANK (3), XRank (15) or TeXQuery (1) it is common to use a monotone decreasing parametric form $decay(g) = \delta^g$, where $0 < \delta < 1$ is a magic decay factor. In Figure 10.13, $decay(g)$ is shown as a strictly decreasing function. However, as we shall see, other shapes of $decay(\cdot)$ may match data more closely.

10.3.1.2 Aggregating over many selectors

Next we need to decide how to aggregate the activation from more than one distinct selector or more than one occurrence of a selector. A selector s can appear multiple times near a candidate; we call this set $\{s_i\}$. If a is the candidate, our generic scoring function looks like

$$score(a) = \bigoplus_s \oslash_i energy(s) \; decay(gap(s_i, a)), \qquad (10.1)$$

where $\oslash$ aggregates over multiple occurrences of s and $\oplus$ aggregates over different selectors. If $\oslash$ distributes over multiplication, we can write

$$score(a) = \bigoplus_s energy(s) \left(\oslash_i decay(gap(s_i, a)) \right). \qquad (10.2)$$

In standard IR, other things being equal, if a query term occurs more frequently in document d_1 than d_2, d_1 gets a somewhat larger score than d_2. In our setting, it is unclear if multiple occurrences of a selector should activate the candidate position any more than a single occurrence. In our experiments, we simply ignored all but the nearest occurrence of each selector, in effect, setting $\oslash$ to max. Sum (Σ) behaves poorly as $\oslash$ because even a low-IDF selector can boost the score of a non-answer candidate token if it appears a few times near the candidate. Apart from max and Σ, it might be worthwhile experimenting with very slow-growing functions of the selector multiplicity. For $\oplus$, sum performs quite well, i.e., we add the activation from different selectors. Here, too, some extent on non-linearity may be worthwhile exploring.

10.3.2 Learning the Proximity Scoring Function

For simplicity, we will limit our attention to the W tokens to the left and right of the candidate position numbered 0 in Figure 10.13. If the word/term at offset o is t_o, we can rewrite (10.2) as

$$score(a) = \sum_{o=-W}^{W} \underbrace{energy(t_o)\ nearest?(t_o, o, a)}_{=x_o} \beta_o = \beta^\top x \qquad (10.3)$$

where $nearest?(t, o, a)$ is 1 if the nearest occurrence of word t to candidate a is at offset o, and 0 otherwise. Ties are broken arbitrarily. In the final dot-product form, $x, \beta \in \mathbb{R}^{2W+1}$.

In our implementation we made a few further simplifications. First, we prevented the candidate token from endorsing itself, even if it was also a selector. Consider the question "Which person designed the Panama Canal?" with atype `person#n#1`. We are certainly not interested in an answer token *person*. Therefore, $o = 0$ is excluded from the sum above. Second, we ignore the distinction between tokens to the left and right of a, i.e., constrain $\beta_{-o} = \beta_o$, and add up x_{-o} and x_o suitably. This means, in our implementation, $x, \beta \in \mathbb{R}^W$.

Suppose x^+ is the feature vector corresponding to a snippet where position a is indeed an answer to the query. Let x^- be a feature vector representing a snippet that does not contain an answer. Then we want our scoring model β to satisfy $\beta^\top x^+ > \beta^\top x^-$. Suppose relevance feedback is available in the form of a set of preference pairs $i \prec j$, meaning that the candidate position i should appear lower in the ranked list than position j. This is now similar to Joachim's RANKSVM setting (21), and we can use his SVM formulation:

$$\min_{s \geq \vec{0}, \beta} \tfrac{1}{2}\beta^\top \beta + C \sum_{i \prec j} s_{ij} \quad \text{s.t.} \quad \forall i \prec v : \beta^\top x_i + 1 < \beta^\top x_j + s_{ij} \qquad (10.4)$$

As with support vector classifiers, C is a tuned parameter that trades off the model complexity $\|\beta\|$ against violations of the snippet ordering requirements.

In our snippet search application, a query may have a handful of positive response snippets and the vast expanses of token segments elsewhere in the corpus are negative examples. Intuitively, to train a good scoring function, it is useless to pick obviously irrelevant snippets. In our experiments, we picked negative snippets that contained at least one selector, and heuristically preferred negative snippets that were most similar to positive ones. This drastically cut down the number of negative snippets. However, the product of the number of positive and negative snippets, which is the size of $\prec$ above, was still very large (see Section 10.3.3). With only 169662 snippets and several million preference pairs, RANKSVM executed millions of iterations with hundreds of millions of kernel evaluations, and failed to terminate in a day on a 3GHz CPU.

Optimization (10.4) can be written as

$$\min_{\beta} \tfrac{1}{2}\beta^\top \beta + C \sum_{i \prec j} \max\{0, 1 - (\beta^\top x_j - \beta^\top x_i)\}$$

which, because $e^{-t} \geq \max\{0, 1 - t\}$, can be bounded by

$$\min_{\beta} \tfrac{1}{2}\beta^\top \beta + C \sum_{i \prec j} \exp(\beta^\top x_j - \beta^\top x_i) \qquad (10.5)$$

We call this formulation RankExp. A somewhat better approximation to the hinge loss $\max\{0, 1 - t\}$ is $\log(1 + e^{1-t})$, leading to the optimization

$$\min_{\beta} \tfrac{1}{2}\beta^\top \beta + C \sum_{i \prec j} \log(1 + \exp(\beta^\top x_j - \beta^\top x_i)),$$

but we did not see practical differences in the accuracy of the learnt scoring function. RankExp may be potentially less accurate than RANKSVM, but allows us to use simpler optimizers such as L-BFGS (28). Moreover, only sequential scans are involved over the training data, which can therefore reside on disk.

By modifying the model roughness penalty from $\|\beta\|_2^2$ to something else, we can encourage β to have some desirable properties. For example, because elements of β correspond to token offsets, we may believe that adjacent elements of β should not differ drastically. This leads us to the modified **locally smooth** formulation

$$\min_{\beta} \sum_{j=1}^{W} (\beta_j - \beta_{j+1})^2 + C \sum_{i \prec j} \exp(\beta^\top x_j - \beta^\top x_i) \qquad (10.6)$$

where we can arbitrarily set $\beta_{W+1} = 0$, because any fixed offset to all β_j leaves the score unchanged.

10.3.3 Experiments

A few thousand questions are available from the TREC 2000 Question Answering Track, annotated with atypes (24). We identified 261 questions for which the answer tokens prescribed by TREC included at least one instance or subtype of the atype of the question. Some other questions had types like *reason* ("Why is the sky blue?") and *recipe* ("How to bake banana bread?") that we cannot handle, or did not have any usable positive answer instances because WordNet does not have a known is-a connection between the atype and the answer token, e.g., WordNet does not know about the vast majority of politicians or quantum physicists living today. For each question, we need positive (answer) and negative (candidate but not answer) tokens, and, to learn their distinction well, we should collect negative tokens that are "closest" to the positive ones, i.e., strongly activated by selectors.

10.3.3.1 Data collection and preparation

Full atype index: We first indexed the corpus. Apart from a regular Lucene (2) inverted index on stems, we prepared a full *atype index* on the corpus, as follows. Each document is a sequence of tokens. Tokens can be compound, such as `New_York`. An annotator module (see Figure 10.2) connects some tokens to nodes in the atype taxonomy, e.g., the string token *Einstein* might be connected to both senses `Einstein#n#1` (the specific Physicist) and `Einstein#n#2` (genius). (Disambiguation can be integrated into the annotator module, but is an extensive research area in NLP (29) and is outside our scope.)

We overrode Lucene's token scanner to look up WordNet once a token was connected to one or more synsets, and walk up is-a (hypernym) links in the WordNet type hierarchy. All synsets encountered as ancestors are regarded as having occurred at the same token offset in the document as the original token. In our running example, given the original token is *Einstein*, we would regard `physicist#n#1`, `intellectual#n#1`, `scientist#n#1`, `person#n#1`, `organism#n#1`, `living_thing#n#1`, `object#n#1`, `causal_agent#n#1`, `entity#n#1` as having occurred at the same token offset, and index all of these as a separate field in Lucene. (This consumes a large amount of temporary space, but we drastically reduce the space requirement in a second pass, see Section 10.4.)

Collecting labeled data for RankExp: We used the full atype index to locate all candidate tokens, and made a generous estimate of the activation from (the nearest occurrence of) each selector. This generous estimate used the log IDF as *energy* and no *decay*, i.e., *energy* was accrued unattenuated at the candidate position. For each query, we retained all positive answer tokens and the 300 negative tokens with top scores. Overall, we finished with 169662 positive and negative *contexts*. 5-fold cross-validation (i.e., 80% training, 20%

testing in each fold) was used.

The next job was to turn contexts into feature vectors. Recall that there must be at least one selector match within W tokens of the candidate a. We set up this window with $2W + 1$ tokens centered at a, and retained only one instance of each selector, the one closest to a. Left-right ties were broken arbitrarily. Obviously, we can also aggregate over multiple occurrences of a selector if ⊘ warrants.

10.3.3.2   RankExp performance scaling

On identical datasets, for $C \in [0.01, 0.3]$ in (10.4) and (10.5), the fraction of orderings satisfied by RANKSVM and RankExp, as well as the MRRs were typically within 3% of each other, while RankExp took 14–40 iterations or 10–20 minutes to train and RANKSVM took between 2 and 24 hours. A more detailed evaluation is shown in Figure 10.14.

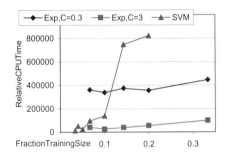

FIGURE 10.14: Relative CPU times needed by RankSVM and RankExp as a function of the number of ordering constraints.

10.3.3.3   Fitting the *decay* profile

The scatter of dots in Figure 10.15 shows a typical β vector obtained from optimizaton (10.5), where β_j gives the relative importance of a selector match at gap j. On smoothing using the optimization in (10.6) instead, we get the values shown as a continuous line. With a suitably cross-validated choice of C, the smooth version of β gave lower test error than the rough version.

We did not expect the clearly non-monotonic behavior near $j = 0$, and only in hindsight found that this is a property of language (perhaps already appreciated by linguists): selectors are often named entities, and are often connected to the answer token via prepositions and articles that creates a gap. This goes against conventional wisdom that spreading activation should monotonically decay with distance.

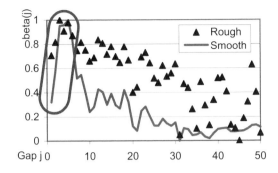

FIGURE 10.15: β_j shows a noisy unimodal pattern.

10.3.3.4 Accuracy using the fitted *decay*

Finally, we plug in the smooth β in place of *decay* and make an end-to-end evaluation of the snippet ranking system. In a standard IR system (39), the score of a snippet would be decided by a vector space model using selectors alone. We gave the standard score the additional benefit of considering only those snippets centered at an atype candidate, and considering each matched selector only once (i.e., use only IDF and not TF). Even so, a basic IR scoring approach was significantly worse than the result of plugging in β, as shown in Figure 10.16. "R300" is the fraction of truly relevant snippets recovered within the first 300 positions. The "reciprocal rank" for a fixed question is one divided by the first rank at which an answer snippet was found. Mean reciprocal rank or MRR is the above averaged over queries. Both recall and MRR over held-out test data improve substantially compared to the IR baseline.

β from	Train	Test	R300	MRR
IR-IDF	-	2000	211	0.16
RankExp	1999	2000	**231**	**0.27**
RankExp	2000	2000	235	0.31
RankExp	2001	2000	**235**	**0.29**

FIGURE 10.16: End-to-end accuracy using RankExp β is significantly better than IR-style ranking. Train and test years are from 1999, 2000, 2001. R300 is recall at $k = 300$ out of 261 test questions. $C = 0.1$, $C = 1$ and $C = 10$ gave almost identical results.

Observe that we used three years of TREC data (1999, 2000, 2001) for training and one year (2000) for testing. The accuracy listed for training year 2000 is meant only for sanity-checking because the training set is the same as the test set. However, the other rows for training years 1999 and 2001, while showing slightly lower accuracy than year 2000, are still far above the IR baseline. We should also note that TREC 1999, 2000 and 2001 questions vary quite a bit in their style and distribution of atypes and words, so Figure 10.16 is also indicative of the robustness of our system.

10.4   Indexing and Query Processing

At this stage we have solved two problems.

- We presented an algorithm for analyzing the question syntax to identify the target answer type from a large type hierarchy.

- We designed a machine learning technique to fit a scoring function that rewards proximity between instances of the desired answer type and syntactic matches between other question words and the snippet around the mentions of the instances.

In this section we address two remaining issues related to system performance.

- We propose a workload-guided system for preparing additional indexes to be used in type-cognizant proximity search.

- We outline the query execution algorithm that exploits the new indexes.

(These are actually interdependent. Index preparation is optimized for the query execution algorithm and query execution is dependent on what indexes are available.)

In Sections 10.2.3.2 and 10.3.3.1, on encountering a token, we pretended that all hypernym ancestors of (all senses of) the token appear at the same token position. In Section 10.3.3.1 we then indexed these together with the original token. Naturally this increases the size of the inverted index; the deeper the type hierarchy, the larger the bloat in index size.

Limited-domain semantic search applications need to index a handful of named entities such as person, place and time. For these applications, the cost of indexing type tags along with tokens is not prohibitive. However, large and deep type hierarchies are essential to support open-domain semantic search. Consequently, the index space required for the type annotations becomes very large compared to the standard inverted index (see Figure 10.17). The overhead appears especially large because standard inverted indexes can be compressed significantly (39).

For a reader who is familiar with large skew in the frequency of words in query logs, the natural questions at this point are whether similar skew

Corpus/index	Size (GB)
Original corpus	5.72
Gzipped corpus	1.33
Stem index	0.91
Full atype index	4.30

FIGURE 10.17: Relative sizes of the corpus and various indexes for TREC 2000.

exists in the frequency of atypes, and whether we can exploit said skew to avoid indexing a large fraction of types that appear in the type hierarchy. In our earlier example of token *CEO* appearing in a document, we may choose to index only a few of its hypernym ancestors, say, `executive#n#1`, `administrator#n#1` and `person#n#1`, because the query log has few or no occurrences of atype `causal_agent#n#1`. The frequency counts in Figure 10.18 seem to corroborate that there is, indeed, a great deal of skew in query atypes.

Freq	Query atype	Freq	Query atype
100	integer#n#1	5	president#n#2
78	location#n#1	5	inventor#n#1
77	person#n#1	4	astronaut#n#1
20	city#n#1	4	creator#n#2
10	name#n#1	4	food#n#1
7	author#n#1	4	mountain#n#1
7	company#n#1	4	musical_instrument#n#1
6	actor#n#1	4	newspaper#n#1
6	date#n#1	4	sweetener#n#1
6	number#n#1	4	time_period#n#1
6	state#n#2	4	word#n#1
5	monarch#n#1	3	state#n#1
5	movie#n#1	3	university#n#1

FIGURE 10.18: Highly skewed atype frequencies in TREC query logs.

However, as is well appreciated in the information retrieval, language modeling and Web search communities, the distribution of query atype frequencies is actually *heavy-tailed*, meaning that a substantial probability mass is occupied by rare atypes (unlike, say, in an exponential tail). This means that, even if we "train" our system over large query logs, we will always be surprised in subsequent deployment by atypes we never saw in the training set, and this will happen often enough to damage our aggregate performance.

Therefore, our first task, in Section 10.4.1, will be to turn raw atype frequencies from the query log into a *smoother* distribution over atypes. Second, in Section 10.4.2 we will formalize our strategy of indexing only a suitably-chosen subset of atypes; in particular, how to adapt to missing atypes at query time. Having fixed the query execution template, we will engage in two modeling tasks: estimating the space saved by indexing only a subset of atypes (Section 10.4.3) and estimating the query time blow-up because all atypes were not indexed (Section 10.4.4). Armed with these models, in Section 10.4.5, we will propose a simple but effective algorithm to choose the atype subset to index. Finally, we will describe experimental performance in Section 10.4.6.

10.4.1   Probability of a Query Atype

The atype subset selection algorithm we propose uses an estimate of the probability of seeing an atype a in a new query, $queryProb(a)$. For WordNet alone, a can have over 18,000 (non-leaf) values, and the skew makes it difficult to estimate the probabilities of rare atypes.

This is a standard issue in language modeling (29). The solution is to reserve and distribute a tiny bit of probability over all atypes not seen in training data. We use the well-known Lidstone smoothing formula to implement this:

$$queryProb(a) = \frac{queryCount(a) + \ell}{\sum_{a'} queryCount(a') + \ell} \tag{10.7}$$

where $0 < \ell \leq 1$ is a parameter to be set via cross-validation. Several times, we randomly split the workload into halves W_1 and W_2, estimate $queryProb(a)$ using W_1 and estimate the probability of W_2 as

$$\sum_{a \in W_2} queryCount_{W_2}(a) \log \left(queryProb_{W_1}(a) \right)$$

Results are shown in Figure 10.19; it is fairly easy to pick off a prominently best ℓ for a given dataset. We shall see later in Section 10.4.6 that ℓ has quite a strong effect on the quality of our index and the query performance.

10.4.2   Pre-Generalize and Post-Filter

Let the full set of atypes be A and imagine that some subset $R \subseteq A$ is **registered**. During indexing, tokens are attached to the type taxonomy (see Section 10.3.3.1) and we walk up is-a links, only registered atypes are included in the index. For example, in Figure 10.20, the heavily-shaded nodes `entity#n#1` and `living_thing#n#1` are in R, but the lightly-shaded nodes are not.

Now suppose we are given an atype index for only the atypes in R, and get a query with atype $a \notin R$. For example, corresponding to the natural language

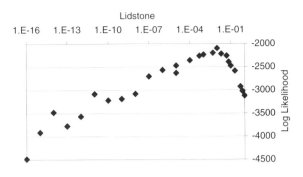

FIGURE 10.19: Log likelihood of validation data against the Lidstone smoothing parameter ℓ.

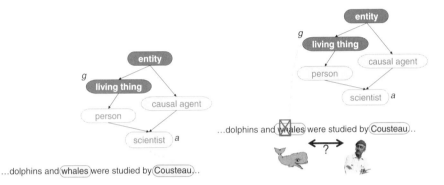

FIGURE 10.20: Pre-generalization and post-filtering.

question "Which scientist studied dolphins," we frame a query in our system of the form `type=scientist#n#1 NEAR studied dolphins`. Here is how we would execute the query.

1. Find the best (defined later) registered generalization g in the taxonomy. In the running example, we may prefer $g = $ `living_thing#n#1` over $g = $ `entity#n#1` because the former, being less general, is presumably rarer in the corpus (but also see commments below).

2. Perform a proximity search using g and the selectors in the query, which ensures recall, but generally lowers precision. Therefore, we must inflate k in the top-k search to some $k' > k$ (more about this later).

3. Use a *forward index*, described in Section 10.4.2.1, to get the actual instance token i of g in each high-scoring response. In our running example, the qualifying snippet may bring forth two candidate tokens, *Cousteau* and *whales*, because both are instances of `living_thing#n#1`.

4. Retain response i if probing a *reachability index*, described in 10.4.2.2, certifies that i is-a a. This consumes some more time and eliminates a fraction of responses. We realize that whales are not scientists (as far as WordNet is concerned) and discard it.

5. In case fewer than k results survive, repeat with a larger k'. This is very expensive and is best avoided.

The central issue is how to choose the registered subset R. Another issue is the choice of k'. We address these issues in the rest of this section.

(While selecting R, we pretend all roots of A are included in R as sentinels, but we can avoid actually indexing these. While processing a query, in case no g can be found, we can pretend every word is a potential candidate, a situation that will essentially never arise given a reasonable algorithm for selecting R.)

In addition to the registered atype index, we need to build two other indices, which we discuss at this point.

10.4.2.1   Forward index

The task of the forward index is to store the corpus in a highly compact format on disk, and, given a document ID and a token offset (or range of offsets), quickly return the tokens or token IDs at those offsets in the specified document, using very few disk seeks. The forward index should occupy no more space on disk than, say, a compressed (using `gzip`, say) version of the original corpus. We cannot just use the original corpus as-is, because it is too large, and ordinary compression inhibits random access.

In a first pass, we build the corpus lexicon, and count the frequency of each token. Next we assign a byte-aligned code to each token. The most frequent 254 tokens get a 1-byte code, the next most frequent 65534 tokens get a 2-byte code, etc. We use codes of sizes that are multiples of 8 bits because decoding variable-length codes that are not byte-aligned, with random access, would be messy. Our codes are suitably escaped so that we can read one byte and decide if we need to read more bytes to complete the code.

The forward index is used for two purposes: to set up the context required for scoring the candidate token, and to report a snippet with every hit in a typical search engine. For these applications, we typically need to access short contiguous token segments. We partition each document into segments of W (configurable at indexing time) tokens.

In the second pass, we dump token codes linearly to a random-access file without regard to their variable lengths. Then we build a persistent map from (document ID, segment number) to begin and end offsets of code bytes in the random access file. If W is configured suitably, 1–2 seeks are enough to retrieve a token segment.

In case of *ad hoc* additions of documents to the corpus, long codes can be assigned to new tokens starting from the end of the allocated range, and once the counts of new tokens get fairly large, codes can be reassigned and the forward index rebuilt.

10.4.2.2 Reachability index

The task of the reachability index is to preprocess A with all its is-a (hypernym) links and all corpus tokens and prepare a small index to be able to quickly answer queries of the form "is type t_1 a generalization or specialization of type t_2" or "is some sense of the string token w an instance of type t." If the index is very small we can store it in RAM, and we prefer to do so. Otherwise it must be on disk.

Reachability indexing is a well-explored area (10; 34). The extreme points of the storage/time trade-off are 1. doing nothing at indexing time and initiating a shortest-path search at query time, and 2. precomputing and storing reachability for all node pairs and answering queries by a table lookup. If the is-a graph on the whole atype set A is a tree, a suitable prefix numbering of nodes (15) enables $O(1)$-time query processing with $O(1)$ storage overhead per node. In case of general DAGs the problem is more difficult, with non-trivial lower bounds (10).

The WordNet noun hierarchy is "almost" a tree. For our prototype we just replicated nodes and numbered them multiple times to effectively make the graph a tree. The blowup of storage was negligible. Figure 10.17 shows the space taken by the forward and reachability index in comparison to the corpus and a regular inverted index. Our overheads are very reasonable. The forward index would be needed anyway by any text search system to be able to provide snippets with query responses.

Corpus/index	Size (GB)
Original corpus	5.72
Gzipped corpus	1.33
Stem index	0.91
Reachability index	**0.005**
Forward index	**1.16**

FIGURE 10.21: Sizes of the additional indices needed for pre-generalize and post-filter query processing, compared to the usual indices for TREC 2000.

10.4.3 Atype Subset Index Space Model

In Section 10.4.5 we will propose a greedy cost-benefit style atype registration approach that will trade off between the extra index space required if an atype r is included in R, against the average query time saved if it is included. In this section we tackle the space cost; in Section 10.4.4 we will consider the benefit of query time saved.

An exact estimate of inverted index size is difficult in the face of index compression techniques (39). The posting list for an atype a (or a token in general) has $corpusCount(a)$ entries in it, so as a first approximation, it takes space proportional to $corpusCount(a)$. Therefore, if subset R is indexed, the space needed can be approximated as

$$\sum_{a \in R} corpusCount(a). \tag{10.8}$$

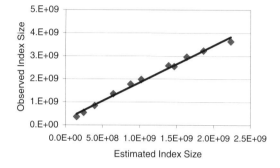

FIGURE 10.22: $\sum_{a \in R} corpusCount(a)$ is a very good predictor of the size of the atype subset index. (Root atypes are not indexed.)

Figure 10.22 shows that this crude approximation is surprisingly accurate. This is probably because, averaged over many atypes, index compression affects disk space by a fairly stable and uniform factor.

10.4.4 Query Time Bloat Model

Next we turn to the considerably more difficult task of estimating the factor by which query execution slows down because only R, not A, the set of all atypes, has been indexed. This is difficult because, in general, the estimate will depend on co-occurrence statistics between all possible atypes and all possible words. In traditional relational database query optimization, where the number of tables and attributes is modest, estimating multidimensional "selectivity" of select and join predicates is a challenging problem (20). Our testbed has over a million distinct tokens and some 18000 atypes in A. Therefore, capturing correlations with any degree of thoroughness is impossible, and simplifying assumptions must be made.

Query bloat happens in two stages: first, scanning the inverted index posting lists takes longer because the posting list of the more general atype $g \in R$ is longer than the posting list of the query atype a; and second, because we are now obliged to screen the results using expensive forward index accesses.

For the first part, we assume that the time spent scanning posting of the atype a and intersecting them with selector postings takes time proportional to $corpusCount(a)$, independent of what the specific selectors are. This is confirmed by Figure 10.23.

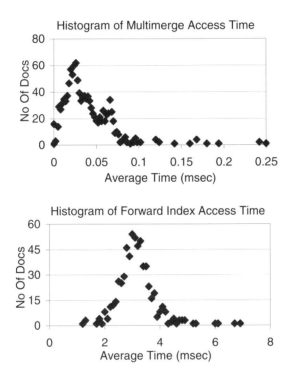

FIGURE 10.23: t_{scan} is sufficiently concentrated that replacing the distribution by a constant number is not grossly inaccurate.

The second part depends on the average time t_{forward} it takes to probe the forward index for one document and do the reachability test, and on k', the number of results sought from the pre-generalized query. Like t_{scan}, t_{forward} is also sufficiently peaked and centered to use a point estimate (Figure 10.24).

The overall query bloat factor is therefore

$$\frac{t_{\text{scan}}\, corpusCount(g) + k't_{\text{forward}}}{t_{\text{scan}}\, corpusCount(a)}$$

Now we come to the question of what k' should be. If we make the crude

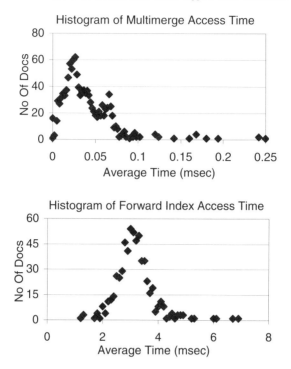

FIGURE 10.24: Like t_{scan}, t_{forward} is concentrated and can be reasonably replaced by a point estimate.

assumption that the selectors occur independently of the candidates, we see

$$k' = k \frac{corpusCount(g)}{corpusCount(a)} \tag{10.9}$$

as a natural and simple choice, using which we can write the query bloat factor as

$$\frac{corpusCount(g)}{corpusCount(a)} + k \frac{t_{\text{forward}}}{t_{\text{scan}}} \frac{corpusCount(g)}{corpusCount(a)^2}.$$

We call this $queryBloat(a, g)$, the bloat because a had to be generalized to a given g. For a given R, we can now write

$$queryBloat(a, R) = \begin{cases} 1, & \text{if } a \in R \\ \min_{g \in R, a \text{ IsA } g} queryBloat(a, g), & \text{otherwise} \end{cases} \tag{10.10}$$

Note that at query execution time the choice of g from a given R is simple, but choosing a good R ahead of time is non-trivial.

   Figure 10.25 shows a study of estimated bloat compared to observed bloat. The fit is not nearly as good as with the other half of our model in Figure 10.22,

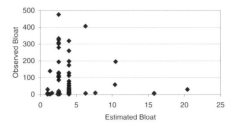

FIGURE 10.25: Scatter of observed against estimated query bloat.

because 1. IO wait times are non-deterministic because of file-system buffering and RAID, and 2. To remain practical, our model ignores the effect of selectors. Similar variability is seen in the Bindings Engine (4, Figure 3, page 447) as well. In the relational query optimizer literature, join size estimates (and therefore CPU/IO cost estimates) are often relatively crude (20) but nevertheless lead to reasonable query plans (14).

Ratio $\leq$	Count	%	Ratio $\leq$	Count	%
.5–1	16	11.6	10–20	110	79.7
1–2	78	56.5	20–50	123	89.1
2–5	93	67.3	50–100	128	92.8
6–10	104	75.3	100–200	138	100

FIGURE 10.26: Histogram of observed-to-estimated bloat ratio for individual queries with a specific R occupying an estimated 145 MB of atype index.

For a specific R picked by **AtypeSubsetChooser** (described next, in Section 10.4.5) and 138 sample queries where $g \neq a$ given R, Figure 10.26 shows the cumulative distribution of the ratio of the observed to estimated bloat. As can be seen, 68% of the queries have observed bloats less than five times the estimated bloats, and 75% are within 10×. The fit of observed to estimated bloats is reasonable for most queries, with only a few queries exhibiting a large difference between the two.

10.4.5 Choosing an Atype Subset

We thus have a bi-criteria optimization problem: given the corpus, query workload W and atype set A, choose $R \subseteq A$ so as to minimize $\sum_{r \in R} corpusCount(r)$ and also minimize the expected query bloat

$$\sum_{a \in A} queryProb_W(a)\, queryBloat(a, R) \qquad (10.11)$$

This optimization problem can be shown to be NP hard via a reduction from the knapsack problem, even when the type hierarchy is a tree. Therefore we look for practical heuristics. We adopt a greedy approach of starting R with only the roots of A^4 and progressively adding the locally "most profitable" atype c. Here "profit" depends inversely on the additional space δS that will be required by the posting list of c, and directly on the reduction δB of expected bloat that will result from including c in R. We use the ratio $\delta B/\delta S$ to pick the best c at every step.

AtypeSubsetChooser(A, W)

1: $R \leftarrow \{$roots of $A\}$, candidates $C \leftarrow A \setminus R$
2: initial estimated space $S \leftarrow \sum_{r \in R} corpusCount(r)$
3: using equations (10.7) and (10.10), expected bloat
     $B \leftarrow \sum_{a \in R \cup C} queryProb_W(a)\, queryBloat(a, R)$
4: **UpdateBloatsAndScores**$(\forall c \in C, \text{commit=false})$
5: **while** R is small and/or B is large **do**
6:      choose $c \in C$ with the largest $score(c)$
7:      **UpdateBloatsAndScores**$(c, \text{commit=true})$

UpdateBloatsAndScores$(a, \text{commitFlag})$

1: $B' \leftarrow B$, $S' \leftarrow S + corpusCount(a)$
2: "cousins" of a to be patched $U \leftarrow \varnothing$
3: **for** each $h \notin R, h \in C, h\, \text{IsA}\, a$ **do**
4:      $b = queryBloat(h, R)$, $b' = queryBloat(h, R \cup a)$
5:      **if** $b' < b$ (bloat reduces) **then**
6:          $B' \leftarrow (b' - b)\, queryProb_W(h)$
7:          **if** commitFlag **then**
8:              $U \leftarrow U \cup \{g : g \in C, g \neq a, h\, \text{IsA}\, g\}$
9: $score(a) \leftarrow (B - B')/(S' - S)$
10: **if** commitFlag **then**
11:      move a from C to R
12:      $S \leftarrow S'$, $B \leftarrow B'$
13:      **UpdateBloatsAndScores**$(\forall u \in U, \text{commit=false})$

FIGURE 10.27: The inputs are atype set A and workload W. The output is a series of trade-offs between index size of R and average query bloat over W.

The pseudocode is shown in Figure 10.27. Once c is included, each

---

[4] Including the roots is only notional. Root types are so frequent in a typical corpus that if generalization takes us to a root type it basically means we must scan the corpus end to end. Therefore, any reasonable R will prevent this event.

descendant h might see a reduction in bloat. If h's bloat decreases, all ancestors u of h must update their $\delta B / \delta S$ scores.

There is a subtle asymmetry in how the code is set up. Here we begin with $R = \varnothing$ and grow R. We cannot, for instance, begin with $R = A$ and discard unworthy atypes with the smallest $\delta B / \delta S$. Initially, all specific atypes will be in R, and more general atypes will appear completely valueless. **AtypeSubsetChooser** will steadily discard any atype that is not directly in the query log. Eventually, when the log is completely processed, we will be cornered into choosing a subset of atypes that directly appear in the log. Therefore, we will not be able to get any benefit out of choosing generalizations that are nearby confluences of many atypes in the log.

10.4.6 Experiments

10.4.6.1 Estimated space-time tradeoff

Figure 10.28 (upper chart) shows the reduction in estimated maximum bloat over all queries as **AtypeSubsetChooser** grows R. Each curve is for a different Lidstone parameter ℓ. The estimated *average* bloat over all queries would be overly influenced by a few outliers (see Figure 10.26). Therefore we discard the lowest and highest 2% of bloats and show a robust average over the rest (lower chart).

The curves in Figure 10.28 show a prominent knee: by the time the (estimated) index size is allowed to grow to 145 MB, the robust average bloat is 7, and it drops to 2 with an estimated index size of only 300 MB ($\ell = 10^{-3}$).

Very low ℓ results in low *queryProb* for atypes not seen in the training set, leading to an excessively aggressive discarding of atypes and consequently high test-set bloats. As ℓ is increased, *queryProb* increases, forcing **AtypeSubset-Chooser** to conservatively include more atypes not seen in the training set.

It is comforting to see in Figure 10.29 that the best trade-off happens for roughly the same value of ℓ that provided the largest cross-validated log-likelihood in Figure 10.19. This need not have happened: maximizing workload likelihood is not the same as reducing query bloat.

10.4.6.2 Observed space-time trade-off

Next we ran multiple queries with various Rs having different index sizes to find actual running times and, hence, actual bloats (Figure 10.30). The average observed bloat curve follows the estimated bloat curve in Figure 10.28 quite closely. In fact, averaged over many queries, our simple bloat prediction model does even better than at a per-query level (see Figure 10.25). With a modest 515 MB atype subset index, the average bloat is brought down to only 1.85.

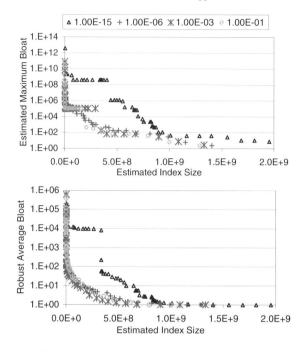

FIGURE 10.28 (SEE COLOR INSERT FOLLOWING PAGE 130.):
Estimated space-time tradeoffs produced by **AtypeSubsetChooser**. The
y-axis uses a log scale. Note that the curve for $\ell = 10^{-3}$ (suggested by
Figure 10.19) has the lowest average bloat.

10.4.6.3   Query execution dynamics

Figure 10.31 shows the average time taken per query, for various Rs with
increasing index sizes, broken down into Lucene scan+merge time taken if
$R = A$ ("FineTime"), Lucene scan+merge time using a generalized g if $R \subset
A$ ("PreTime") and the post-filtering time ("PostTime"). As can be seen,
there are regimes where scan time dominates and others where filtering time
dominates. This highlights why the choice of a good R is a tricky operation:
we cannot assume cost estimates that are any simpler.

10.5   Conclusion

10.5.1   Summary

In this article we have described the IR4QA (Information Retrieval for
Question Answering) project. Our starting point was to recognize that

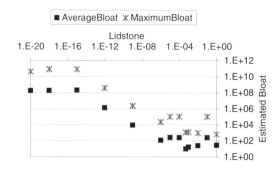

FIGURE 10.29: Estimated bloat for various values of ℓ for a specific estimated index size of 145 MB. The y-axis uses a log scale.

questions with one target type and one or more keywords to match represent a very common class of information need. In Section 10.2 we described the subsystem that interprets a natural language query into a semistructured form, comprising one target answer type and a set of keywords to match. In Section 10.3 we described a machine learning approach to learning a scoring function that rewards proximity between instances of the target type and keyword matches. In Section 10.4 we described those modules of IR4QA that are responsible for index management and query execution. IR4QA is public-domain code that is available for non-profit use.[5]

10.5.2 Ongoing and Future Work

Since 2004, when we proposed (5) and began initial work on the project reported here, significant advances have been made by several groups at building systems for entity search. The RADAR project at CMU[6], the Haystack project at MIT[7] and desktop search offerings from several companies represent entities and relations in personal data (people, places, files, emails, addresses) in a relational or graphical format and enable type-oriented entity searches. There are even whole workshops (11; 22; 19) dedicated to ranking in databases and novel IR systems.

The EntityRank project at UIUC (9) is a recent development that is especially noteworthy. EntityRank allows multiple atypes in a query, which are to be collectively bound to form a record-like structure. For example, to find the customer service phone number of Amazon.com, one may use the query `ow(amazon customer service #phone)`, where `#phone` is the atype and `ow` enforces that the selector tokens appear to the left of the mention of the

---

[5]To get code access send email to `soumen@cse.iitb.ac.in`

[6]`http://www.radar.cs.cmu.edu/`

[7]`http://groups.csail.mit.edu/haystack/`

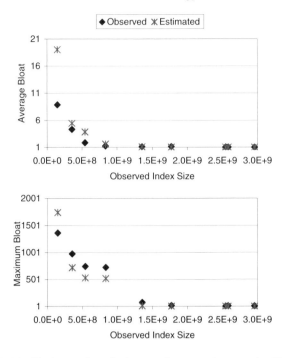

FIGURE 10.30: Estimated and observed space-time tradeoffs produced by **AtypeSubsetChooser**.

phone number. As another example, the query (`#professor #university #research=database`) compiles, from unordered annotations, a table of professors, their affiliations and their research interests, provided the last contains the word *database*. While extending to multiple atypes and ordered and unordered windows is straightforward in our system, EntityRank's main contribution is a novel ranking function that combines uncertainty in type annotations and redundancy of information across multiple mention sites.

The first generation of entity search systems is all focused on the "is an instance of" relation. EntityRank regards textual juxtaposition as evidence of (unknown) relationship, but relations other than "is-a" are neither tagged nor directly searched. Our system described here cannot search over other relations yet. "Is an attribute of" seems like the most important relation that we would like to address after "is-a." In a research prototype (6) for Searching Personal Information Networks (SPIN), we have explored the "activated twigs" paradigm for searching graph-structured textual databases. For example, one may look for a twig "person a works in Microsoft, sent me an email, and also wrote paper p" where the instantiated entities a and p are strongly activated by words *XML* and *indexing*. Being able to express such small structures, ranked by generic keyword proximity, may be the next

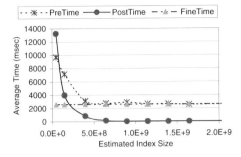

FIGURE 10.31: Average time per query (with and without generalization) for various estimated index sizes.

important step forward in entity and relation search engines.

References

[1] S. Amer-Yahia, C. Botev, and J. Shanmugasundaram. TeXQuery: A full-text search extension to XQuery. In *WWW Conference*, pages 583–594, New York, 2004.

[2] Apache Software Group. Jakarta Lucene text search engine. GPL Library, 2002.

[3] A. Balmin, V. Hristidis, and Y. Papakonstantinou. Authority-based keyword queries in databases using ObjectRank. Toronto, 2004.

[4] M. J Cafarella and O. Etzioni. A search engine for natural language applications. In *WWW Conference*, pages 442–452, 2005.

[5] S. Chakrabarti. Breaking through the syntax barrier: Searching with entities and relations. In *ECML/PKDD*, pages 9–16, 2004. Invited talk.

[6] S. Chakrabarti, J. Mirchandani, and A. Nandi. SPIN: Searching personal information networks. pages 674–674, 2005.

[7] S. Chakrabarti, K. Puniyani, and S. Das. Optimizing scoring functions and indexes for proximity search in type-annotated corpora. Edinburgh, May 2006.

[8] P. K. Chan and S. J. Stolfo. Experiments in multistrategy learning by meta-learning. In *CIKM*, pages 314–323, Washington, DC, 1993.

[9] T. Cheng, X. Yan, and K. C. C. Chang. EntityRank: Searching entities directly and holistically. September 2007.

[10] E. Cohen, E. Halperin, H. Kaplan, and U. Zwick. Reachability and distance queries via 2-hop labels. *SIAM Journal of Computing*, 32(5):1338–1355, 2003.

[11] G. Das and I. F. Ilyas, editors. *Ranking in Databases*, Istanbul, 2007.

[12] T. G. Dietterich and G. Bakiri. Error correcting output codes: A general method for improving multiclass inductive learning programs. In *National Conference on Artificial Intelligence*, pages 572–577. AAAI Press, 2002.

[13] S. Dumais, M. Banko, E. Brill, J. Lin, and A. Ng. Web question answering: Is more always better? In *SIGIR*, pages 291–298, 2002.

[14] G. Graefe. Query evaluation techniques for large databases. *ACM Computing Survey*, 25(2):73–170, 1993.

[15] L. Guo, F. Shao, C. Botev, and J. Shanmugasundaram. XRANK: Ranked keyword search over XML documents. In *SIGMOD Conference*, pages 16–27, 2003.

[16] K. Hacioglu and W. Ward. Question classification with support vector machines and error correcting codes. In *HLT*, pages 28–30, 2003.

[17] S. Harabagiu, D. Moldovan, M. Pasca, R. Mihalcea, M. Surdeanu, R. Bunescu, R. Girju, V. Rus, and P. Morarescu. FALCON: Boosting knowledge for answer engines. In *TREC 9*, pages 479–488. NIST, 2000.

[18] E. Hovy, L. Gerber, U. Hermjakob, M. Junk, and C.-Y. Lin. Question answering in Webclopedia. In *TREC 9*. NIST, 2001.

[19] V. Hristidis and I. F. Ilyas, editors. *Ranking in Databases*, Cancun, 2008.

[20] Y. E. Ioannidis and S. Christodoulakis. On the propagation of errors in the size of join results. In *SIGMOD Conference*, pages 268–277, 1991.

[21] T. Joachims. Optimizing search engines using clickthrough data. ACM, 2002.

[22] T. Joachims, H. Li, T.-Y. Liu, and C. X. Zhai, editors. *Learning to Rank for Information Retrieval*, Amsterdam, 2007.

[23] D. Klein and C. D. Manning. Accurate unlexicalized parsing. In *ACL*, volume 41, pages 423–430, 2003.

[24] V. Krishnan, S. Das, and S. Chakrabarti. Enhanced answer type inference from questions using sequential models. In *EMNLP/HLT*, pages 315–322, 2005.

[25] C. Kwok, O. Etzioni, and D. S Weld. Scaling question answering to the Web. In *WWW Conference*, volume 10, pages 150–161, Hong Kong, 2001.

[26] J. Lafferty, A. McCallum, and F. Pereira. Conditional random fields: Probabilistic models for segmenting and labeling sequence data. In *ICML*, 2001.

[27] X. Li and D. Roth. Learning question classifiers. In *COLING*, pages 556–562, 2002.

[28] D. C. Liu and J. Nocedal. On the limited memory BFGS method for large scale optimization. *Math. Programming*, 45(3, (Ser. B)):503–528, 1989.

[29] C. D. Manning and H. Schütze. *Foundations of Statistical Natural Language Processing*. MIT Press, Cambridge, MA, 1999.

[30] G. Miller, R. Beckwith, C. FellBaum, D. Gross, K. Miller, and R. Tengi. Five papers on WordNet. Princeton University, August 1993.

[31] D. Moldovan, S. Harabagiu, M. Pasca, R. Mihalcea, R. Goodrum, R. Irji, and V. Rus. LASSO: A tool for surfing the answer net. In *TREC 8*, 1999.

[32] G. Ramakrishnan, S. Chakrabarti, D. A. Paranjpe, and P. Bhattacharyya. Is question answering an acquired skill? In *WWW Conference*, pages 111–120, New York, 2004.

[33] G. Salton and M. J. McGill. *Introduction to Modern Information Retrieval*. McGraw-Hill, 1983.

[34] R. Schenkel, A. Theobald, and G. Weikum. HOPI: An efficient connection index for complex xml document collections. In *EDBT Conference*, pages 237–255, Heraklion, Crete, Greece, 2004.

[35] F. Sha and F. Pereira. Shallow parsing with conditional random fields. In *HLT-NAACL*, pages 134–141, 2003.

[36] A. Singhal, S. Abney, M. Bacchiani, M. Collins, D. Hindle, and Fernando Pereira. AT&T at TREC-8. In *TREC 8*, pages 317–330. NIST, 2000.

[37] K. S. Jones, S. Walker, and S. E. Robertson. A probabilistic model of information retrieval: Development and comparative experiments. *Information Processing and Management*, 36(1–2):1:779–808 and 2:809–840, 2000.

[38] V. Vapnik, S. Golowich, and A. J. Smola. Support vector method for function approximation, regression estimation, and signal processing. In *Advances in Neural Information Processing Systems*. MIT Press, 1996.

[39] I. H. Witten, A. Moffat, and T. C. Bell. *Managing Gigabytes: Compressing and Indexing Documents and Images*. Morgan-Kaufmann, May 1999.

[40] D. Zhang and W. Lee. Question classification using support vector machines. In *SIGIR*, pages 26–32, 2003.

[41] Z. Zheng. AnswerBus question answering system. In *HLT*, 2002.

Index

Page numbers in italics indicate figures and tables.